DATE DUE

AUG 0 3 2000		
DE1 5 00		
MR 12 02		
AP 1 02		

QUICK RESPONSE

Life is making us abandon established stereotypes and outdated views. It is making us discard illusions. The very concept of the nature and criteria of progress is changing. It would be naive to think that the problems plaguing mankind today can be solved with means and methods which were applied or seemed to work in the past ... .

Today we face a different world for which we must seek a different road to the future. In seeking it, we must, of course, draw upon the accumulated experience and yet be aware of the fundamental differences between the situation yesterday and what we are facing today.

Mikhail Gorbachev (1988)

QUICK RESPONSE

Managing the Supply Chain
to Meet Consumer Demand

BOB LOWSON
Cardiff Business School, UK

RUSSELL KING
North Carolina State University, USA

ALAN HUNTER
North Carolina State University, USA

JOHN WILEY & SONS, LTD
Chichester · New York · Weinheim · Brisbane · Singapore · Toronto

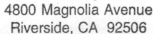

Copyright © 1999 by   John Wiley & Sons Ltd,

, England

9777
l3 779777
stomer service enquiries): cs-books@wiley.co.uk
http://www.wiley.co.uk
http://www.wiley.com

Other Wiley Editorial Offices

John Wiley & Sons, Inc., 605 Third Avenue,
New York, NY 10158-0012, USA

WILEY-VCH Verlag GmbH, Pappelallee 3,
D-69469 Weinheim, Germany

Jacaranda Wiley Ltd, 33 Park Road, Milton,
Queensland 4064, Australia

John Wiley & Sons (Asia) Pte Ltd, 2 Clementi Loop #02-01,
Jin Xing Distripark, Singapore 129809

John Wiley & Sons (Canada) Ltd, 22 Worcester Road,
Rexdale, Ontario M9W 1L1, Canada

Library of Congress Cataloging-in-Publication Data
Hunter, Alan, *1930–*
    Quick response : managing the supply chain to meet customers demand
/ Bob Lowson, Russell King, Alan Hunter.
      p. cm.
    Includes bibliographical references and index.
    ISBN 0-471-98833-2 (cased)
    1. Business logistics. 2. Just-in-time systems. 3. Inventory
control. 4. Physical distribution of goods. 5. Customer services.
I. King, Russell. II. Hunter, Alan. III. Title.
    HD38.5.H86   1999
658.5—dc21   99–24152
                                                      CIP

British Library Cataloguing in Publication Data
A catalogue record for this book is available from the British Library
ISBN 0-471-98833-2

Typeset in 10/12 Times from the authors' disks by
Mathematical Composition Setters Ltd, Salisbury, Wiltshire
Printed and bound in Great Britain by Biddles Ltd, Guildford and King's Lynn
This book is printed on acid-free paper responsibly manufactured from sustainable forestry,
in which at least two trees are planted for each one used for paper production.

CONTENTS

PREFACE

This book is about the rapid growth of consumerism on the one hand, and the attempts of both management theorists to understand it and industry to meet its customers' demands on the other. By consumerism, we mean the increasing power of the buying public to demand variety and value on the retail shelves when they want it. From the points of view of the manufacturing and retailing processes, such demands have called for a total re-thinking of the ways in which industries operate. We say industries because very few of them are immune. Food, pharmaceuticals, electronics and automobiles are just as affected as the more obvious apparel industry and its supply system.

The birth and development of consumerism is for others to document. It seems, though, that anyone growing up before 1960 did so in an environment of manufacturing driven choice; sedate department stores with limited selections, and discernible fashion trends. It could be that the first real sign of things to come was the sudden appearance of the mini-skirt in the mid-1960s. Shortly afterwards, innovative marketers began to offer the levels of product diversity in color, style, flavor and size that today's public regards as perfectly normal.

We will describe, at least in outline, the responses of industry and management thinkers to these consumerist shifts. Within the time span we are discussing, the changes are almost heroic in scope and scale. Paradigm shifts in management thinking and practices occur almost annually, and yet there seems to be only a faint light at the end of the tunnel.

We maintain that consumer/industry interaction in the last 5–6 years has benefited from technological development to the point where it is possible to implement strategies that are practicable, and quantifiable (we have made every effort to quantify our assertions about the benefits of QR management). In saying this we argue strongly for the following:

- The diversity of consumer wants has approached the chaotic. This implies that attempting to forecast demand, using trend analysis or any other method, is not possible. Desires will emerge from the complex mix of offerings and expressed preferences, but too late for them to be of much use to the buyer, especially when it is realized that retailers are having to target more and smaller markets.

- Despite the best estimates of planners, designers and buyers, the only firm datum occurs when a consumer puts down his or her money at the cash register and expresses clear approval of a certain Stock Keeping Unit (SKU) at a particular price. This point of sale (PoS) information, when properly analyzed and acted upon by the entire supply system, allows customer demand to be met under most circumstances.

- We can do much to counteract the present, destructive cycles of sales promotions, and discounts that depress end-of-season economics, provided the supply pipeline is sufficiently responsive in terms of time from order to on-shelf availability of merchandise. Shorter product development times, smaller pre-season inventories, continuous re-estimations of demand level and product mix, and frequent small reorders on suppliers that are met by small lot, flexible manufacturing procedures, permit tailoring of in-store inventories to meet demand at the SKU level throughout the season.

The above practices are embodied in one of the most promising industrial innovations to come along in the last 10 years or so. Quick Response (QR) Manufacturing and Marketing offers ways to satisfy consumers while improving the performance of the supply pipeline. Here we note that many variations on the term QR have surfaced in the past few years. However, a name change means little and we stay with the original nomenclature.

The book has a number of objectives. First we place QR in a broad framework of business thinking, e.g. Supply Chain Management. Despite the obvious benefits of practicing QR, industry has been slow to adapt and we will show why this is so. Next, we quantify the benefits of QR and suggest procedures for implementation, using examples from industry as well as computer simulation. Finally, future research directions are discussed and we provide some clues to successful operation in the 21st century.

The retailer has a thankless task. He is the interpreter of consumer desires and must pass these on to his suppliers. Still, he has great difficulty in knowing what is happening in his stores; for example, how many customers are walking out unsatisfied because of stock-outs, the real cost of markdowns, and the impact of different sourcing and markdown policies. We offer ways of looking at these and other problems and describe a sophisticated computer model of the retail operation—Sourcing Simulator that allows examination of the impacts of various strategies on financial and other performance measures.

We hope that this book will have appeal to senior managers in a number of industries that are faced with increasingly complex, dynamic and volatile demand patterns. Similarly, students, particularly at post-graduate level, will find contributions to the disciplines of strategic and operations management,

Supply Chain Management and logistics, industrial engineering, operations research and systems dynamics.

There are three authors. We have made every effort to meld styles, spelling and the like, but our omissions will show. One of us is British and business-oriented (Lowson), one is American and an Industrial Engineer (King) and the third has a background in the Textile and Apparel industries (Hunter). We believe that the three backgrounds and disciplines are necessary to cover adequately the topics addressed in the book.

Bob Lowson is Research Director of the Quick Response Research Programme (QRRP) based at Cardiff Business School, Cardiff University. This is a European initiative aimed at improving the flexibility, responsiveness and diversity of manufacturers and retailers in a number of Fast Moving Consumer Goods (FMCG) industries. Prior to this appointment, he spent several years in various industry sectors, involved with QR, Supply Chain Management and logistical improvement projects.

Russell King is Professor of Industrial Engineering at NCSU, Raleigh, North Carolina. He is the Director of the NCSU Logistics Center. He has worked for the apparel industry on Quick Response systems analysis, automotive industry, the US Navy on problems of maintenance scheduling, and for the furniture industry centered in North Carolina. He has also consulted extensively on QR-related matters and is the author of several papers and articles on QR.

Alan Hunter, a UK citizen, spent much of his career as a senior manager in the US Fiber/Textile/Apparel/Retail complex. He was one of the developers of QR in the early 1980s, taught at North Carolina State University (NCSU), and helped establish the research program underlying this book. He is currently a Visiting Professor with the College of Textiles, NCSU, and a consultant to the QR program at the university. He resides in Montreal, Canada.

INTRODUCTION AND EXECUTIVE SUMMARY

Quick Response was developed as a way for domestic North American and European industries to become more competitive in the face of increasing imports from low wage countries. If traditional pipeline supply times could be shortened as a result of flexible and responsive production techniques, it was discovered that a very different set of operational procedures could come into play using newly emerging technologies. Simultaneously, there came the realization that consumerism was growing by leaps and bounds and had reached the point where forecasting of demand trends was virtually impossible. These two aspects of the new business world can be made to fit together by means of the intelligent use of Point of Sale (PoS) data. If consumer demands and preferences can be identified early in the life cycle of a class of merchandise and re-estimated at regular intervals, if initial store or manufacturer inventories are kept low, and if the supply system is responsive to frequent, small replenishment reorders, then a supply pipeline can be operated in a different way. Subsequent work on what became known as Quick Response has shown that its advantages include not only increased customer service levels, and satisfaction, but much greater financial success because of fewer lost sales, and substantially better end-of-season markdown performance.

Initially, QR was developed by and for the textile and apparel industries. However, anyone connected with a supply pipeline that serves the consuming public will be absorbed by the material we provide. Food, shoes, toys, electronics, furniture, home furnishings, appliances and even the military would all show improved performance if they were to adopt a QR approach to business. This is not, however, another management book peddling another 'fad' or another one-minute wonder! Quick Response, unlike many other management paradigms, is quantifiable and measurable, its implementation, progress and development can be accurately circumscribed.

The application and implementation of QR in a number of industries is at the cutting-edge of innovation; it is quite simply a new paradigm for senior and operational managers, business schools and theoreticians—one that offers a distinct route to more competitive strategies. Yet it is not catholic in its application. We will describe how the generic form of QR recognizes a changing consumer world and brings benefits to many sectors operating in volatile environments. But, we are realists. QR is not a universal panacea. It is not a 'best practice' that will apply to every organization in every industry—beware those that claim such power. QR has, we believe, remarkable benefits when used and adapted circumspectly. Despite the strength of its underlying philosophy, different components of QR will work in contingent contexts, circumstances and settings.

The apparel or clothing industry is, perhaps, the most demanding QR application—hundreds of colors, thousands of styles and millions of SKUs on the retail shelves at any one time. Further, as we shall discuss, the average shelf lives of these merchandise items shorten with each passing year.

A couple of examples may help the reader to understand the complexity of the apparel business and why QR is so important. Suppose sardines were to be offered in cans of a dozen or so sizes, in at least as many shapes, and 30–40 colors. Worse, every three to four months, the cans not sold would have to go on sale because they are now out of style. That is not even close to the diversity and complexity of the clothing business.

It is with this in mind, together with the history of QR, that necessitates the inclusion of many examples from the Textile and Apparel industry. The reader will soon appreciate the applicability of many QR concepts to other sectors, and later chapters demonstrate its inter-industry transferability. To aid such visualization, case studies or vignettes will be provided from different applications both in Europe and North America.

Now, another aspect of QR. Consider shoes. Two to three times per year, residual stocks are placed on sale racks in shopping malls the world over. The tragedy, for retailer and consumer alike, is that no one wants the very small or the very large sizes, but there is nothing else on sale. In the same way, marked-down toys or apparel is usually a 'white elephant' sale of unwanted lines, colors, sizes and styles.

QR has much to say about how to handle the growing complexity and unpredictability of product lines, to prevent these and similar occurrences. As noted in the preface, the basic premise is that all forecasts made before a selling season are wrong. The truth only occurs when the consumer puts down money for a specific SKU and registers what we shall call a PoS preference. As noted above, the QR methodology is based on accumulating these data points and turning them into information for use by a responsive manufacturer and his suppliers. It is basically simple but very complex to put into practice.

Of course, each industry supply chain has its own characteristics. Some are dominated by the retailer (the modern grocery industry is a prime example), some by the primary supplier (the mobile phone sector, steel and chemicals), and others where assembly operations control the system, e.g. the automotive industry. Textiles/apparel is unique in a very important aspect—the actual assembler of the finished product is, with a few exceptions, financially insignificant. There are some 14 000 apparel manufacturers in the US, 8000 in the UK and 67 000 in the European Community. In the US, over half of these have fewer than 20 employees, and the largest sector, Women's and Misses apparel, with 9200 establishments, averages sales of US \$2.3 million per year. Thus, the garment manufacturer is caught between large and powerful textile producers and even larger retailers. Under these circumstances, he cannot be expected to lead any pipeline restructuring such as that required by QR. Contrast this picture with that of the automotive industry.

The problems facing the implementation of QR in differing circumstances will be examined in more detail in Chapter 6, but despite these difficulties, in the last 2–3 years there has been an increasing interest in the methodology. In Europe, the better companies are looking at ways to implement QR and, finally, business and research funding is being made available (the Quick Response Research Programme being one such example).

In the US, the National Textile Center has provided funds for research under the aegis of the Department of Commerce, and the Department of Energy has, since 1993, been investigating improved information and business architectures under the banner of DAMA—the Demand Activated Manufacturing Architecture project of the AMTEX Partnerships.

The book is divided into four parts, and we beg the indulgence of those readers who wish to dive immediately into QR. We believe it is important to set the stage for QR by examining in some detail the development of modern management thinking. In this way we hope that QR will emerge naturally as the successor to earlier attempts to understand the complexity of supply systems.

Part I—The Business World—provides the theoretical underpinning for QR. In Chapter 1 we look at the business environment in which we live, one which is dominated by a growing consumerism—a proliferation of goods. A cursory examination of products at the supermarket will reveal a massive choice of foods compared with even five years ago. Such variety has to be backed by enormous inventories, especially when shelf life is germane. For the last 30 years or so, the buying public has become increasingly accustomed to greater value, and industry has had to discard many of its earlier practices—those based on the teachings of Ford and Taylor—and focus instead on flexibility.

We examine these new philosophies, briefly, in Chapter 2. A number of industry initiatives are reviewed, including those in grocery, automotive, and apparel trades, together with new ways of looking at strategy, flexible specialization, agile manufacturing, lean production, and time based competition, among others. This chapter also contemplates the development of Supply Chain Management in its various guises.

Chapter 3 brings us up-to-date on the current theories of management specialists: supply chain and pipeline organization, partnerships and alliances, global sourcing, benchmarking, information technology, managing change, and the newly emerging implications of chaos theory. However, many of these fail to be quantitative, and little guidance is given on how to implement the new ideas. Our aim at the outset has been to mix classic qualitative management thinking with quantification—the 'how-to' and 'how-much' are as important as the 'why'. In this chapter we also single out Supply Chain Management for constructive analysis and criticism—something many commentators have been loath to contemplate in the face of a tidal wave of popularity. It is at this point that we introduce the methodologies of Quick Response and their pertinence for an organization's strategy, operations and culture.

Part II describes QR within the organization. It covers the history and application of QR methodologies in the business environment. In Chapter 4 we first review the origins of QR, and the basic ideas involved. The second part of the chapter takes a look at why QR has taken so long to be adopted when its advantages are so clear cut. We believe that the ideas behind it were well ahead of their time—technologies had still to be developed, and questions about who should lead the changes went unanswered. The time now seems ripe for pushing ahead with methods that have so much to offer, even though a great deal remains to be worked out; details such as inventory responsibility, and margin sharing among the pipeline participants. The third part of Chapter 4 examines the key role of the Small and Medium-sized Enterprise (SME). We include reports on surveys of 64 companies in the UK and four companies in Quebec, Canada. These have thrown new light on the problems of SMEs and point to possible solutions, so far as QR is concerned. The economic health of SMEs is vital for the simple reason that these companies are the backbone of many industries, whether they are 'tied' suppliers, independent, or contractors. Because they are, for the most part, deprived of retail PoS information—the 'mole' syndrome—they are obliged to carry excessive inventories of raw materials and/or finished goods if they are to satisfy their customers.

Chapter 5 deals with QR applications; how goods can be categorized by their logistical attributes, their volatility understood and their influence upon the pipeline measured and controlled. It is at this point that we consider potential applications in other fast moving and dynamic industries such as food, footwear, furniture, home furnishings and even the armed forces. For these we suggest ways in which QR application could improve operating performance.

In Chapter 6 we provide what the practitioner may feel is the heart of the book: QR implementation. Clear and prescriptive guidelines for an organization whether it is concerned with retailing, operations or supplying raw materials—the three primary pipeline stages.

Part III covers the important approach of pipeline modeling. In earlier sections, we refer to the exorbitant costs of full-scale supplier/manufacturer/ retailer QR trials. Here we have used simulation techniques to explore the impact of QR methodologies. In Chapter 7 we introduce a simple graphical method for understanding and evaluating the impact of QR on a complicated supply system. This is followed in Chapter 8 by a description of a powerful stochastic computer simulation model of the retailing function. The program, which is arousing a great deal of interest, details the internal logic, inputs, outputs and algorithms for the re-estimation of demand at the SKU level and the resulting reorders on the manufacturer. We also give the more important results obtained by exercising the model under a variety of scenarios, and using a number of retail strategies. Included in these are estimates of the financial losses to retailers who fail to measure accurately the preferences of their customers.

In Chapter 9 we look at the retail buyer's sourcing decision, including off-shore production, and the justification for the choice. This involves an examination of the performance yardsticks behind the selection, and we show that often no financial or customer service measure supports such a sourcing approach. We also introduce a new concept in sourcing. This we call 'Mixed Sourcing'.

One of the requirements of QR is that the manufacturer, and other up-stream suppliers, respond quickly to retail reorders during the selling season. These reorder lead times are not as critical for Basic (year round) or Seasonal goods (2–3 seasons per year), but more volatile or short season merchandise, with short shelf lives often requires lead times of less than 1–2 weeks. In Chapter 10, therefore, we look at the kind of manufacturing systems that can provide the necessary flexibility and speed of response. This work is still in progress, but the scope and direction of the research are important parts of the QR story.

Part IV of the book is concerned with the research directions and implementation paths that seem to us to be important.

Chapter 11 includes some ideas on short season or volatile products, i.e. that class of goods with a very short shelf life. Under pressure from both the consumer, and the retailer trying to maintain a distinctive image, it is now possible to discern a trend toward something approaching seasons of 1–2 weeks, with new products landing on the shelves as soon as they are developed: perhaps nothing new to the retailer of fresh and chilled foodstuffs. Such a trend calls for totally new ways to estimate and manage requirements.

The second research direction has to do with the interactions between Service levels (e.g. back-orders), order Lead-times, Inventories (no matter where in the pipeline) and Process times. We refer to this as SLIP modeling, and believe it to be extremely important.

The *total* logistics of most pipelines are simply not understood. In Chapter 11, we look at some of the implications of this and identify research that will clear up an important area of costing and the equitable sharing of profits.

Chapter 11 also breaks new ground. For many years, one of the top managerial 'buzz' phrases was Management Information Systems (MIS). Less is now heard of this concept, probably because it is a one-way street. The senior manager is fed data in a pre-digested form, with little or no opportunity to ask questions. Should he or she do so, it takes an age to provide the answers. Our interest is in Interactive MIS. Using 'high level' models of the enterprise, questions can be asked, and answers obtained immediately, using such technologies as Neural Networks. Examples include rapid estimations of the impact on inventories of enlarging the number of products offered to customers, and the implications for manufacturing of shortened order lead times.

Finally, Chapter 11 concludes with some promising, if slightly more obscure research areas, such as the QR Domain. These are little understood at present, but may in the future provide the next paradigm shift.

Throughout the book we make generous use of tables and figures. This is deliberate. Our aim is to reach the widest possible audience—CEOs to factory managers to systems analysts to students from many disciplines—for which there is no single language. More prose would have lost some of the audience; more detail on the algorithms employed in the models could present difficulties for others. We have tried to achieve a middle ground.

ACKNOWLEDGEMENTS

We wish to acknowledge the work of Doctors Henry Nuttle, Fang Shu-Cherng, James Wilson and Gordon Berkstresser III at NCSU. They are the other members of the research team supported, most recently, by the National Textiles Center under US Department of Commerce funding. We are also grateful for the support of the European Union funding agency, European Regional Development Fund, for supporting the research into UK operations, and the advice of Professor Roger Mansfield and Sally Earney at Cardiff Business School and Ian Brodie at the Open University.

Among the many students who have worked with us, we wish to thank the following: Leigh Ann Brain, Daryel Brown, Joseph Chen, Sowmya Gottipati, TC Hall, Woody Hewitt, Julie Hinshaw, David Hung, Robert Maddalena, Claude Martin, Lynn McGoogan, Amy Pinnow, Martha Poindexter, Ken Powell, Issa Rafidi, Steven Reynolds, Alex Sands, Laura Semproch, Shelly Shippy and Pete Wu.

Members of industry who gave us a great deal of necessary advice and help include: Michelle Benjamin, Peter Butenhoff, Chad Horne, Barbara Mazziotti, Steve Freudenthal and Ken Watson.

Anne-Marie Lopes and Helen Louise also deserve our thanks for their help, support and infinite forbearance, as does Gloria Supino who gave so much of her time to helping prepare the draft versions of the book.

PART I
THE BUSINESS WORLD

Modern industrial man needs goods for the same reason as the tribesman: to involve other fellow consumers in his consumption rituals. They need goods to commit other people to their project. The fact that, in the course of these rituals, food gets consumed, flags get waved, and clothes worn, is incidental.

Mary Douglas (1982)

The distinguishing characteristic of modern civilization is an indefinite multiplicity of human wants. The characteristic of ancient civilization is an imperative restriction upon, and a strict regulation of these wants.

Mohandas (Mahatma) Gandhi
(Attenborough, 1992)

1
A NEW ENVIRONMENT

1.1 UNUSUAL TIMES

Few would deny that we live in rapidly changing times. We are witnessing far-reaching and unprecedented shifts in our culture, politics and economic life. As we move toward the millennium, society is undergoing changes that will affect the foundations of our current beliefs concerning human behavior patterns and the world about us. Sociologists and anthropologists attempt to understand and classify these changes, and all they infer, using a variety of models and frameworks. Perhaps the most far reaching is the description of a massive change from a 'modernist' society to one of 'post-modernism'.

These are hotly debated concepts and we do not intend to enter into the current discussion. However, no matter which terms are used to describe recent events there is no denying their impact; especially on consumer industries such as food, electronics, electrical appliances, textiles and clothing; and the organizations that comprise them.

What is the essence of this post-modern society? Of what relevance is it to consumer industries, the firms operating within them, and their management? What changes will these companies have to undergo to continue to prosper in such a setting? Will a radical rethinking of managements' approach to business be necessary? It is these, and similar questions that this book will confront. We will describe this new environment, and the direction of its evolution, and offer a picture of the future and what it will mean for these industries. Finally, a recipe for change is suggested; a practical implementation path which will provide many organizations with a route to re-establishing their competitive edge.

This new era is typified by a society in pursuit of individualism and the increasing fragmentation of traditional social groups. Hierarchy in its many forms is in decline and institutional authority questioned. Deference is frowned upon. Change is accepted as the norm, and the so-called meta-narratives[1] are being eroded and destroyed. This new post-modernist world is marked by acceptance of ephemerality, fragmentation, discontinuity, chaos, and pluralism. But for our purposes, it is the changes in consumer behavior that are of most interest: consumer-purchasing patterns are increasingly diffuse and fragmented[2], with a diversity of products and services being offered.

Goods, whether they be clothes or basic foodstuffs, are no longer merely products with utilitarian values, but represent a patina of symbols, signs, images and statements of difference. Their symbolic meaning is often of more importance than any other, and it is created, reinforced and sustained through the mechanism of branding. The brand assumes the status of a 'bundle of meanings' in support of a lifestyle, and serves as a signpost through the confusion and clutter of post-modern life. The value of products becomes less their ability to satisfy primary needs and more the way they function within society to show who we are and our position or status in life. Staple items such as bread, butter and toasters are not immune, and even the music business has seen the 'superbands' of the 1980s replaced by a less integrated scene. These signs take on a life of their own, referring not to a real world outside themselves, but to their own 'reality'—the system that produces the signs.

Some examples may serve to illustrate our contention: the survival of what were originally designed as working class overalls—simple Levis to designer jeans; the brand power of sports shoes such as Nike; the cache of designer clothes all the way from Liz Claiborne to Armani; 'retro' fashion of the 50s, 60s and 70s; the military boot which fashioned Dr. Martens footwear; cars like the VW Beetle and the Mini; designer foods from all corners of the globe; and the globalization of brands, in remote corners of the world, such as McDonald's, Mars Bars, Snickers, etc.

If we accept this picture of a splintered society with its growing fragmentation and increasingly diverse consumer requirements, it will have profound implications for retailers and their manufacturing suppliers in trying to satisfy that demand. We also believe that the changing patterns we are now seeing are only the tip of a very large iceberg upon which many of today's successful firms may well founder tomorrow.

In summary, readers, especially those working in the consumer industries, may well identify with the scenario we are about to address:

Consumer demand upon retailers in many industries is displaying piecemeal, disjointed and unsystematic tendencies and thus becoming increasingly difficult

---

[1] Large-scale theoretical interpretations purportedly of universal application like the 'Victorian work ethic' and a 'social consciousness'.

[2] The term 'mass-customization' is often used to encapsulate this phenomenon and contrast it with 'mass-production'.

to satisfy. Consumer purchases are more than ever a reflection of a lifestyle or fashion statement rather than the satisfaction of a basic need, and this is only the beginning. To this has to be added the complexity of instantaneous, electronic, world-wide communication, and an information explosion that has served to educate the average shopper beyond any level seen to date.

To meet these changing demand patterns, retail outlets are proliferating and having to react more speedily, while at the same time avoiding the penalties associated with increasingly volatile demand. Often, the only way that such responses can be achieved is at the expense of large stockpiles.

Logic dictates that the onus of satisfying much of these new demands will fall not only upon the retailer, but also on the supplying manufacturer or vendor. Such a supplier can adopt one of three strategies. First, total compliance with the dictates of a retailer, despite their increasing and onerous cost; second, bargaining and confrontation with the retailer in order to attempt to reduce the burden; this risks loss of business. Third, he can seek a more flexible and responsive posture; one that allows the freedom to satisfy, profitably, whatever is demanded in an atmosphere of joint co-operation. It is this third strategy, a very futuristic strategy, which forms the basis for this book.

The new environment described above is also unique in the diverse and disparate linkages it contains. Determinism and deterministic outcomes become rarer as the association between cause and effect becomes more tenuous; a single case now involves multiple and open-ended outcomes. Foresight is no longer plausible and forecasting, despite the sophistication of the system employed, is almost worthless; no longer can futuristic projections be built around a repetition of past events. The future becomes open-ended, chaotic and out of control. Prior planning and design fail to produce the desired results; these more often than not arrive through a process of spontaneous self-organization. It is from this increasingly disorganized, dynamic, diverse and somewhat disorderly state of affairs that new organizational forms must develop.

The descriptions of this new environment are many and varied, but for us, of more interest is how the organizations that live in this new and burgeoning world have tried to cope with its current demands. We need to appreciate some of the recent concepts and frameworks that have been introduced, in an attempt to capture the meaning of these changes, before any new dimension can be added. For an exposition of the ways in which an approaching chaotic environment affects strategy formulation, Ralph Stacey's article in the journal *Long Range Planning* (1996) is of considerable interest:

> The new science of complexity leads us to see organizations as complex adaptive systems. Such systems are creative when they occupy a space at the edge of disintegration, and here their specific futures cannot be foreseen. The price we pay for creativity and free will is an inability to foresee and intend future outcomes.

1.2   NEW THEORIES

In this section we examine some of the intellectual concepts that have been employed to describe how organizations transform themselves in the face of these new demands. The theories described are used to show how many industrial sectors seek to change in an attempt to meet new challenges.

1.2.1   Flexible Specialization

In a study of Italian manufacturing regions, Sebastiano Brusco (1982) identified what he described as the beginnings of a new era. He wrote of:

> the emergence since the mid-1960s of a significant demand for more varied and customized goods, produced in short series ... which will only be satisfied by a new form.

He recognized that in the face of these new consumer demands, many small manufacturers within this industry were operating in a unique manner. This new method of working was described as 'flexible specialization'. Theorists saw these changes as a unique industrial concept and likened them to a move away from traditional manufacturing patterns or 'Fordism' toward what they referred to as 'post-Fordism'.

The Fordist organization was based upon the premise that the greater the scale of production and technological introduction, the larger the return on investment (the more black cars that were made, the more efficient the producer; a strategy that succeeds providing black is the only color demanded). It was, and still is, a system unparalleled in its ability to deliver standard goods cheaply and on a mass scale using the methods of work developed by Frederick Taylor. However, the market for mass produced goods is finite, and is often subject to large and rapid changes in taste, fashion and demand. Eventually, if the changes become large enough there develops a 'crisis in demand' when traditional ways of operating are no longer sufficient.

In the past, various solutions to such crises have been described as neo-Fordist or post-Fordist. They have included various coping strategies such as diversification into new products and markets, geographic internationalization and technological intensification. However, these remedies often prove short-lived as the crises have deepened and included chronic stages of unemployment and slow growth. Examples include many traditional industries such as steel, coal and shipbuilding.

One of the remedies most often employed to satisfy these new consumer demands has been that of 'global Fordism'. Here, production is de-centralized, not simply nationally but internationally, by removing it to low wage regions of the world while design and control remain in the West. So, post-Fordist elements in the First World co-exist alongside classic Fordist and 'peripheral' Fordist in the Third World.

Proponents of post-Fordism argue that many of these so-called coping mechanisms are nothing more than a temporary alleviation of the problem. For them, there needs to be a total re-appraisal of approach—a complete change in direction to counter the growing consumer requirements of diversity and customization. Such changes, they argue, will alter the essence of competition and strike at the very heart of 'Fordism'. They describe such shifts as a move toward 'flexible manufacturing'.

Fordists organized production so as to combine maximum specialization of workers with maximum standardization of product. The new flexible firms, reacting to rapidly changing market demand, seek to generalize the skills of workers so that they can adapt to a wide range of tasks and produce an expandable range of highly specialized products. Fordism relies on economies of scale and was made explicit in the Boston Consulting Group 'experience curve theory'. The latter concept is a wonderful insight into the relationship between unit cost and cumulative production: its fatal flaw is that the product has to remain constant (for example, cement and aluminum ingots). When product diversity rears its head, the whole thing becomes more complicated. By contrast, in flexible manufacturing, economies of scope become increasingly more important.

A further attempt to conceptualize these changes was made by Piore and Sabel (1984), applying the term 'flexible specialization'. What they describe is a rejection of Fordism and a return to a craft form of production, based upon the use of information technology and customized, short-run manufacture, in a network of small firms operating in niche, segmented, markets.

It should be noted that the supporters of Fordism disagree with much of this theory. For writers such as Gramsci (1971), and more recently Clarke (1990 a,b), there may be crises, but the response of industry is not a movement away from 'Fordism' but merely a continuing evolution of it.

> Fordism was not just a new technology; it was the systematic application of new techniques—social as well as scientific in the technical sense—to the organisation of production in all its spheres,' (Clarke, 1990a)

Thus, Fordism cannot simply be equated with inflexibility; it is a constantly evolving operational principle and can become more flexible if and when required.

1.2.2   Evolution and Natural Selection

Since its publication in 1859, Charles Darwin's *The Origin of the Species by Means of Natural Selection* has had few rivals in terms of its impact on both scientific and popular thinking. Naturalists of the 19th century were preoccupied with questions about both the *adaptations* of organisms and the enormous *diversity* of living things. Darwin's seminal contribution to this debate was to produce two simple explanations that would account for both these problems. The first was to demonstrate that modern species are descended from earlier species, i.e. species had evolved. The second contribution was to show how a process of natural selection could explain this method of descent.

Evolution—The Madagascar Lima

The Madagascar Lima is an interesting example of evolution through natural selection. The Lima of this island has evolved to deal with the dominant vegetation: cacti. In order to jump between the plants their toes have curled in a particular way to wrap around the thorns. Unfortunately, unlike other species of Lima, they have almost lost the ability to walk on all fours and shuffle in a most ungainly manner.

It is instructive to think of industrial development (evolution) in Darwinian terms. The industrial enterprise is an organism or entity facing immense competition in a changing environment. Of course time scales are much compressed, compared with evolution of natural species, but what we think of as a modern manufacturer is an *adaptation* only possible due to the initial invention of agriculture. Since that time there has been a gradual and steady change in the environment faced by such manufacturers: new metals, new forging processes, new energy sources and not least new markets, as transport and communication improve.

These incremental developments followed the Darwinian model of evolution. But in addition to these relatively small and steady changes, there have been two sudden shifts or large step changes in the environment of the manufacturer: the Industrial Revolution and the Information Revolution[3].

The first of these led to mass production, repetitive processes, lowered cost, the production line and the adoption of new technologies. Those entities that did not adapt to these challenges died. A similar process is evident in contemporary production systems—the drive to adopt Supply Chain Management (SCM), Just-in-Time (JIT), Material Requirements Planning (MRP), Manufacturing Resource Planning (MRPII), Total Quality Management (TQM), Enterprise/Distribution Planning (E/DRP), etc. all culminating in what we now consider to be the modern producer. However, virtually all of these improvements are manufacturing or distribution related and merely pay lip service to genuine consumer demand.

---

[3] In 1972 a paper appeared with the daunting title *'Punctuated Equilibria: An Alternative to Phyleticgradualism'* by Eldredge N and Gould S J. The authors argued that while evolutionary development may well have occurred in tiny steps as Darwin had suggested, there were times when much more significant changes transpired. This contention is still being debated, but for our purposes, it seems that the Industrial and Information Revolutions fit well with the idea of such discontinuities.

The second major shift is still occurring and is a result of the development of the computer coupled with the growth of consumerism. It is our contention that Quick Response is the new paradigm for examining and responding to the Information Revolution, in which the wants of the final consumer are paramount and drive all industrial activity.

1.2.3   Population Ecology and Organizational Ecology

The next set of macro perspectives regarding organizations and how they are required to change, concerns survival and the use of flexibility and responsiveness to adopt niche positions.

The population ecology viewpoint is also based on Darwin's theory of evolution. The arguments are as follows. Organizations, like organisms in nature, depend on their ability to acquire an adequate supply of resources for survival. In doing this they face competition from others[4]. As in nature, only the fittest survive. The environment influences survival by selecting which resources are available and which organizations succeed and fail; the most robust prosper at the expense of the weak. As Darwin noted, for selection to occur there must be variation between the individuals. This entails a cyclical model of variation, selection, retention and modification of individual characteristics; the fitter varieties standing a better chance of selection.

For the study of organizations, the focus shifts from explaining how individual organizations adapt to their environment, to one of understanding how different species rise and fall in importance, and what influences this success or failure. As changes in the environment occur, new populations of organizations emerge to take advantage of these opportunities and other populations decline and disappear. Organizations make changes in the hope that they will evolve and survive. Failure to do so can bring about their extinction and that of their industry sector, replaced by more adaptable species (the rise of the supermarket at the expense of specialist stores is a typical example). Command of resources and their proper utilization, combined with awareness of the need to innovate and change, is crucial; the choice of strategic direction is fundamental to success if the environmental conditions demand flexibility, speed and adaptation.

The organizational ecology perspective sees organizations as existing in a complex ecosystem, evolving with the environment, and not entities separate and isolated from it as in population ecology. It is the whole ecosystem that evolves. It is evolution of a pattern, a fit with the environment, not adaptation to it: 'survival of the fitting' not just the 'fittest'. The organization and its environment are inseparable and both influenced by and influencing of it. In addition, the environment is comprised of other organizations, which can often

---

[4] We should think of resources in this sense as not merely land, labor, capital and information, but also to include customers, investors, suppliers, knowledge, etc.

link their activities as in a network. Each organization can rely heavily upon such linkages; they become a route by which the organization can influence its own environment, to shape, and, to some degree, alter the future.

An organization's environment or 'domain' (comprised of other organizations, and similar to a planetary system in which some elements are closer or more important than others), holds many opportunities for inter-organizational collaboration. As in nature, collaboration, or more correctly symbiotic relationships, are surprisingly common between both private and public sector firms. Partnerships, joint ventures, alliances, learning networks, technological development groups and the like, are strategic obligations in this frame of reference, where altruism is a necessary precursor to profit.

Both 'population ecology' and 'organization ecology' place a strong emphasis upon the role and influence of the environment, both operating and macro. In both concepts, organizational change, and indeed survival, depends upon the interaction with this environment.

1.2.4   Transaction Cost Economics and Theory of the Firm

The final theory examined here comes from the discipline of economics and involves the allocation and distribution of resources at the organizational level. Theories of the firm attempt to understand and explain how inputs to the organization (raw material, energy, skills, etc.) are transformed into outputs (products or services), and the resultant outcome should internal changes be made as a reaction to the environment.

It was R H Coase (1937) who first speculated about the 'make or buy' decision in any firm. This is the decision whether to use an administrative relationship (inside—'make') or use a market relationship (external—'buy'). According to Coase, the key to this decision is the cost of the 'transaction'[5]: firms judge whether or not to make or buy based on minimizing the cost of the transactions involved. Such calculations provide important insights into the boundary of the firm.

Williamson (1981) further developed transaction theory. He based the theory and its analysis upon two 'behavioral assumptions' and three 'principles of organizational design'.

Behavioral Assumptions

Bounded rationality. Decisions are intended to be rational. However, they fail in this objective due to factors such as limited information about the situation or a limited ability to deal with the information should it be possessed. This

---

[5] Transaction costs are those not related to the costs of material and labor, etc. They refer to the costs, often hidden, of managing and controlling the transaction as well as those associated with uncertainty and risk.

contrasts with many other economic models that assume logical decision making based upon perfect knowledge.

Opportunism. There is a 'hidden agenda' behind any decisions made on behalf of the organization. Williamson called this 'self interest seeking with guile'.

Principles of Organizational Design

Asset specificity. Resources such as skills and equipment become specialized and will have little or no value outside their particular production context. This applies mainly to organizations such as suppliers who will focus on one particular input to a larger product. For example, firms that produce plastic bottles and supply major soft drink manufacturers will have high degrees of asset specificity, and competition is reduced to a few specialists.

Externality. Agents, or any bodies representing the firm in the market-place, will have private goals often inconsistent with those of the organization.

Hierarchical decomposition. This rather ugly term describes the most effective management structure. In terms of transaction costs, the advantage of carrying out transactions internally within an organization clearly depends on the efficiency with which the organization manages its activities. At the time Williamson was writing, the predominant organization form was the U-form (unitary form), whereby each function reported vertically to an executive board. As businesses grew, this structure became ill-equipped to cope with the increasing complexity of decision making. Accordingly, more decentralized structures evolved, e.g. the M-form (multi-divisional form). Thus, we see that hierarchical decomposition refers to delegation of decision making within the organization.

A 'transaction' occurs when a good or service is transferred across a distinct and separable interface; for example, the purchase of plastic bottles by the soft drink manufacturer. When such a transaction takes place, there are costs involved—whether they be part of an implicit or explicit contractual arrangement. Any organization will try to minimize the costs of its transactions. Decisions as to whether the transaction takes place within the organization (under 'hierarchical governance') or in the market (under 'market governance') will depend on the lowest cost and will determine the boundaries of the firm.

What determines lowest cost? The behavior of individuals has a bearing. Decision makers will have 'bounded rationality', especially in the market-place, and this will increase costs. For transactions taking place within the organization, there may be more control and flexibility with reduced costs.

Similarly, 'opportunism'; e.g. individuals cheating for their own gain, may be lower internally due to control and greater information levels. Where there is 'asset specificity', a strong case will also exist for keeping the activities within internal control, under internal management. Uncertainty of supply and exploitation by a few suppliers can be controlled by backward integration—bringing the transaction within hierarchical governance, that is, 'make' rather than 'buy'. In addition, 'externality' will increase costs, especially in market situations. The distribution of products is a classic example; if a manufacturer sells his products to independent retailers, and the logistics between the two is handled by a third party specialist, the lack of control and distance from the consumer can result in costs greater than mere distributional efficiency.

'Hierarchical decomposition' is critically important, as the optimum structural efficiency of the organization will influence the transaction cost. There is little point in bringing activities in-house, under hierarchical governance, that is 'make', if the firm does not have the structure necessary to support these activities.

The theories of Williamson offer some insights into where organized boundaries are drawn, and why changes in these boundaries may occur due to alterations in demand and transactions costs. Other environmental influences can also change such decisions. The growth of the 'outsourcing' of various non-core activities, such as logistics and distribution, to specialists is a recent example.

According to Williamson, all things being equal, it is more efficient for an organization to use the market to carry out its transactions. Transaction cost is lower because the market offers:

- Scale economies. Specialist suppliers focusing on one activity such as producing plastic bottles.
- Risk pooling. A supplier can spread the risk over many customers.
- Economies of scope. A supplier with many customers can offer variety.

However, these market advantages can disappear for a number of reasons and then it may make sense to bring them in-house; the soft drink manufacturer producing his own bottles, for example.

Transaction cost theory, although it has other applications, is a useful tool in the strategic analysis of firms seeking to become more flexible and responsive. In the past, organizations tended to focus on sets of core activities, described variously as 'core competences' or 'critical success factors', that were the basis of competitive advantage. Other non-core activities were 'outsourced'. A focus upon activities and operations is not of itself sufficient in the new competitive climate; it neglects demand variety and brings about a form of tunnel vision unsuited to new demands.

Theories such as transaction cost ignore one crucial element: cost and cost efficiency may cease to be the sole determinants of success and the prime goal. Performance measures to do with quality, responsiveness and flexibility may become overriding factors. For example, if a firm grows and supplies fresh produce to Marks and Spencer, speed and quality will ostensibly be more important than mere cost factors.

Efficiency as a major performance objective may be important for some firms, e.g. large, vertically and horizontally integrated bureaucracies, having a standardized, high volume product remaining unchanged over a long period of time. However, in the new demand era, there will be very few successful organizations fitting this description. For survival in the new environment, firms will have to adapt rapidly to shifts in technology and become 'first movers' into new markets and products. These will be the new performance measures for the new environment[6]. Efficiency and cost will retain some importance, but not to the exclusion of the real determinants of successful operation.

Some of the theoretical concepts that are being used to describe the new environment and the typical responses of the various players within it have now been described, albeit in rather a perfunctory manner. The remaining part of this chapter will examine one particular type of organization; one that has had no choice but to manage this new milieu.

1.3   NEW RETAILERS

A new environment creates the need for different organizational responses. For many firms operating in this new era, especially manufacturers and service providers, the challenges and problems constantly facing them are a direct result of retailer requirements. The retailer is frequently the most powerful and demanding player in the supply pipeline. Often producers regard these retailer exigencies as being overly stringent and exacting, and a confrontational relationship ensues. For others, the retailer is merely the agent of the consumer and facing the same environmental challenges as the rest, the only difference being that he bears the brunt of these consumer pressures and has to pass on such mandates to the rest of the pipeline[7]. Whatever the viewpoint, the demands are real, and a new breed of retailer has evolved in the face of such challenges.

1.3.1   Evolution of Retailing

In the UK, the Romans introduced the concept of a fixed site shop nearly 2000 years ago; manufacturing and selling in one of a series of places. This proved to be inflexible, however, and by the Middle Ages, craft fairs and markets were the only form of distribution system for merchants who both bought and sold a variety of products.

The industrial revolution of the late 18th and 19th centuries, with its increased urbanization, purchasing power, and transportation, brought about

---

[6] Later chapters will develop the ideas of new performance measurement systems.
[7] The authors tend to agree with this latter interpretation of events. Space will be devoted to this aspect later.

the first milestone in retailing, the widespread separation of retailing as an activity from manufacturing[8]. However, the system relied heavily upon wholesalers. With the development of mass communication, marketing, and cost pressures, manufacturers gradually eroded the wholesalers' position and drove out the 'middleman' in order to establish a loyal following for their brands.

By the turn of the 20th century, multiple retailers, as we now know them, had continued to grow. Indeed, by the 1970s they became the largest industry sector; retail growth and power had exploded. The sector is now well established with a number of large players. Strategically, competition is fierce and many now attempt to differentiate themselves using non-price factors, while at the same time having to compete on price with the so-called 'discounters' or 'warehouse clubs'.

Retailers now comprise some of the world's largest companies. Wal-Mart is a company whose sales and profits have grown at an average rate of 25%/year since 1962 when the first store was opened in Arkansas. At its current annual growth rate of 18%, its sales of some $100 billion are forecast to double by the year 2000. This unsurpassed expansion of retailing is not merely a rise in consumer spending, it is a fundamental change in the way goods and services reach the consumer, for this is at the heart of retailer power[9].

1.3.2   The Power of the Retailer

Retailers derive their dominance from the utilization of a number of crucial weapons, the effects of which have culminated in the manufacturer losing control over the distribution channel[10]. Below are some of the major contributing factors that have led to this retail authority.

The Supply Chain

The retailer faces increasing demands from a well-informed, intelligent and 'smart' shopper. There is, however, a major compensation—he is the interface with that consumer; the voice, the agent and the representative. No longer does a retailer try and sell what is produced. A retailer now has to supply what the customer demands, no matter how bizarre. Micro-merchandising at ever more focused levels is crucial, as is the ability to get close to, and understand, how

---

[8] Interestingly, with the rise of retailers' 'own label' or 'private label' products, they become quasi producers. In contrast, some traditional manufacturers are contemplating a reversion to the retail function. Hence, the growth of factory shops in both Europe and North America.

[9] This size disparity, compared to other organizations in the supply channel, is important and a subject which will be addressed later.

[10] Suppliers now have regard for both the retailer and the end-consumer as the customer. However, the very fact that often a retailer's 'own label' goods will be the manufacturer's largest competitor does cause a certain identity crisis, and will have profound implications for the purists who argue in favor of partnerships and alliances between the two.

the shopper thinks. In management terms, retailers now provide a conduit through which the product stream is pulled.

Increasing Variety—Dressed for the Occasion

Once upon a time a basic salad, certainly in the UK, consisted of lettuce, tomato and salad dressing—usually salad cream or mayonnaise. Now salad is pre-cut, pre-washed and can be bought in bags with a diverse range of salad greens—on the next visit to the supermarket just add-up the salad variety. But, you've got to put something on your salad; dressing. Now we have honey, mustard, blue cheese, Ranch, Italian, Thousand Islands, Paul Newman, Caesar, French, Greek, vinaigrette with olives or oregano, vinaigrette with lemon, parmesan cheese based, with balsamic vinegar, white or red wine vinegar, tomato and bacon, roasted garlic and numerous other combinations based upon different herbs and marinades, fruits, roasted vegetables etc., etc., etc. Multiply this by the other dimensions such as low fat, low sodium and then by the different brand names. This amounts to huge variety and subsequent complexity as all of these products compete for the same, limited, shelf space. 1997 saw the introduction of 247 varieties. So far, this year a further 80 have been added. Sales of pre-prepared commercial dressing have risen from 6.3 million gallons in 1950 to almost 60 million gallons in 1998. Sales in the USA of pre-packed salads in 1993 amounted to $287 million. Last year they had almost quadrupled to over $1 billion.

In addition, the power of the retailer is related to size. Becoming bigger and more efficient allows increasing economies of scale through bulk purchase and the ability to influence choice, and dictate convenience, service, price and quality.

The use of 'own' or 'private label' goods. As price competition intensifies, retailer brands become more important for two reasons. First, they are produced at lower total cost than the manufacturer's equivalent—thus providing a better margin, lower risk and better cash-flow. Second, 'own' label strengthens the retailer's image.

Image has been a fundamental key to the retail success story. Since the early 1980s, differentiation using non-price factors has been the main thrust of a retailing strategy. 'Own' brands are now marketed with a quality emphasis: a covert promise of similar quality to that of leading manufacturing brands, but slightly less expensive. A retailer's strategic positioning rotates around the adoption of an overall image, one that strives to satisfy the consumer by ensuring that all brand characteristics (manufacturers as well as their own) support the overall trading appeal[11].

The next step would seem to be the use of packaging design of 'own' label products to reinforce the communication of a retailer's distinctive brand values. Hence 'own' label products and traditional brands have increasingly used similar packaging designs and are deliberately positioned next to each other[12]. In many cases, retailers welcome the brand name; designer clothes is a example, but best selling lines are often replicated by 'own' label when they are established.

'Private' or 'own' label is a growth area that some analysts believe will amount to 30% of retail sales by the end of the decade. Not only are food, household and clothing sectors affected; it is conceivable that even more traditional industries may be vulnerable. For example, Europe and the USA are witnessing a growth in 'own' label financial packages (major retailers offering credit cards and bank loans), and an 'own' label car cannot be in the much too distant future.

Information systems technology. The application of Information Systems Technology (IST) to all aspects of store management, logistics and the distribution chain, has, and will continue to have, a profound influence upon retail power.

Sophisticated systems now provide retailers (K-Mart and Wal-Mart were pioneers) with detailed information on what is selling, where, and to whom; even decisions regarding product positioning in store, its shelf height and optimal time of day for display, are made with the input of sales data. Clearly, through greater integration of supply chain systems and increasing use of sales data, the stocking burden is now being pushed further up-stream as the control over the shelf space becomes more rigorous.

There are many examples of this development, and here we will mention only five:

- One of the greatest innovations in retailing sprung from the backwoods of Arkansas, USA, in the early 1970s. It was here that Wal-Mart first began to harness the power of Point of Sale (PoS) information. Now common in all large retailers, the laser scanning and bar-code systems at the till recorded sales and reduced stock holding instantaneously. The Wal-Mart innovation was the integration of these PoS systems with others in the supply pipeline to track stock movements from manufacturer, through distribution warehouses, to store, even to the point of employing satellite

---

[11] This has become known as 'ghost branding'. A manufacturer's brands are chosen and promoted in such a way that supports the retailer's overall image. Retail buyers will often influence packaging design in order that this takes place.
[12] It also serves to induce us into buying the retail equivalent of what we think is a major brand.

technology. These innovations have moved Wal-Mart closer to 'real-time' continuous replenishment than any other retailer. Unique partnerships with suppliers such as Proctor and Gamble have led to the sharing of information, through Electronic Data Interchange (EDI), and joint category management of products. Both firms benefit as activity is tailored to demand[13].

- In the UK, top retailers such as Marks and Spencer, Tesco and J. Sainsbury are also investing huge sums of money in information systems and information technology. The benefits are already apparent, with Tesco for example, able to cut its stock in the distribution chain to just two weeks, with a future objective of continuous flow, driven by powerful modeling and simulation systems. If one adds to this picture the growing amounts of consumer profile data that are collected through the medium of loyalty cards and catalogues, one begins to see the power of information.
- In the clothing industry, firms such as The Limited use IST to link their PoS systems to manufacturers in Hong Kong. Together with the use of air freight and computer-aided design, this has cut the lead time, from fabric and pattern cutting to store, to three weeks. Such developments allow faster adjustments of sizes, colors and patterns in accordance with actual sales levels.
- Levi Strauss are also beginning to harness the power of IST to customize products using a 'personalized pair' approach to women's jeans. This service scans the customer and relays the exact measurements to the manufacturing site. Similar developments are to be found in France and Japan.
- Many retailers are also considering the introduction of 'smart-tags' which will contain all the information about an individual garment; not only the washing instructions, but data regarding where and when made, by which retailer it was sold, and conceivably, who bought it, and where the item was eventually recycled.

Amid all these glowing reports of the power of technology, there is a downside. The rapid growth of cheaper and faster computer hardware[14] has led to a massive 'shake-out' of the manufacturing industry. Retailers are radically pruning their supply sources in order to concentrate on geographic locations using specialist global manufacturers. In addition, there is still major incompatibility between technological approaches, with many retailers and manufacturers having disparate and incompatible systems both internally and externally. To the casual observer this is somewhat surprising given the many

---

[13] These arrangements have not always been entirely conflict free. As will be discussed later, there needs to be much more in place than mere rhetoric as to the sensibility of such partnerships and alliances.

[14] It is estimated that if the automotive industry had developed at the pace of the micro-processor, we would be driving cars capable of travelling at the speed of sound for thousands of miles on a thimble full of fuel; at a cost of around $100.

third party service providers (General Electric et al.), ready and willing to establish the necessary linkages (see Chapter 4).

The importance of data. Competitive advantage does not come from the possession of technology, it is the use to which it is put. The main advantage for retailers of their combined pipeline position, and the application of technology, is their ability to collect and 'mine' more and more information about the customer. The possession of this information is power and is often the reason why it is not readily shared with the suppliers. Today, retailers may not only know what and when goods are selling, but also are getting better and better at profiling to whom.

Database marketing is the next source of conflict between manufacturers and retailers. Customers are no longer segmented into groups, they can be treated as individuals. Huge amounts of information can be accrued about buying habits and lifestyles in order to target each individual or household through the use of schemes such as loyalty cards. But, how much of this information should be shared with the rest of the supply pipeline under the guise of Supply Chain Management and other partnership initiatives?

1.3.3   Retailing Strategy

The face of retailing is changing. New breeds of retailer are relentlessly driving diversity into operating channels. Traditional department stores (Debenhams, John Lewis Group, etc.) are losing ground to the chain stores (Burton Group, Next, J C Penney), while specialist chains (The GAP, River Island and The Limited) are in the ascendancy. Niche retailing (La Senza, Sweater Shop, Mango, et al.) continue to fulfil a need, and boutiques still flourish. Strange mutant retailers are appearing; for example, the growth of designer boutiques on the department store floor, the firms that cross product lines such as Marks and Spencer and Asda, and the manufacturers that now rent retail space to sell their wares[15].

The task of managing the marketing mix has grown considerably over the past decade as retailers constantly seek to create and sustain unique trading images that attract and maintain customers. Competition is no longer between products, but encompasses all elements of this mix, including: product offer and positioning, store location, customer service, quality, retail design and store image, retail promotion, retail advertising, and price points. The successful retailer of the next century will have to adopt core strategies that:

- Build an individual identity for each store product; one that consumers

---

[15] Sam Walton, the founder of Wal-Mart, was the first to suggest this concept. Many manufacturers are viewing this possibility as a way to get closer to the customer and keep the shelves stocked. This type of quasi-retailing lends itself particularly well to those products made in store; bread, for example.

perceive as a brand in its own right. Everything in the store, or connected with the store, has this brand value underlying its philosophy.

- Provide a higher value than any competitor, but at a lower cost.
- Offer unique products and services.
- Supply a unique customer service through convenience and added value.

Many will feel that these goals are too ambitious, yet these strategies will be pursued utilizing all the power at the retailers' disposal. The approach adopted does, however, raise a number of other issues. How will these goals and objectives be attained? Will they be accomplished through co-operation or conflict with suppliers? Will these same suppliers remain free agents with their own brands, or become 'captive' producers of 'own' label goods? Given that excellence today is standard tomorrow, what is the next stage in the retailer evolution path? It is to these questions, and more, that we will provide partial answers during the course of this book.

We wish to outline one more scenario. The retailer is facing unprecedented requests from an increasingly sophisticated consumer for variety, quality, cost and availability. To meet such demands, while striving for a unique image and avoiding the penalties associated with stockouts and excessive markdowns, the retailer must learn to handle diversity in new and innovative ways. How is he going to go about the task?

The first steps are already being taken. Under the label of 'adding value', suppliers are being asked to use EDI for all communications with the retailer. This provides an electronic 'beachhead' from which the retailer can mandate revolutionary strategies such as: individual market differentiation; continuous market-driven stock replenishment; quick and flexible response to orders; vendor managed, and often owned, inventory replenishment up to point-of-sale; pre-ticketing; floor ready drops; advanced ship notices; cross docking and consolidation of distribution programs; in-store style testing and flexible adjustment to response; single unit delivery direct to store; new and faster product development cycle times; electronic markets; and numerous other time and money saving options.

However, there is little unanimity among the major retailers (often the group responsible for this new thinking and large enough to force through the change) about the protocols, procedures, timing and formats needed to compete in this new era. Thus, the manufacturer is faced with having to satisfy diverse product demands, from diverse retailers, with a disparate yet limited range of processes, systems and structures, often designed around the needs of mass production. The new and different retailer mandates are often addressed by suppliers with the same received wisdom and the same rigidity, instead of appreciating that there is now a need to change fundamentally the way organizations operate in favor of flexibility, specialization and diversity.

Retailers recognize the new imperatives of the industry, and they continue to force radical changes along the supply channel, though seemingly with little consistency. The supplier is more than ever asked to assume the management and ownership of what was previously the retailer's inventory. Yet, he often does so with the structures, systems and processes designed for a bygone industrial era. This leads to significant increases in the manufacturer's finished goods stock, penalization for unnecessary mark-downs, as well as punitive action for allowing a retailer to become out-of-stock.

It is doubtful whether many retailers have really thought through the consequences of reducing their inventories to such low levels. At present, customer service levels (if expressed as the percentage of times customers find what they are looking for) are far from satisfactory in many consumer sectors. The thoughtless slashing of inventories, and the pushing of responsibility and cost further up the supply chain, will ultimately have serious consequences for retail performance.

This short-term 'fix', measured by inventory levels, may look attractive to management, financial accountants and shareholders alike. However, longer-term, the effects of such a trade-off in the face of increasingly stringent and diverse consumer demand will have adverse consequences for competitiveness; unless, of course, more intelligent approaches are developed and enacted. Unfortunately, despite having access to real-time data, many retailers have a very limited appreciation of future sales and the correct SKU mixes; evident in the high proportion of stock-outs, despite more than adequate stock levels.

It is these aspects of business that have underscored the need for a complete re-shaping of the supply pipeline. Manufacturers and retailers must make fundamental changes to the way they operate if growth in the consumer sector is to continue. The bottom line is finding a new and revolutionary way of doing things that combines both their abilities—a way that produces a 'paradigm shift'. That way, we strongly believe is through the new strategies, practices and systems we discuss in this book.

1.4   COMMENTS

This chapter has attempted to set a scene. Society, especially consumer society, is radically changing. Change has a habit of encroaching by small degrees. Unnoticeable and incipient, change inexorably broadens the gulf between consumer demand and organizational response. Eventually, a massive strategic difference can ensue between the needs of the consumer and the goods offered by the producer.

The new consumer society, with its new demands, is the tune to which modern retailers now dance as the fundamental rules of competition change. The problem lies, we believe, in the fact that manufacturers or suppliers to these retailers are ill-equipped to even begin to react to these massive and complex changes. Alternative methods of organization and operation are required for both producers and retailers. Figure 1.1 attempts to summarize the

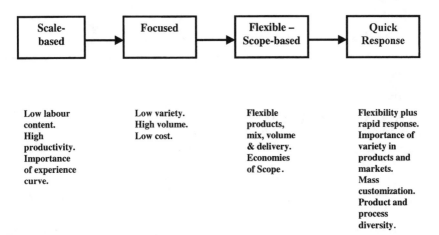

Figure 1.1   Changes in responses to consumers' demands

ground covered in this chapter and the steps that must be taken to reconcile industry and the consumer.

The next chapter begins to explore some of the more practical and pragmatic remedies that have been used to help firms cope with the changes they are witnessing, and will discuss their utility for the future.

2
NEW FORCES

The next two chapters are about new ideas, particularly new ideas in management, organization and business administration. The last 20 years have seen a marked change in approach to the way management strategies are conceived, organizations operate[1] and business cultures are formulated. Many of these changes now recognize that firms do not function in isolation; they are part of, and dependent upon, a larger system. For the purposes of this chapter, such notions will be classified under the heading of Supply Chain Management (SCM).

In Chapter 1 it was observed that retailers have to make radical changes to the way they operate. Similarly, manufacturers have realized that transformations are necessary, but for a number of reasons, they are finding it hard to adapt.

2.1 NEW MANUFACTURERS

Some of the conceptual responses recently developed by manufacturers when faced with growing demand pressure merit examination. Whether or not a crisis is pending, manufacturers and producers have begun to modify their operations at a pragmatic and practical level. The question is whether such approaches provide only a partial answer.

By the turn of the 20th century, manufacturing was characterized by an emphasis on mass-markets, high volume and the use of interchangeable parts. When the principles of scientific management, as promulgated by Frederick Taylor and his disciples, were also adopted, it produced a new era of industrial power that was eagerly exploited by the likes of Henry Ford, Isaac Singer and Andrew Carnegie.

---

[1] In an academic sense, we would have to admit to an error of reification here. Despite its inaccuracy, it is seemingly common to talk of and regard organizations as having an independent ability existing above and beyond the individuals that compose them.

The dogma was clear. For utmost efficiency in any factory: divide work into the smallest possible components; assign the tasks to specialists; appoint managers to supervise and make decisions, leaving workers free to concentrate on manual tasks; reduce variation to a minimum; standardize all inputs and outputs to reduce defects; exercise control through a rigid hierarchy which channels communication in the form of exception reports upward and directives downward; measure performance by cost, scale, experience and length of production run; and employ forecasting systems in order to anticipate any possible changes.

It soon became apparent that organizations operating in this manner were unable to cope with one particular demand: variety. Fundamental and radical new approaches to organization and management of manufacturing were needed once the demand for diversity reached a critical level.

2.1.1   Flexible Production Systems

Before discussing flexibility, an understanding of its forerunner, the focused factory, is required. Wickham Skinner (1974) proposed the idea that manufacturers have to learn to focus their plants (or even departments within plants) on a limited range of technologies, volumes, markets and products, and that strategies, tactics and services should all be arranged to support that focus. The maxim was that a factory that succeeds in focusing its activities will outperform one that does not. Costs would be lower than in unfocused operations due to experience curve and scale benefits, consequently focus provides competitive advantage.

There are, however, always trade-offs with such an approach; for example, low cost and flexibility are inappropriate bed-fellows. If the market demands greater variety and diversification, the focused factory comes under considerable strain, often alleviated only at the expense of high inventory levels.

This is when flexibility becomes important. Flexible manufacturing describes the idea of combining general purpose capital equipment and skilled, adaptable workers to produce a wide and changing range of semi-customized goods—matching the variety of goods produced to the variety in demand.

Flexible manufacturing reverses the principles of mass production. Its many components include: customization of products, creation of additional product features, rapid development times, short throughput times and frequent delivery of small batches. In short, flexibility of:

- Products
- Product volumes
- Product mix
- Product delivery schedules.

The objective is flexibility and market responsiveness; being able to tailor activity to sales trends and develop new market niches by adapting products to customer needs.

To return to the possible 'crisis in demand' discussed in Chapter 1, the supporters of flexible manufacturing would argue that existing systems of production are under considerable strain through their inherent rigidity in the face of increasingly complex, changing and uncertain markets. Rapidly changing customer requirements and increased competition are thus forcing many organizations to be more market and customer oriented.

Flexibility revolves around having the ability to identify market trends before competitors, producing a variety of different products on the same line, switching between lines rapidly at lowest cost, concentrating on short runs, and developing new and modified products faster than the rest of the industry. In short, synchronization of production in proportion to demand.

Flexibility and Response—South Australia State Cricket Club

Traditionally the game of cricket was divided into specialities. None more so than bowling, with specialist fast, medium and slow bowlers. Colin Miller from South Australia was the top wicket taker in the 1998 Sheffield Shield season. He bowls a mixture of medium paced 'seamers' and slow 'offspin'. The batsman has great difficulty in detecting each delivery as it is often produced with the same run-up. As he pointed out when asked why he has been so successful: 'it's a flexible response to each situation—every ball is different to meet the demands'.

Perhaps one of the most celebrated examples of flexible manufacturing and the ability to manage change is that of Benetton, the highly successful Italian clothing company. Benetton operates in an information-rich environment, utilizing data from both up- and down-stream sectors of the supply pipeline. The rapid and flexible operations it performs are triggered as a direct result of consumer demand and market preference, and are reflected in the use of PoS data and the use of such technologies as garment dyeing that allow greige garment production with dyeing reserved for the last minute. The structure of the company, with its network of small subcontractors and franchised retail outlets, provides an integrated and flexible system capable of responding rapidly[2] to fashion demand through flexibility of volume and product mix.

---

[2] Benetton is famed for its ability to gear its production to changing style demands from different subcultures and age groups. Its integrated system of flexible production is reputedly capable of response to new market demands within 10 days.

It should, however, be noted that, despite Benetton's use of flexible production methods and undoubted adaptation toward greater differentiation and individualization in products and markets, they still follow many Fordist principles[3].

Flexibility in manufacturing, whether it be called 'flexible production', 'flexible manufacturing' or 'flexible specialization', is an essential element for an optimal response to retailer and consumer. The philosophy underpinning flexibility is that an organization, no matter what it produces or creates (whether tangible products or services), must weld all its activities[4] to three fundamental environmental forces or 'drivers':

- the demand of the market and consumer
- the volume and rate of consumer and market demand
- the variety of that demand.

All forms of organizational activity must be linked to demand patterns, both in terms of products and product volume as well as mix. The first driver listed is common sense: the firm must only make products that are in demand. The second dictates that a company should not make more products than are demanded. The third requires that the variety of products and rate manufactured should match the variety and rate required.

An example may help. If a firm produces only cans or tins of baked beans in mustard sauce when the market wants baked beans in rich tomato sauce, then it is in trouble. Once it begins providing cans of beans in rich tomato sauce, it should only do so at the rate of demand, it should only produce every day or every week the volume that is actually selling. If, however, it also makes cans of artichoke hearts in Aioli sauce (that sell at the rate of a case a month) as well as beans in rich tomato sauce (that sell at the rate of many cases a day), then that is exactly the frequency at which it must arrange for delivery of raw materials and manufacture them; the variety of demand matches the variety of activity throughout the whole organization.

These simple notions have been welcomed by many management writers who have re-packaged them using impressive oxymorons such as 'uniform variety', 'repetitive flexible supply' and 'rigid flexibility'[5].

---

[3] The Benetton operation closely resembles what has been described as the 'world car model' (designed locally and procured globally to utilize low labor costs).

[4] This applies not just to manufacturing but to every company activity. For example, The Kao Corporation, Japan's biggest soap and cosmetics company, boasts an ability to deliver goods within 24 hours to any of 280 000 shops, whose average order is just seven items. Its information networks track every product and, following a new launch, they target who is buying and its likelihood of success. Kao declares an ability to virtually eliminate the lag between buying a bar of soap and the arrival of the news at company HQ.

[5] Such seemingly paradoxical approaches usually combine the application of simplicity and discipline in factory practices so as to attain flexibility. Responsiveness and constant market adaptation are achieved via a clinical 'establishment of simple, spartan and foolproof operating environments in which manufacturing procedures are carried out in a disciplined and dedicated fashion'. Seemingly there is little room for the messy business of creativity and innovation in this well-oiled machine! For further details on this see Collins and Schmenner (1993).

The use of flexibility in operations will be covered in more depth later. At this point, it is necessary to briefly cover one or two other manufacturing or production concepts that, many argue, are really euphemisms for the same basic group of theories.

2.1.2   Alternative Manufacturing Approaches

As with the theory of flexibility, most of these are noteworthy and of importance but, as we shall see later, they are insufficient on their own to cope with the complex and dynamic forces we are beginning to witness. A more robust and holistic strategy is fundamental to any organization's continued survival.

World-class Manufacturing

> World-class manufacturing symbolizes the level of manufacturing performance which is exhibited by the top manufacturers in the world. (Giffi et al., 1990)

This rather tautological definition is deliberately chosen to show that, despite the popularity of world-class manufacturing in the literature, there is much argument as to its exact meaning. Further, there is some doubt as to its efficacy for the very reason that its successful proponents are loath to reveal their true standards and then provide benchmarks for their competitors.

Nevertheless, there is substantial support for the concept. Hayes et al. (1988) identified its key attributes as being:

- becoming the best competitor
- growing more rapidly and being more profitable than competitors
- hiring and retaining the best people
- developing top-notch engineering staff
- being able to respond quickly and decisively to changing market conditions
- adopting a product and process engineering approach which maximizes the
- performance of both
- continually improving—kaizen.

There is little new in these components. Perhaps the only elements missing are the notions of total quality management (which include elimination of waste, excess and unevenness); Just-in-Time (JIT) manufacturing; and people involvement and empowerment. Hayes (1981) neatly epitomized the approach of 'world-class manufacturing' when he declared that:

> Japanese success came about by doing simple things well and continually improving their productivity.

Lean Production

The concepts and principles of 'lean production' were first widely introduced by Womack et al. (1990). Drawing upon the experience of Japanese production systems (Toyota mainly), and world-wide research into the motor industry, the authors promoted the principles of 'lean production', as an element of fast and flexible response, which they claimed leads to efficiency with half the resources.

Lean production uses:

> less of everything ... half the human effort in the factory, half the factory space, half the investment in tools, half the engineering hours to develop a new product in half the time. Also, it requires keeping far less than half the needed inventory on-site, resulting in fewer defects ... (op. cit.)

Indeed, the authors affirm that such principles:

> can also be applied equally in every industry across the globe (op. cit.)

as long as companies adopt the necessary structures and practices to promote diffusion.

'Lean production' soon developed into 'lean purchasing', 'lean supply' and the 'lean enterprise'. The transferability of key 'lean principles', both geographically and between industry sectors, is promoted with much zeal. More recently, 'lean techniques', 'lean thinking' and the steps toward 'lean organization' have been added in a veritable 'bulimic' binge of Japanese management techniques[6] and organization methods.

There is much criticism of such 'best practice' models. In particular, they revolve around an assumption of implicit simplicity in transferring stereotypical ideas of homogeneous, static systems from one organization or industry to another. Complexity and dynamism are often conveniently side-stepped as the proponents apply their techniques in established industries exhibiting relatively stable demand patterns. In practice, we believe that very few industries will display these characteristics in the future; the majority will be attempting to cope with multiple differentiation through rapidly changing value chain configurations.

Agile Manufacturing

Agile manufacturing contradicts many of the fundamental principles of the 'Japanese' approach. Its proponents believe that systems such as lean

---

[6] What are now known loosely as 'Japanese management techniques' were developed by the Toyota Motor Company as far back as the late 1930s. Those interested should read *Toyota Production System: Aiming at an Off-Scale Management* by Taiichi Ohno (1978). The system is described as being born out of the need to manufacture automobiles of many different kinds in small volumes with the same process.

production are no longer able to cope with the new competitive environment we have already described; indeed, they cite the current (1998/99) difficulties being experienced by the Asian manufacturers as support for this contention.

The Japanese management techniques developed out of an inability of the mass production system to cope with increasing variety. However, consumer demand has evolved even further—from a wide range of standardized products to custom-made goods and services. It is this unpredictability that is causing a complete re-adjustment of the contemporary manufacturing approach.

The agile manufacturer aims to produce highly customized products at a cost comparable with mass production and within short lead-times. The tailoring of products to demand includes a higher element of service and thus, greater added value. A flexible workforce, structure and production technologies (especially through the use of computer-integrated manufacturing) are all contained within a learning culture. While externally, the concepts of vertical integration and long-term partnerships are replaced with short-term, flexible contracts and horizontal outsourcing that allow rapid response through an expansive system of communication networks.

Agile Manufacturing has gained much popularity in North America and is widely promoted by bodies such as the Textile/Clothing Technology Corporation[7], [TC][2], as an answer to increased consumer demand for uniqueness and customization. Agility in this context is described by Fralix and Off (1994) as:

> being able to make information driven decisions at the last possible moment in time, prior to the need to execute the decisions by a flexible and empowered workforce.

The idea of agile manufacturing as a production, management and engineering philosophy was widely introduced as a direct consequence of an industry-led consortium chartered by the US Secretary of Defense MANTECH Program Office and facilitated by the Iacocca Institute at Lehigh University. This initiative included many Fortune 500 companies such as AT&T, Boeing, Air Products, Chrysler, FMC, GE, IBM, Motorola, Texas Instruments, TRW and Westinghouse. Further details of this work can be found in Nagel and Dove (1991a,b)[8].

Agile manufacturing was developed for specific application in the apparel industry at a time when manufacturing was a lengthy cycle, often in excess of 12 months, and retailers bought well in advance for lengthy selling seasons in which consumer choice was limited to what was available.

---

[7] [TC][2] was created in 1981 to conduct long-term research and development for the automation of apparel manufacturing. It is a non-profit collaboration of fiber, apparel and sewn-product industries, as well as retailers, labor unions, government and academic institutions.
[8] Additional information concerning the application of agile manufacturing is also available in Hamel and Prahalad (1990) and Goldman and Nagel (1993).

[TC]² has a technology 'teaching factory' in Cary, North Carolina, USA and has achieved remarkable success in developing a flexible and agile production system using some of the latest technological advances in the textile/clothing industry. It has state-of-the-art, integrated equipment, which ranges from Computer-Aided Design (CAD), Computer Numerically Controlled (CNC) laser cutters, and modular/team manufacturing facilities. It regularly produces batches of garments (e.g. slacks and T-shirts) which are shipped to a major department store.

It is undeniable that these advances are crucial to the manufacturer of the 21st century; nevertheless, as we will explore in future chapters, there are still a large number of vital ingredients missing.

Virtual Organization

The 'virtual organization' or 'virtual factory' deserves a brief comment for completeness as it is a direct development of the ideas discussed above. Since 1984, Insead in France have carried out a bi-yearly survey of European manufacturing and practice. De Meyer (1992) reported that many manufacturers implementing various Japanese and 'lean' techniques had discovered that improvement on the factory floor had not been translated into increased profits and competitiveness. The firms taking part in the survey indicated an increased dependence upon their supply pipelines as relationships and dependencies were being formed externally. In what many may regard as a large leap of faith, the compilers of the report suggested that this was a trend toward the 'virtual factory'. A factory where networks of outside resources are mobilized and con-figured for a particular task and then disbanded or re-configured. The concept was also applied to logistics, process engineering, suppliers, marketing, sales, and it seems that even customers can become virtual!

Certainly, during the late 1980s, there was a growing trend toward forms of 'outsourcing', as firms shed employees and functions; many firms becoming less vertically integrated and more specialized; actively focusing upon core skills or competences while externally 'outsourcing' anything that does not add-value. As Quinn et al. (1990) describe:

> a concentration on identifying those few core service activities where the company has—or can develop—unique capabilities. Then aggressively seeking ways to eliminate, limit, or outsource activities where the company cannot attain superiority, unless those activities are essential to its chosen areas of strategic focus.

The key is to identify which activities are core and which can be sourced externally to the experts while at the same time retaining a degree of control. Today the most common examples include the devolution of responsibility to 'partners' for the provision of warehousing, transportation and information technology services. In the future, the proponents of the 'virtual organization' believe it will be possible to combine organizational modules as and when needed only to discard them when demand changes.

The theoretical approaches of 'outsourcing' and the 'virtual organization' can be attractive. However, the practical and pragmatic difficulties of co-ordination of such unstable entities, as well as loss of control of a potentially important function to a third party, are serious concerns.

Time-based Competition

Kenichi Ohmae (1982) described the aggressive product development strategy of Casio in watches and pocket calculators. It aimed to turn customers' desires rapidly into new product designs that would bring about faster obsolescence, even of its own products.

Since that time, management literature has continued to abound with exhortations regarding the use of time as a competitive weapon. Many proposed that time-based competition was one of the major factors in the success of Japanese industries; it was an extension of Just-in-Time (JIT in manufacturing to the whole 'value chain' or supply channel; Abbeglen and Stalk, 1985).

Many firms now base their strategies on rapid response, including such Japanese corporations as Sony, Matsushita, Sharp, Toyota, Hitachi and Toshiba; Western exponents such as Benetton, The Limited, Federal Express, Domino's Pizza and McDonald's are also practitioners. In the service industry, particularly the financial sector, speed is becoming of fundamental importance. Loans and mortgages applications are processed in minutes rather than weeks. Mail order companies such as Lands' End and LL Bean offer 24-hour delivery, when not long ago the plea to allow 4–6 weeks for delivery was commonplace.

Time-based strategies are seen as one way to cope with the increasing demand for variety. The *Wall Street Journal* comments:

> Quality in US industry may be up and costs down, but American companies like Xerox are getting sideswiped by foreign competitors who get new and improved products to market faster. The edge those competitors get from shorter development cycles is dramatic: not only can they charge a premium price for their exclusive products but also they can incorporate more up-to-date technology in their goods and respond faster to emerging market niches and changes in taste.[9]

The use of time as a strategy involves more than just speed of response. It is concerned with reducing delays throughout all business cycles, reducing reliance on long lead-times and, most importantly, the need to produce to forecast. In addition to rapid response, time-based competition requires expanded variety, flexible manufacturing and increased innovation. Stalk and Hout

---

[9] 'Speeding Up: Manufacturers Strive to Slice Time to Develop Products' (23.2.88), *Wall Street Journal*.

(1990) suggest that any strategy involving time as a crucial element should seek to reduce its influence in all areas of operations, such as: time-based manufacturing (shorter and more frequent production runs, increasing product mix and customer response while reducing scheduling complexity); time-based sales and distribution (cutting delays in sales and distribution and speeding information flow in order not to dissipate gains made in production); and time-based innovation (reducing time in new and improved product development cycles).

The reckless pursuit of time reduction can, however, pose threats. The Japanese experience is again enlightening. Here, time contraction exercises and initiatives in many organizations have become a treadmill in search of an ever-faster response for its own sake—ignoring the lessons that activity must be linked to demand. Increasing effort, commitment and resources are often used in producing an ever increasing variety of products in a self-destructive competitive race; products that may not be wanted in the first place. In Tokyo, and probably many other major cities, for example, it is possible to buy 250 varieties of 'walkman' type products, 55 varieties of coffee makers, 127 types of personal computers and refrigerators in 24 different colors. The variety is staggering, but as Stalk and Webber (1993) recently commented:

> hardly anyone is making any money.

This time-strategy can often miss that all-important link to the customer: connecting activity to demand in regard to both the volume of products, and also the type.

The real value of competing, using time, is the creation of a close interface with the customer. Merely introducing an infinite variety of products can turn the brand into a commodity and miss what is the real purpose of time as a strategy: creating value for the consumer and eroding the boundaries between the organization and its environment.

The various manufacturing approaches discussed thus far have contributed much to discipline and, at the very least, ensured that the function is viewed as a weapon of positive competitive advantage rather than an unnecessary evil. However, in isolation, these concepts are insufficient to meet increasing consumer demand. As noted, an external holistic viewpoint is needed, and this is why attention has begun to shift toward a wider view of the organization and, in particular, its links with others in its environment.

2.2   THE RISE OF SUPPLY CHAIN MANAGEMENT

Since the early 1950s, the 'systems approach' has assumed increasing importance in various scientific disciplines. Bertalanffy (1950, 1956), one of the earliest contributors, revealed the importance of the notion of a system being open or closed to the influences of its environment. Since then, much has been

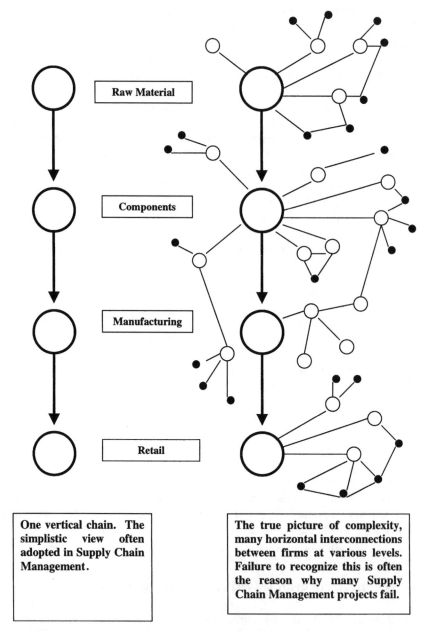

One vertical chain. The simplistic view often adopted in Supply Chain Management.

The true picture of complexity, many horizontal interconnections between firms at various levels. Failure to recognize this is often the reason why many Supply Chain Management projects fail.

Figure 2.1   The supply pipeline: Horizontal and vertical connections

written on the subject; though there has also been some criticism. Today, these ideas pervade many subjects, not the least management, with the use of terms such as 'synergy', 'emergent property', 'holism' and 'gestalt theory' [10]. The importance of these developments is the fact that most managers and students of management recognize an organization does not exist in a vacuum; its success or failure is very much dependent upon other bodies and individuals in its environment.

From these systemic concepts came the understanding that an organization performs as part of a wider group or supply chain (also referred to as a channel or pipeline). Such a chain is only as strong as its weakest link, although it has to be said that the earlier proponents limited the theory to one vertical chain of organizations without any particular horizontal connections. Figure 2.1 contrasts these approaches in diagrammatic form.

Supply Chain Management describes the management of the entire chain of activity from raw material supply to final consumer in order to minimize the time taken to perform each activity, eliminate waste and offer an optimal response by maximizing value. An organization does more than merely manage its own supply part of the chain, the process should involve suppliers, customers and consumers as well as ancillary organizations. Further, Supply Chain Management is not merely concerned with logistics. Information provision, materials, relationships, strategies and cultures are all crucial elements. The complexities of many such chains are immense. Like the firing of neurons in different directions along different routes of a network of synapses, communication, goods, services and other activities are constantly being generated. In fact, the use of the word 'chain' is misleading; many companies form part of many pipelines from mother earth to consumer. Different parts of the same organization can become elements of different systems and membership of any one pipeline is a temporal and a fluid activity.

At this point it is instructive to consider the evolution of the supply system as portrayed in Figure 2.2. The first stage, (a), depicts the industry situation at the turn of the century. Here the participants considered themselves as separate and autonomous industries with no influence, reliance or interconnection with each other. For example, textile manufacturers made yarn and fabric products for the dry goods store. Women bought the fabric and produced their own clothes. The second stage, (b), shows the effect of 'off-the-peg' clothes and the rise of the department store. Interdependence is now recognized and the supply chain is born. But, industries remain manufacturing- and product-driven. In (c) we see the current situation (theoretically); with Electronic Data Interchange (EDI) beginning to form an interface between industries in a pipeline responding to consumer pull. Upon reaching (d), we have a future vision. The

---

[10] The debate between the reductionist application of many physical sciences and a more systemic approach has raged in the social and natural sciences for many years.

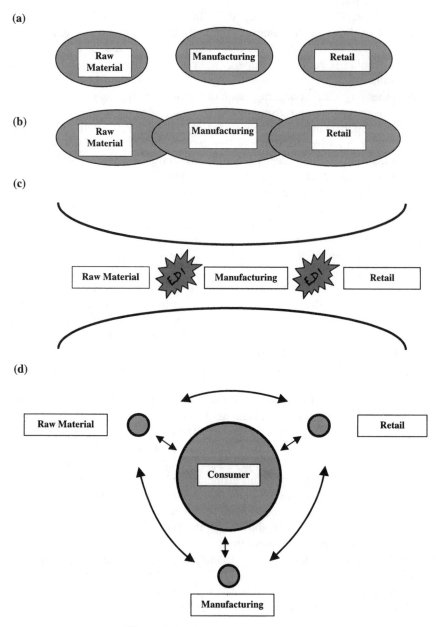

Figure 2.2   Supply system evolution

consumer is dictating and driving all activity, and all entities are responding. Consumer groups are constantly changing over time and organizations are involved in many different simultaneous supply systems at any given point. Further, these types of interactions are necessary for the implementation of 'mass customization', a topic to be introduced in Chapter 3.

The exact origin of the term 'Supply Chain Management' (SCM) is unclear, although during the late 1970s and early 1980s, the notion of integrating functional areas within a firm to obtain synergy became popular. One of the earliest influences upon this school of thought was Michael Porter (1985), who described an organization's 'value chain' as being embedded within a 'value system' comprising suppliers and buyers. The linkages within this chain or system provided the building blocks of competitive advantage.

The term 'value-added chain' comes from the field of microeconomics, where it is used to describe the various steps a good or service goes through from raw material to final consumption. Economists conceived these transactions as being either arm's-length relationships, or hierarchies of common ownership. Conversely, supply chain management involves partnerships that are developed between organizations performing adjacent steps in the chain. The supply chain is viewed as a whole rather than a set of fragmented parts in order that activities, the basic units of competitive advantage, can be configured, confined and performed in different ways to rival chains (Porter, 1996).

At this point we should digress to include logistics in our discussion of SCM. In the field of logistics, many of the tenets of Supply Chain Management have been practiced since the early 1960s. Drucker (1962) wrote:

> Physical distribution is today's frontier in business. It is one area where managerial results of great magnitude can be achieved and is largely unexplored territory.

This view of distribution had, in fact, been identified by Borsodi (1927) some 40 years earlier:

> ... in the 50 years between 1870 and 1920 the cost of distributing necessities and luxuries has nearly trebled, while production costs have gone down by one-fifth ... what we are saving in production we are losing in distribution.

And in 1988, Johnson and Lawrence suggested that advantages could be gained by:

> a set of independent companies that work closely together to manage the flow of goods and services along the entire value-added chain ... we term such arrangements 'Value-Adding Partnerships' (VAPs).

The early meaning of logistics was simple—it referred to the cost of having things where you want them to go, with the major components being transportation and warehousing. Later, it was realized that the term should include both the suppliers' costs, or inbound logistics, as well as the costs of storing and moving goods within the company; the internal logistics.

Thus, the Total Logistics Cost (TLC) could be equated to the sum of the following:

- Transportation costs—incoming, within the company, and out going.
- Facilities costs—warehousing, DCs, and handling equipment.
- Communications costs—order processing, invoicing, information systems.
- Inventory costs.
- Material handling costs.
- Packaging costs.
- Management costs.

In this regard, the US Council of Logistics' definition is admirable:

> the process of planning, implementing, and controlling the efficient flow and storage of goods, services, and related information from point of origin to point of consumption for the purposes of conforming to customer requirements.

We maintain, however, that even the most sophisticated view of logistics does not make it anything but a sub-set of SCM, which is a more holistic concept. SCM involves not only the cost elements of logistics, together with its value-adding aspects, but also the intangibles of a complete system—the human, or partnership, sides of the business.

With SCM, the era of 'chain reaction' and 'consumer pull' was born. This spawned a cascade of terms and theories with grand sounding names, including: 'information partnerships', 'relationship marketing', 'extensive vertical integration models', 'sourcing systems and networks', 'customer–supplier relationship tools' and 'symbiotic and competitive co-operation'. Others are discussed below.

Nor was the public sector immune: 'inter-organizational networks' or 'clusters' of voluntary organizations and government agencies were suddenly discovered to be pooling resources and collaborating for the good of their clients.

Today, Supply Chain Management and logistics are seen as a strategic capability encompassing all organizational activities. In many organizations they are accorded a degree of planning and co-ordination necessary to ensure added-value, reduced cost and the requisite customer service levels. Recently the emphases have turned toward: speed and shortening product life-cycles; strategic information flows; customer partnerships and relationships; cross-functionality; flow-through distribution; and business processes rather than functions. Indeed, the province of supply chain management is now widely recognized as overlaid and spanning all other functional hierarchies within the organization (see Figure 2.3).

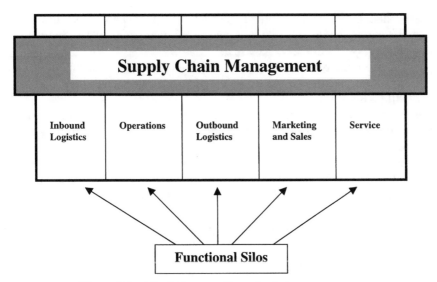

Figure 2.3   The influence of supply chain management

As noted, the term Supply Chain Management is synonymous with a mixed bag of concepts, theories, terms and tools that apply to more than one industry. The overall proposition is quite simple, however; it has been made unnecessarily complex by various diverse and disparate 'movements' and 'schools of thought' within different industries.

SCM covers a number of activities (some of which are more value-adding than others), having numerous interconnecting branches and distinct staging posts (the analogy of a subway or underground system is useful). However, it appears that the myriad of terms encountered in the literature in fact equate to a short list of common sense axioms:

- An organization is an open system, existing in a wider environment and influenced by it.
- Organizations, as systems themselves, have inputs that they transform into outputs using a variety of energy sources.
- For their inputs and energy sources, they nearly always rely upon other organizations[11], likewise for the sale or transfer of their outputs.
- These other organizations, upon which they are reliant, are part of a wider supply chain, channel or pipeline.

---

[11] As Michael Porter expounded, we prefer to think of value systems and supply chains as not merely suppliers and customers. An organization's supply channel can be made up of firms and institutions from other sectors; for example, banks supplying financial services, governments providing incentives, other manufacturers with whom an organization shares capacity or 'outsources' in a horizontal manner, etc. A good example of this wider thinking is the Japanese Kyoryoku kai (co-operative circles) or keiretsu (a system of interlocking companies in different industrial sectors whose relationships are often cemented by equity holding).

- Products, services and value-added activities form part of the currency of this supply chain and they are constantly generated, traded, bought and sold.
- The more the parties in a supply pipeline align their focus upon the end-consumer and the necessary value-adding services, the more profitable will be the venture.
- A common agreement is needed between the members of a supply channel, as to exactly what does and does not add value, and how this is to be measured.
- Effective and open communication is essential.
- Unlimited flows of data and information are necessary, travelling both forwards and backwards, to which each organization has unrestricted access.
- If the parties in any particular supply chain recognize their joint dependence in what is a symbiotic relationship, it is a first step to improving the performance of the total entity. Should they then form closer working partnerships as a result, so much the better.
- A commitment to continually improve the whole pipeline activity is mandatory.

2.3   THE WIDER THEORY OF SUPPLY CHAIN MANAGEMENT

There is a large and growing literature surrounding the best way to organize or manage, and an even more dazzling array of terms used to describe what is Supply Chain Management, or at least a sub-set of it. For example, a cursory scan of the library shelves reveals:

- 'Value-adding Partnerships'
- 'Strategic Alliances'
- 'Inter-organizational Networks'
- 'Inter-organizational Systems'
- 'Trans-organizational Strategic Alliances'
- 'Inter-organizational Strategic Alliances'
- 'Supplier–Retailer Collaboration' (SRC)
- 'Lean supply'
- 'Partnership sourcing'
- 'Pro-active and Strategic Purchasing'
- 'Supplier–Customer Relationship'
- 'Time-based Distribution'
- 'Co-makership'
- 'Demand Activated Manufacturing Architecture' (DAMA).

Plus, the term 'supply chain' is often replaced by 'supply channel', 'supply pipeline' or 'value stream', to say nothing of logisticians who prefer their own vocabulary. The flow of jargon from various 'schools' is unremitting, with many new phrases which are often no more than a re-packaging of old themes. Emphases vary from physical product flow, through supply chain feedback loops, and the supply chain as an 'extended enterprise'. The rapidity of change in these management practices is astounding—what used to take a generation, now arrives in no time, and there is even a new discipline and field of study in the 'management of change'. Yet, within all these different approaches, each striving to prove 'dantotsu' (the best of best practices), there has been, we contend, little meaningful progress over the last 10 years[12].

2.4 INDUSTRY INITIATIVES

In addition to the general terms in common usage, many industries have developed their own language. It is now necessary to consider three of these contributions to the discipline without attempting to offer a comprehensive review.

2.4.1 Food and Groceries

In North America and Europe, the power of the retailer has led to many new initiatives in Supply Chain Management, none more so than in the grocery industry. Here, supply chains are being transformed by quantum leaps in technology, rapidly changing consumer demand and the need to take a global viewpoint. Taiichi Ohno (1978) of Toyota credited the supermarket organization as an inspiration in his development of the Toyota Production System, later known as the Just-in-Time system:

> In 1956, I toured US production plants at General Motors, Ford, and other machinery companies. But my strongest impression was the extent of the supermarket's prevalence in America. For this reason, by the late 1950s, at Toyota's machine shop that I managed, we were already studying the US supermarket and applying its methods to our work.[13]

The early 1980s began with many autonomous retailer initiatives. Independently they began to seek out what was called a 'preferred supply base' with which they could build supply chain programs. Under the heading of

---

[12] Thomas Kuhn (1962) in a seminal work, described this as 'normal science', that being, tinkering or incremental experiments within a known past scientific achievement. It is only when gestalt or major change comes along that whole scientific direction alters: a paradigm shift.

[13] Interestingly, with the Japanese stock market and the yen currently (1999) at their lowest point in years, consumer prices are falling all over the country. This has brought an influx of warehouse type cost cutting stores and American retailers such as The GAP, LL Bean and Toys 'Я' Us.

partnerships, retailers undertook propaganda initiatives in an effort to persuade their larger suppliers to adopt new methods of operation. Electronic Data Interchange (EDI) was in vogue and the new 'preferred suppliers' were encouraged to introduce compatible EDI systems and bar-coded product identification in order to handle transactions with ease and speed. However, the development was piecemeal, with different retailers having differing approaches (and often systems). It was at this point that retailers began to develop more strenuous and robust frameworks by which to measure their suppliers' performance, beyond merely delivery and quality.

This period saw a huge expansion and investment in information technology in order to reduce cost of transaction handling, enhance stock control, give greater cross-functional retailer/supplier communication, and, disappointingly in our view, build even more sophisticated sales forecasting systems. Despite these major improvements, manufacturers continued to harbor suspicions as to the motives behind many of these moves. Were such programs a covert and deliberate plan for retailers to pass on more and more of the cost of operation? Was this a way to reduce the power of manufacturer brands in favor of 'own' label goods? Would all this promised new data and information be freely available? And, most importantly, who would be sharing the promised benefits accruing from these new methods of operation—how would the savings achieved be shared with suppliers?

The vision driving these moves was a seamless interface from consumer purchase to manufacturing schedules. This is still a distant vision for many. In Chapter 4, we will explain why, we believe, the dream of a decade ago has not been fully accomplished.

Change in the UK Food Industry

The UK grocery industry is worth about £25 billion. The supply pipeline holds about one week's excess stock—this represents approximately 230 million pounds that QR and ECR could liberate. Total stocks in the system total about three weeks. Saving two weeks would free-up about £460 million. For every £100 million of manufacturers' sales turnover this might mean about £3 million liberated and perhaps £1 million possible profit. This might explain why the country is littered with an ever growing number of gleaming vast warehouses storing merchandise waiting hopefully on consumers' choice and the right weather. One day, soon, we might have to make them all redundant and return to direct store delivery for many more products, bypassing the DCs—that will shake everyone up!

CEO, Reckitt & Colman plc, UK

More recent developments in the food industry have been on a larger and more intensive scale. As industry growth slowed during the late 1980s and early 1990s, and margins were squeezed as prices were reduced to compete with discount stores, relationships between trading partners began to take on a more adversarial nature; both sides seeking to secure market share at the expense of the other (a 'zero-sum game'). Eventually, following the prompting of Kurt Salmon Associates, 1992 saw the establishment of a joint industry (retail and manufacturing) task force or working group called Efficient Consumer Response (ECR). The aim was to analyze the grocery supply chain and identify potential opportunities for enhanced operation. ECR was defined as:

> ... a responsive, customer-driven system in which distributors and suppliers work together as business allies to maximize consumer satisfaction and minimize cost.[14]

It was estimated that applying ECR concepts could save US $30 billion on 41% less inventory. Table 2.1 outlines its core strategies and objectives and Figure 2.4 its major processes spanning pipeline players (Kurt Salmon Associates, 1993). The processes were allied to two important aspects of the

Table 2.1   ECR strategies and objectives

ECR strategies	ECR objectives
Efficient store assortments	Optimize the productivity of inventories and store space Increased sales and gross margin per square foot, increased inventory turns
Efficient replenishment	Optimize time and cost in the replenishment system. Automated retail and warehouse ordering, flow-through logistics, reduced damages, reduced supplier and distributor wholesale inventories
Efficient promotion	Maximize the total system efficiency of trade and consumer promotion. Warehouse, transportation, administrative and manufacturing efficiencies; reduced forward-buy (investment buy), supplier inventories, and warehousing expense
Efficient product introductions	Maximize the effectiveness of new product development and introduction activities. Fewer unsuccessful introductions and better value products

[14] The similarities to Quick Response and Supply Chain Management are immediately apparent and, as will be discussed shortly, the whole initiative resembles a similar textile/apparel project undertaken a decade ago in the USA.

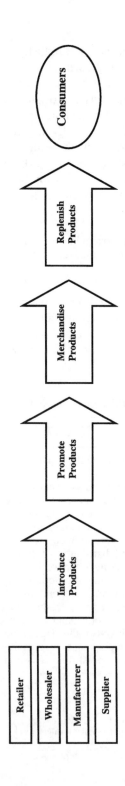

Figure 2.4 ECR processes

grocery business: category management (a holistic view of a total category or consumer/customer group) and the use of PoS data.

The guiding principles of ECR include:

- Constant focus on providing better value.
- Driven by committed business leaders—committed to achieving 'win/win' alliances.
- Provision of accurate and timely information.
- Maximization of value-adding processes throughout the whole supply chain.
- A common and consistent performance measurement that focuses on the effectiveness of the total system.

Figure 2.5 demonstrates the ECR improvement concepts as outlined in The Official European ECR Scorecard (1997). This shows the importance of the linkage between demand management and supply management that is enabled by enabling technologies.

It was initially envisaged as having two phases:

- Phase I—Implementation of Best Practices (achievable in 0–2 years).
- Phase II—Full ECR Implementation (achievable in 2–4 years).

ECR committees, conferences and surveys continue to date with the latest focus being tailored ECR; there is even a new acronym, ACR (Automated Consumer Response)[15], and a slightly clearer direction:

- Linking through alliances and information technology.
- Optimal sourcing strategies (not just lowest cost).
- Cutting cycle times in replenishment and product development.
- Improving distribution systems.
- Building new, integrated information architectures for merchandising, micro-merchandising and forecasting.
- Category management.
- Better targeting of consumer needs.
- New performance measurement systems.

However, despite these laudable intentions, the ultimate objective of a consumer driven supply system with total retailer/supplier collaboration over availability, information sharing, least cost, maximum product innovation, and shared profits, be it the grocery or any other industry, is still rather distant.

---

[15] *Vision for the Millennium … Evolving to Consumer Response*, KSA Report, 1996.

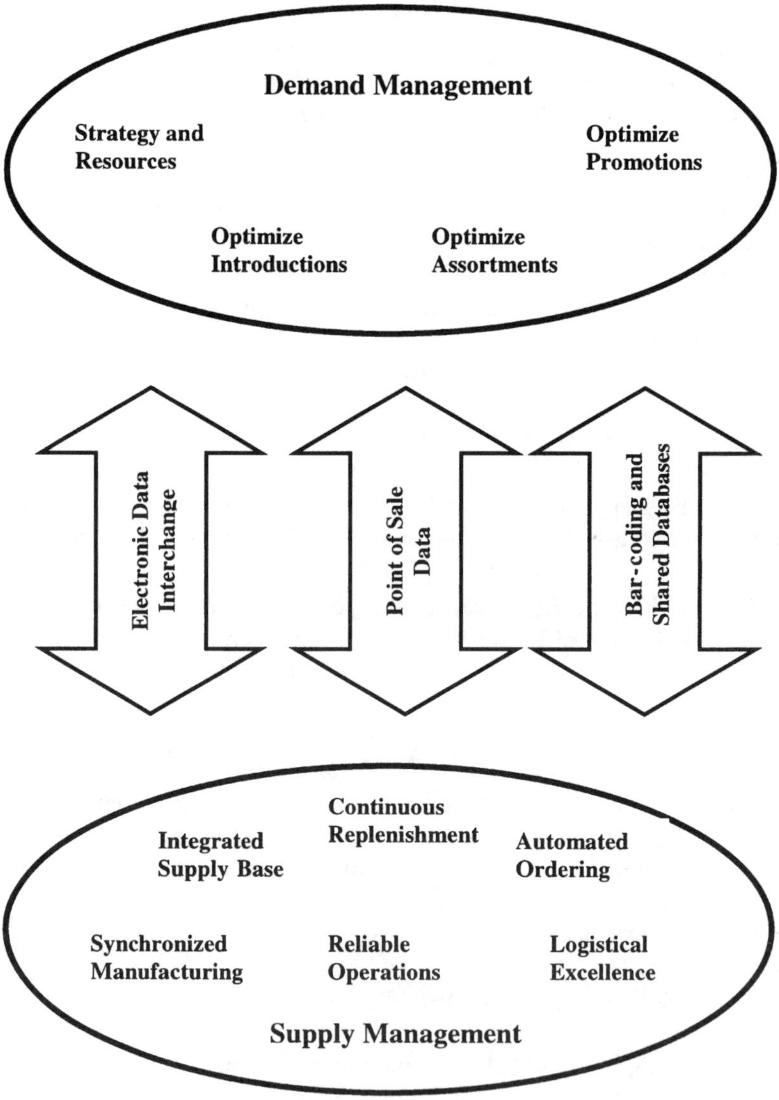

Figure 2.5 ECR improvement

The Forrester Effect—Colmans of Norwich

Colmans of Norwich (now Robinsons Britvic) produce soft drinks under the Robinsons brand name that are sold to all the major supermarkets. These products suffer from extremes of seasonality usually caused by the vagaries of the British climate. Sales rocket one week only to plummet the next and the swings were amplified the further upstream in the pipeline. In the early 1990s senior management were becoming increasingly alarmed at the high cost and waste associated with these patterns. Was all this activity really due to the consumer purchasing patterns? Or, were other factors at work that were not as yet understood?

A large research program was launched in order to try to analyze and appreciate demand patterns. Leading retailers became involved and products flows were scrutinized over a period. As the graph below shows, individual products were tracked and the PoS data from retailers was used to demonstrate the seasonality of the product. However, the orders placed by retailers upon Colmans were even more extreme and the manufacturing activity worse still. This is a classic example of the Forrester Effect, where volatility increases in oscillation the further away from its source. But other strange influences also became

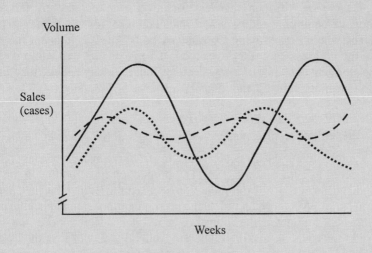

Manufacturing Activity

Vendor Sales to Retailer

PoS Data (Consumer Demand)

continues

apparent. For example, the retailers would often indulge in a forward purchase or investment buy. If a product was being promoted by a cut in price over, say, a week. The retailers would often place a spot purchase—they would order 2–three months of their usual requirement in one week then nothing more for the next three months. To the manufacturer this was consumer demand gone mad. Overall, the exercise enabled Colmans to better understand demand and to obtain advance information of investment buys. It opened the channel of communication between them and their retailing customers. In addition, they began to link their internal activity to external demands of unique product flows and customer behavior by producing and delivering every product every week or day in-line with actual sales to consumers (this aspect is detailed in Section 3.10 of Chapter 3).

The food market is saturated and any increase in market share will come only at the expense of a reduction elsewhere—a competitor. Complexity is increasing, especially in the growth of promotional deals, and new global competitors have appeared who specialize in warehouse clubs and deep discounting. Certainly some advances have been made in such areas as efficient replenishment, cross-docking and integrating EDI. However, much is yet to be done and there are still many barriers. Achievements thus far still fall a long way short of equipping retailers and manufacturers for the demands of the future. The whole Fast Moving Consumer Goods (FMCG) industry has failed to make the progress necessary over the last 10 years that will equip it to deal with the stringent demands of a new century. Indeed, many believe that the gulf between consumer demand and industry response is widening.

2.4.2   Automotive

Today's automotive industry takes its origins from the system of mass production pioneered in 19th century USA. The production line dominated the work ethic and became a byword for alienation, as exemplified in Charlie Chaplin's 'Modern Times'. Mass production had a moronic purpose: to banish the craftsmen who had dominated the industry. In its place, Henry Ford and others employed thousands of unskilled laborers from all walks of life; the assertion being that in reducing every job to its simplest tasks and making them repetitive, any worker could perform them optimally with little prior training.

The approach ensured consistency of product and spared the need to find and train skilled employees; it also allowed payment of the lowest possible wage. Foremen and managers who used the threat of summary dismissal as a major bargaining tool controlled these workers. For more than half a century such factories prospered. However, as described in Chapter 1, diversity and variety became increasingly popular; consumers wanted meaningful rather than superficial choice. In the face of such demands, many monolithic organizations employing mass production principles struggled to find the flexibility and response necessary[16].

It was at this point that the Japanese showed variety was possible while still retaining low cost and high quality. Their system became known as 'lean production'.

In 1950 Toyota, originally a loom manufacturer, saw opportunities in car production. Eiji Toyoda, a descendant of the founder, spent months in the USA studying Ford's manufacturing operation. He returned to Japan and set about building a production system that recognized a changing demand pattern and profitably made small numbers of different types of cars using a minimum of stock and a highly trained and skilled workforce. The Toyota philosophy was to produce small batches in line with demand using a fast machine tool changeover. Stock levels were kept to a minimum and faults became immediately apparent, thus improving quality. Workers were empowered with responsibility for tasks, quality and planning—the production line mentality disappeared.

Other important developments from the industry have included:

- Just-in-time (JIT)—in its four basic forms (a production scheduling system often referred to as kanban, a method of reducing inventory, a way of increasing throughput, and a philosophy for driving continuous performance improvement—kiazen).
- The sub-contracting networks or 'kieretsu'.
- Supplier associations or kyoryoku kai and partnership sourcing.
- Simultaneous or concurrent product engineering.
- Cell manufacturing.
- Set-up time reduction (e.g. single minute exchange of dies).

The automotive industry has been responsible for many important advances in methods of organization—particularly in the fields of engineering, robotics and materials management. These have contributed to a vastly different and modernized approach.

2.4.3 Textiles and Clothing

Quick Response (QR), the subject of this book, grew out of the textile and clothing industry. Contemporary North American and European textile and

---

[16] For those interested in this phenomenon, Rosabeth Moss Kanter's book: *When Giants Learn to Dance* (1989), Unwin, provides an excellent account.

apparel industries suffer immense competition from foreign producers. As early as the mid-1980s, imports were estimated to account for close to 50% of consumption. The primary response of governments and industry had been legislative protection with heavy investment in new equipment. Thus, by the mid-1980s, the textile and apparel sector was the most protected in the USA.

Despite such measures, imports continued to grow unabated and it was quickly realized that protectionist actions and new technology alone were not likely to be sufficient to preserve the industry.

In 1984, a number of industry leaders gathered together to form 'Crafted with Pride in the USA Council', under the leadership of Roger Milliken. Its mission declared:

> The Crafted with Pride in the USA Council Inc is a committed force of US cotton growers, labor organizations, fabric distributors and manufacturers of man-made fibers, fabric, apparel and home fashions whose mission is to convince consumers of the value of purchasing and promoting US made products.

By 1985, the Council had begun an advertising campaign that was to raise significantly consumer awareness of the country of origin label on apparel and the consequences of buying imported garments. Under the direction of its Competitiveness Committee, they set about research into ways of improving the long-term profitability of the industry. One of the earliest tasks was to determine the true cost to the retailer of importing garments. The analysis, carried out by the Boston Consulting Group, was completed in early 1985.

In parallel, Kurt Salmon Associates were commissioned to conduct a supply chain analysis. These reports subsequently revealed that although individual parts of the system, such as simple knit goods, were relatively efficient, the overall supply chain performance was far from optimal. In seeking to minimize costs independent of each other, the separate stages of the supply channel (fiber, textile, apparel and retail) were in fact pursuing strategies that added huge costs to the overall pipeline. The degree of this cost was startling as was the average lead time from raw material to consumer: up to 66 weeks! (Hunter, 1990).

Losses in the supply stream were projected at some $25 billion (two-thirds of which occurred due to unplanned markdowns and stockouts). Of the 66 weeks lead-time, only 11 weeks comprised manufacture, while nearly 40 weeks was time spent in warehouses or transit, with a final 15 weeks in-store. These costs were compounded by a system that relied on long-term forecasts. Further, as if to add insult to injury, it was established that despite all the effort and waste, many customers still left the store unable to find the garment, color or size they required. The subsequent research undertaken and the improvement projects implemented led to the development of Quick Response methodologies.

2.5   COMMENTS

This chapter expanded the notion of a new business environment and covered some of the methods of operating that have been witnessed recently. Some are generic, others specific to particular industries. All have their value and are worthy of analytic consideration. However, care should be taken; dramatic claims for globalized, utopian and linear models are to be treated with suspicion. Often the application of the new principles will vary depending upon the industry, the supply pipeline position, and even the firm; failure to at least recognize this point is dangerous.

One of the crucial difficulties with many of the concepts offered to date is that of practicality and pragmatism. How should such theories be converted into practice? How can they be used to introduce changes within the organization? What are the action steps and implementation paths necessary?

Recently, creative and innovative ways of understanding organizations have begun to emerge. For instance, viewing such systems in a non-linear form utilizing elements of 'chaos theory'. Many of the traditional foundations of management and organizational thinking, developed over the last 50 years, are being steadily replaced. New ideas are being introduced that would have seemed heretical only five years ago. Often, when viewed in isolation, many of these changes are but a piecemeal collection of small and isolated tinkerings; a grab-bag of alternative strategies and operational developments in different industries. Nevertheless, once combined, a pattern emerges which possibly sets the scene for a very new approach. It is to this deeper understanding to which we now turn in Chapter 3.

3
NEW THINKING

This chapter is dedicated to recent thinking about organizational theory, management and business. There is, nevertheless, a 'health warning': it was never the intention of the authors to provide a comprehensive work, thoroughly reviewing all the latest concepts. What follows is more an account of our thought processes and their development, than it is a critical assessment of the disciplines involved. The starting point was the new environment and consideration of organizational approaches during the last 20 years. It was only when an exploration began into the most recent concepts that a realization grew of an underlying structure; a pattern amid the chaos.

Many new and exciting developments in the disciplines of management and organizational theory have been witnessed recently. Organizational structure is seen as a shifting flux that is far from stable. Organizations are designed from the 'outside in'. Endless innovation and creativity are obligatory for continual regeneration of form. No longer machine-like, nor organic, they resemble chaotic systems with the potential for immense flexibility but at the same time the fragility of crystalline structures.

These new abstractions pervade many facets of modern business, including its strategy, structure, systems, style of management and culture. Some of these features require elaboration.

3.1 MODERN STRATEGY

Traditionally, an organizational strategy was contained in annual financial projections prepared by the strategic planning department and based upon forecasts. The next 12 months would be spent in rigid adherence to the plan, attempting to steer the business in accordance with the directions previously declared (the analogy of trying to force the toothpaste back in the tube springs to mind). In times of stability, this method of developing and implementing a strategy had the advantage of precise control and was secure in the knowledge that there would be little, if any, change. Today, even the most established company cannot risk such a degree of rigidity and rationality in trying to plan for the future.

There is a growing contention that strategy per se is ineffective in a rapidly changing world. 'How can a strategy be developed and deployed in a world that is increasingly unpredictable and dynamic?' Strategies can indeed be deliberate, rational and intended; traditionally these types predominated in the more stable environment. At the other end of a continuum, they can be interpretive, emergent, incremental and adaptive—more applicable to dynamic situations. Whittington (1993) went some way to developing a taxonomy of strategy types:

- Classic strategies. Rational planning methods found in most textbooks, devised by a confident and inspiring management, able, in theory, to direct the business to its desired outcomes.
- Evolutionary strategies. Less rational and less confident in the all-embracing powers of management to steer from point A to B. This type adheres to the concepts of natural selection and biological evolution, but in a fairly orderly environment where there is some predictability.
- Processual strategies. Strategies emerge from chance and confusion. A pragmatic viewpoint acknowledging messy confusion and incremental movements toward a desired goal.
- Systemic strategies. Success and failure of the strategy is dependent upon, relative to, and embedded within, the environment and social systems (both internal and external). The strategy attempts to negotiate the various pitfalls by planning with an awareness of possible future events.

The point is that it may be a mistake to view the organization environment as either stable or totally random. These are extremes. For each situation there will be differing layers or strata in-between. Each strategic decision must assess the degree of complexity and turbulence involved and invoke a suitable strategy. The external environment of the enterprise has many levels of complexity. Strategies need to be developed that are tailored and customized to address each circumstance (just like products). Just as most of our businesses have more than one customer, supplier, product and service, so we must have multiple strategies for a multiple environment.

Perhaps the best way to approach the strategic question is to examine the actual nature of strategy—'What is a strategy?' Many textbooks have been devoted to this subject and time does not permit full discussion, but one practical guideline came from Jack Welch, Chief Executive Officer of GEC, who referred to strategy as:

Understanding where the business is, at the moment. Having a clear vision about where it wants to be in the future. And, working out, through wide-scale debate, how it will reach its future destination. (Jack Welch, *The Guardian*, 22 February 1993)

Expanding on this, any strategy must contain three basic elements:

- An *ability* to understand the current standing of the business, its markets, resources, products and unique capabilities. An audit of what adds value and what does not.
- A *vision* of where the organization wishes to be in the long term, again through the auspices of its markets, products, resources and capabilities.
- A *plan* of how the transition from the current position to the desired future is to be brought about.

3.1.1   Ability

Ability in this context alludes to an holistic and systemic aptitude, rather than merely the capability as a leader, marketing manager or manufacturer, important as these may be individually. Strategic ability provides an in-depth understanding of organizational resources and their best configuration in order to meet the singular needs of the customer. These resources enable and facilitate the unique activities undertaken by the firm; the activities are the basis for competitive advantage if they can be tailor-made and fashioned to meet the demands of the customer as an individual.

Resources include people, knowledge, plant, machinery, capital, sources of supply, availability of raw materials, and accessibility of customer segments (even a segment of one). In addition, and of equal strategic import, is the resource of data and information. However, the increased provision of data and information from modern technology can provide an overload. The ability to analyze and shape data to provide information support for a changing resource configuration, which in turn 'drives' differentiated activities, is the key to operating in a volatile, fast-moving environment and achieving a competitive advantage that is hard to match.

3.1.2   Vision

Vision of direction probably precedes 'ability'. The organization must be clear about its position vis-à-vis its customers. What exactly are its offerings to its purchasers? How are these different from its competitors? Once these questions can be adequately answered, resources can be directed into performing activities that not only satisfy demands, but do so in a way that the competition cannot easily copy. Such inimitable activities must involve the whole of the organization and include, for example, how the product is derived and delivered, and not just the product itself.

Vision is a constantly moving target. It is not something that can be developed at a set time of year or by an elite group of management. Strategy is no less creative than writing a book, painting a landscape picture or developing new products. It is not the process of financial extrapolation using linear projections and forecasts of profit and costs constrained by shareholder or financial market expectations. True strategic development is a rich experience utilizing intuition and imagination, romanticism and even fantasy, and not an ability that can necessarily be summoned at will. The vision of a continuing direction or future is an unfolding scenario, constantly adjusted in line with events, a continual process, gaining impetus from a myriad of inputs, not least from the environment and each person within the organization. Quite possibly, a management's faculty for 'strategic listening' is its most important attribute.

3.1.3   Planning

The resultant plan returns the process to a more practical level. Here, concern will be:

(A) for current resource capability,
(B) for activities currently performed,
(C) for strategic vision of the desired future and the diversity of change involved, and
(D) to accommodate the new position indicated in (C), what changes will be required in both (A) and (B), and how will they be achieved.

Once these factors are known, the plan must look at the costs/benefits and the trade-offs between various activities, while still remembering not to lose sight of the unique organization of these activities as part of the essence of competitive edge.

3.2.   OPERATIONAL EFFECTIVENESS

Once the strategic process is underway, the organization will be able to isolate the core activities and their performance parameters that constitute 'operational effectiveness'. At this juncture, consideration needs to be given to the exact nature of this term.

To begin, the subject of 'organization analogies'. These phrases are used to convey a message, to add an emphasis to communication. Over the last 30 years, they have ranged from the organization as a machine to the biological metaphor. Supply channels have been described as chains, pipelines with various flows, and organic bodily systems. More recently, whole industries have been likened to human physiology; the brain acting as a guide to conceptual, management and operational thinking (Cunning et al., 1995). Alternatively, groups and mutual networks of organizations in supply systems are often compared with cellular structures with dependencies and connections similar to those between synaptic knobs and dendrite spines in the brain.

Unfortunately, many analogies place emphasis upon the structure of a firm or network of firms in a rather static environment. With the importance and prominence of operational flexibility, new parallels are required—ones that convey a fluid and dynamic picture, capturing the customization of activity flows and organizational modules. Many modern analogies are severely limited and recourse may be needed to more illusory sources of inspiration, such as dreams[1] and fantasies, in order to describe adequately new virtual organizations and their high degrees of operational efficiency. New metaphors must also take into account the many radical and contemporary concepts of organization and management, such as outlined below.

3.2.1   Diversity

In the future, organizations will have to place a far greater degree of importance upon the diversity of their markets, products and processes. At a strategic level, the successful appeasement of these diversification forces will assume a high priority. Diversity can be viewed as 'related' (new products in existing markets) and 'unrelated' (new products in new markets).

The whole question of diversification is currently 'hot'. Many companies have seen it as a way to solve their problems, without really thinking over what is involved. We maintain (Lowson and Hunter, 1996) that until the present business has reached 'cutting edge' status, enterprises are in no position to contemplate diversification. And when they are prepared, the choice of diversification targets is daunting. Figure 3.1 shows the possible diversification candidates for, say, a blouse manufacturer. It gives some idea of the possibilities involved in taking the current business into new fields.

The influence of 'consumerism' and the omnipotence of 'mass customization' are set to gather pace. Indeed, many commentators believe that the idea of 'personalization' in consumer goods, from refrigerators to clothes, and the allied shortening of product 'lives', will become an escalating tendency. The flexibility and responsiveness necessary to meet this Zeitgeist is something organizations will have to build as part of their strategy for organizational effectiveness.

3.2.2   Evolution

Methods of operation are rapidly evolving. A firm must scrutinize its environment for changes that can radically affect its very existence. Two examples serve as an illustration.

---

[1] As WB Yates declared: 'In dreams begins responsibility'. *Responsibilities* (1914), epigraph.

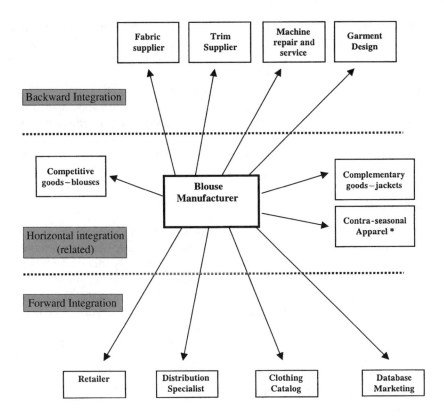

* Apparel goods demanded in a different season from existing lines (e.g. Winter versus Summer tops or jackets)

Figure 3.1   Diversification alternatives (adapted from Johnson and Scholes, 1997)

Grocery

Logistical systems have turned full circle in this industry over the last 25 years. At one time, suppliers had to schedule delivery of nearly all products directly to store. This was complex and expensive in terms of handling for both retailers and manufacturers, and the concept of central warehousing was developed. Retailers built new warehouses to accommodate deliveries from manufacturers, which in turn could be re-packed and re-delivered to store[2]. The warehousing systems expanded and became increasingly centralized[3].

---

[2] More recently, the techniques of 'backhauling' and 'cross-docking' have further advanced this type of system.
[3] A well-known international retailer and manufacturer recently embarked on an extensive project to build one enormous warehouse in France serving the whole of Europe! At the last minute the plan was abandoned when the cost to flexibility and response was computed.

'Outsourcing' was the next logical step, giving control to the logistics experts. More recently, the trends have been reversed, with leading retailers actively considering a return to direct store delivery for many ambient products in addition to the chilled and fresh.

It is recognized that the flexibility and response necessary to support micro-marketing and customization cannot be achieved in any other way (apart from, that is, holding large amounts of stock). The direct delivery phenomenon will eventually include volatile Stock Keeping Units (SKUs) such as fashionable clothing ranges, soft drinks and any products that sell in high volumes at a particular time of year.

Apparel

In the garment industry, the relationship between retailers and manufacturers is rapidly changing. At one time the traditional method of sale was to order all the items of clothing in advance of the selling season. This incurred immense waste in the form of manufacturers' inventories and of stockouts or unplanned end-of-season markdowns at retail. At the same time, retailers realized the cost of holding large amounts of stock in order to retain high levels of customer service, and developed the 'call-off' system that placed the burden further up the supply pipeline. Thus, despite most of the manufacturing taking place before the start of the season, the manufacturers stockpiled finished goods and delivered them in accordance with demand in a form of 'EDI replenishment'. The obvious inadequacy of both systems has led to the development of strategies such as Quick Response (QR)[4].

3.2.3   Management

Managerial concepts are changing at an increasing rate[5]. At a strategic, tactical and operational level, management has to become more externally focused in consideration of alliances, partnerships and the supply chain.

The unique alignment and configuration of a firm's core activities through-out its supply channel is a fundamental contributor to competitive advantage. It does, however, necessitate trade-offs, and it is these trade-offs that are perpet-ually changing. Some examples will serve to illustrate these new influences upon the discipline of management:

- Added Value Assessment (AVA). Many retailers have developed propri-etary systems to measure suppliers' activity and the degree to which it adds value to the retail operation. Likewise, some larger manufacturers

---

[4] We will later contend that despite concepts such as Quick Response, Efficient Consumer Response, Accurate Response, Mass Customization, Lean Manufacturing, and Agile Manufacturing, the performance of many supply chains remains sub-optimal.
[5] Managers seem increasingly of the opinion that they are also becoming of less practical use.

have developed systems that assess retailers in a similar vein. There is also some evidence that joint, mutually agreed approaches exist. However, few appreciate the trade-offs involved at a holistic pipeline level, that is, the costs and benefits concerned when local changes are made. In addition, there is little indication of any successful measurement and reward system being used that motivates all parties in the supply channel.

- Service levels, order Lead-times, Inventories, and Process times (SLIP). As part of the supply chain system, retailers and manufacturers measure attributes such as lead-time, inventory and customer service level. Nevertheless, do the parties concerned actually understand the trade-offs involved? What are the quantifiable effects of changing one of these variables? How do such modifications influence other variables?

- Total Logistics Costs (TLC). Logistical operations involve a number of elements, including transport facilities, communications, inventory, material handling, packaging and management. How many organizations appreciate which of these add value, to what degree, what costs are involved, and how minute, localized changes can influence the broader picture? What are the trade-offs between such costs? How will changes at these levels modify a firm's unique positioning vis-à-vis their operational effectiveness?

- Sourcing. Many retailers and manufacturers now import products from low wage economies. However, we suggest that there are hidden costs that are not always considered. These can include Irrevocable Letters of Credit charges, delays at the port, last minute use of air freight, expensive administrative air travel, quality problems, and early manufacturing commitment before sales trends are clear. In addition, and perhaps more important, this method of operation utilizes a rigid sales plan or forecast; changes cannot be made in the light of later demand information. These costs, as well as costs of lost sales, reduced levels of customer service and markdown expense of products left unsold, are rarely computed as an activity trade-off[6].

3.3 PARTNERSHIPS, ALLIANCES AND NETWORKS

The new and emerging organizational forms are heavily reliant upon external influences. In both the wider and the operating environments, a firm will naturally form many partnerships, alliances and coalitions. These dependencies will affect all operations and can both constrain and enhance those unique activities that are the basis of competitive advantage.

---

[6] We discuss a possible method to model these costs in subsequent chapters.

The QR approach operates using a web of relationships; a mutual network of knowledge sharing. This horizontal and vertical structure is far more complex than the supply pipeline or chain, although of course it encompasses these participants. The linkages between the organizations in this web vary in intensity and duration; some distant and fleeting, others semi-permanent, open and highly symbiotic. But all cemented by joint objectives and a value added exchange of information sharing.

The management of this arrangement is also complex. Multiple contacts at all levels of core process of the business, both cross-functional, and multi-disciplinary, requires a new breed of management and control system. Firms are beginning to recognize the intricacy required for successful operation, but at the same time understand the resource implications. Staff and whole departments will in the future be dedicated to the co-ordination of this inter-organizational role.

At a strategic level, few organizations have attempted to map the various linkages, and thereafter quantitatively determine the degree to which they add value. Without this ability, the core activities of the firm cannot be assessed as they all, to differing degrees, will rely upon some form of outside agency. Once such outside influences are identified, it is possible to address important questions. Whether or not to proactively seek partnerships and alliances, and with whom? What steps should be taken? What resources should be dedicated?

3.4   MEASUREMENT AND BENCHMARKING

Performance measurement, in the form of various ways of benchmarking, is currently in vogue. Successful companies rely upon performance measurements which reflect not only internal activities, but also external, for example, in the supply pipeline. Within many industries there is an almost total lack of common terms and 'yardsticks'. Many measurements of so called success are totally inadequate, especially in external situations—this we call the 'fruit syndrome'[7]. For more on this whole subject, see Chapter 11.

The activity of an organization can be viewed as discrete cycles. For example, manufacturing, product and process development, logistics, marketing, distribution and information systems can be measured in a number of ways, including time involved. In a seminal contribution to the measurement debate, Kaplan and Norton (1992) suggested that any system of measurement should be balanced, and view the organization from four perspectives:

- How do our customers see us?
- What must we excel at? (The internal perspective which considers unique activity configurations.)

---

[7] There is little point in using 'fruit' as a measurement of performance when most customers are demanding apples that are rarely in stock. A successful performance in terms of 'fruit' which does not take into account customer service levels for apples and pears is of little use.

- Can we continue to improve and create value? (An innovation and learning perspective.)
- How do we look to shareholders? (The financial perspective.)

We suggest that two further dimensions will add to the power of such a frame-work:

- How well do we perform in our supply channel relative to the other organizations therein?
- How well are our suppliers and customers performing relative to us?

Within each of these dimensions there will be many individual 'goals' and 'measurements', and of crucial importance is the linkage between 'unique activity architectures', their 'management' and their 'cost/benefit trade-offs' both internal and external—see Figure 3.2.

The latest developments in performance measurement include new 'pipeline methods'. Here, suppliers and retailers evaluate each other and the total business they are in. Retailer systems to measure their suppliers and vice versa are, as we have seen, nothing new. What is particularly innovative is the new form of 'Added Value Assessment (AVA)' now beginning to emerge. This concept brings together the participants in a supply chain as equal partners[8]. A

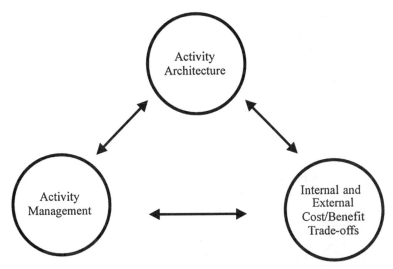

Figure 3.2   Links between activities, management and cost

---

[8] It is important to recognize that individual configurations of value adding activities will often be unique to each particular product. Thus, our earlier exhortation to customize value channels or pipelines by individual product if necessary.

methodology is then applied to identify activities that:

(A) add value,
(B) do not add value, and
(C) are necessary at the moment, but not adding value longer term.

An agreed financial scoring system is evoked to provide the motivation for continual improvement. Consequently, any player who performs an added value activity will be financially rewarded. Likewise, any participant persisting in non-adding value actions will be penalized.

The new breed of 'pipeline' measurement systems places a high degree of emphasis upon activities in the organizational environment. The successful competitor of tomorrow must excel in activities such as:

(1) Decision making
  - decision cycle time
  - time lost in decision making
(2) Processing and production
  - product creation and manufacture
  - inventory turnover and work in progress levels
  - quality and conformance to specifications
  - asset utilization and plant efficiency
  - cycle times
  - quality levels
  - workforce turnover
  - product and process flexibility
(3) Category management
  - category strategy
  - category measures
  - category processes
  - category capabilities
  - data/information requirements
  - category relationships
  - activity based costs
(4) New product introduction
  - market/segment research
  - number of new introductions
  - design for manufacture rating
  - percent first into the market
  - assessment of effectiveness
  - development and execution
  - time from idea to market
  - rate of introduction
  - new vs. existing sales levels

(5) Product merchandising
- managing product categories
- developing brand propositions
- managing trade sales
- managing store operations
- managing channel strategies
- retailer and supplier levels of Gross Margin Return on Inventory (GMROI)

(6) Product promotion
- program planning
- execution
- forecasting and deployment
- assessment

(7) Replenishment
- management of store inventory and orders
- material procurement
- order fulfillment cycle times
- logistics performance
- product records
- on time shipment

(8) Distribution
- flow-through distribution
- shipping cycle time
- floor ready units
- percent auto replenishment
- direct to store delivery
- shipping accuracy
- cost of shipping
- inventory accuracy
- cross docking capabilities

(9) Electronic data interchange (EDI) and bar-coding technology
- degree of electronic data interchange adoption in supply channel
- percentage of products bar-coded
- percent of Universal Product Code (UPC)
- SKUs on electronic catalog
- depth of EDI implementation
- EDI integration
- percent shipping cartons with UPC container code

(10) Customer service
- response time
- deliveries on-time
- order lead-time
- line fill and order fill

(11) Quality and reliability
- adherence to quality procedures
- quality failure level (internal and external)
- level of customer/consumer input through Quality Function Deployment (QFD)
- quality performance
- accuracy of interpretation of customer needs and requirements
- customer satisfaction with product life-cycle and new product introduction.

As discussed, the way these activities are performed, or actually formed into an architecture, must be unique to provide competitive edge. Further, as with strategy direction, the configuration of activities is an evolving, dynamic and fluid enterprise. These functions or tasks, like the resources that support them, must be constantly renewed and changed as they continue to change. Any list, as in the one above, is merely an outline or sketch of the business at one moment in time. Constant vigilance is required to detect shifts in demand which will require new activity and resource frameworks; like the 'fruit syndrome', it is pointless continuing to measure something that is no longer important to the customer or consumer.

3.5. DATA, INFORMATION SYSTEMS AND INFORMATION TECHNOLOGY

The structuring and sharing of information between individuals or groups of varying sizes are devices used in a business culture for coping with complexity. Boisot (1994) described information as displaying two distinct variables: *codification* and *diffusion*. The higher the codification of the information the less the 'richness' of the content, but the easier the transmission or *diffusion* and the wider the possible audience. Compare the verbal description of an individual with the use of a photograph. The latter has a lower level of codification and is richer in information (a picture is worth a thousand words); the former is easier to convey to a wider audience (through speech for example) but contains less detail.

A firm's internal and external activities and their performance rely heavily upon information systems[9]. A unique task configuration requires a matching information framework by way of support. Figure 3.3 demonstrates how the Information System sits as a filter across the organization. Figure 3.4 is a section of Figure 3.3 showing a more detailed level.

---

[9] It is important to remember that information systems at this level are nothing to do with computers and technology. An information system can be a filing cabinet or a chat at the office coffee machine!

Often data are freely available to all players in a particular market-place. However, the type of information extracted and the way it is used, in the form of knowledge, is the crucial element. The traditional Middle Eastern story told in the box throws some light on this situation.

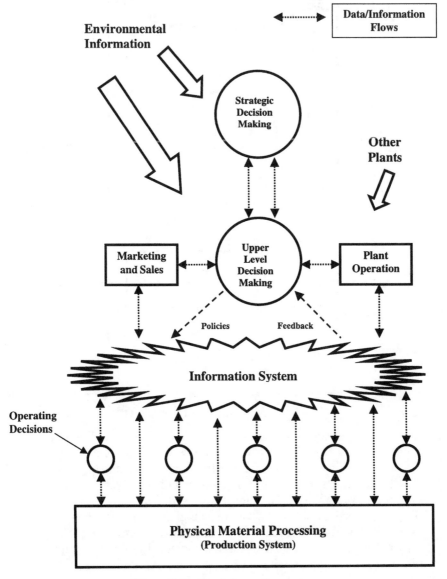

Figure 3.3   The information system

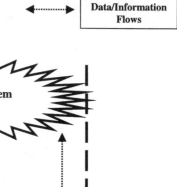

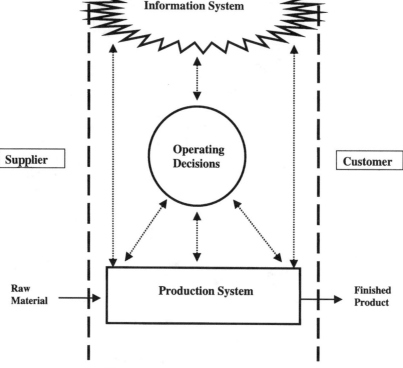

Figure 3.4 Information system detail

The Four Men and the Interpreter

Four people were given a single piece of money.
The first was a Persian. He said: 'I will buy with this some angur.'
The second was an Arab. He said: 'No, because I want inab.'
The third was a Turk. He said: 'I do not want inab, I want uzum.'
The fourth was a Greek. He said: 'I want stafil.'
Because they did not know what lay behind the names of things, these four started to fight. They had information but no knowledge. One man of wisdom present could have reconciled them all, saying: 'I can fulfil the needs of all of you, with one and the same piece of money. If you

continues

honestly give me your trust, your one coin will become as four; and four at odds will become as one united.'
Such a man would know that each in his own language wanted the same thing, grapes.

It is impossible to be prescriptive over what data are needed in any particular circumstance. The organization must treat information as a resource, have a strategy for it, and a close link between its unique activities and the vital information to support them.

The mere possession of the latest technology is insufficient. It is the application of that technology and the particular information derived that is important. Successful organizations now realize that responsive and flexible strategies are built on an information platform that accommodates all members of the supply channel. Internally, information is needed to drive activities such as:

- Co-ordination
- Time to market
- Management control
- Organizational learning, creativity and innovation.

Externally, however, the new environment requires vastly different information flows. Influences such as:

- Dissolution of trade barriers
- World-wide information networks
- Lifestyles which transcend traditional boundaries
- Alliances and partnerships
- Global customers
- Increasing customer expectations
- Customization of products to meet local needs
- Information-intensive products
- Global competition
- Database marketing.

These are just a few of the fundamental trends any company must be aware of and seek information about.

In addition, within the firm's operating environment—its supply pipeline—effective performance will require information sharing and rapid data flow. Timely information provides the basis for accurate planning of activities linked to demand and, in so doing, eliminating waste. The data sharing necessary for optimal operation of supply chains will only be possible if all parties have access to industry-wide data sources that provide retail sales levels and stock holding, as well as manufacturing schedules and inventory levels. It is highly likely that third party providers, such as General Electric, will eventually run such database operations and supply a brokerage service to the firms concerned in any supply pipeline situation.

The technologies needed to support the new networked organizational structures are already very advanced. The major difficulties arise in the linking of various separate islands of technology and ensuring that there is an open sharing. Any supply channel operation will require a well integrated and unified database technology, developed standards for universal product codes (UPCs), electronic data interchange (EDI) communications, shipping container bar-codes, full access to point-of-sale (PoS) and inventory data, and a well developed multimedia technology.

3.6   TOTAL QUALITY MANAGEMENT (TQM)

Quality is a vital ingredient of Quick Response. The shift from traditional quality assurance practice to total quality management has confirmed that the approach is customer-driven and involves the commitment of every employee, as internal customers themselves, to provide quality products and services that satisfy complex demands.

There are many excellent publications covering the subject of quality. It is not our intention to review them here. Nevertheless, total quality management has produced a number of core concepts that are at the heart of QR:

- Customer focus. Quality is seen from the perspective of the customer. Products and services conform to customer specifications.
- Error prevention. Rather than detection. A system and management discipline that prevents defects.
- Cost of quality. Understanding the cost of not producing products or services that are 'fit for use'. Appreciating internal and external failure costs, and prevention and appraisal costs.
- Right first time or zero defects. A target to achieve defect free work most of the time.
- Acceptable quality levels. These are no longer tolerable. This implies that a level of failure is acceptable.
- Competitive benchmarking. Measurement of performance (products and services, business processes and people). A continuous cycle of improvement, feedback and measurement (both internal and external).
- Involvement of everyone. Everyone is involved in producing quality goods and services and cutting costs of quality. The quality of the final good or service supplied to the consumer relies on a long chain of

activity. As such, the customer–supplier chain is only as strong as its weakest link. The concept of the internal customer recognizes this inter-dependence and the fact that everyone in the organization is both a customer and a supplier.

- Synergetic partnerships and teamwork both internal and external. The combined output is greater than each of the inputs taken separately and also greater than the sum of the total inputs.
- Ownership. Psychological ownership. People own the problems, investi-gations, processes, solutions and successes.
- Management as a role model. A commitment to TQM comes from the top.
- Recognition and reward. An appropriate system of recognition and reward is vital to stimulate TQM improvements.
- Quality delivery. Awareness of quality and how processes can con-tinually be improved.
- Design. Design for quality, use or manufacture has ensured an under-standing of quality issues at the point of delivery. We advocate an exten-sion of this: design for Quick Response. Collaborative efforts between functions and multiple companies in a mutual network are an essential ingredient for producing QR products and services that are designed close to the selling season.

3.7 CHAOS

Any discussion of contemporary thinking in business and organization would be incomplete without a cursory examination of the contributions of chaos, complex systems theory or complexity theory.

The approach to the management task within an organization should recog-nize the role of chaos. The chaos of which we speak is not the management state of 'constant chaos' or 'fire-fighting', nor chaotic work patterns resulting from poor time management; most of us have first-hand knowledge of these sit-uations. Chaos theory has far deeper ramifications and influence, and is much more complicated.

It is an oversimplification, but the study of complexity theory begins with two notions:

- systems
- non-linearity.

Systems can be defined as the understanding of the relationship between interacting elements. More than just a set, the term system implies a relation-ship. A car or Concorde is a mechanical system; the universe is made up of natural systems; bridges, tools and computers are designed systems; and a factory is a human activity system. Systems can be modeled and often mathematics is the tool that is used.

Non-linearity is connected with the process of understanding the mathematical models used to describe systems. Traditionally, these models were analyzed as though they were linear systems (plotted on a graph using a straight line). We think of a factory as a linear system with certain inputs, transformations and predicted outputs: the system is deterministic. In actuality, a factory is non-linear, as with most in nature, and outputs are not easy to predict using straight lines on graphs. This is the reason why the use of performance indicators and benchmarking is much more haphazard than many textbooks would have us believe. For an entertaining look at linearity, organization, and much more, see Burrell (1997).

Science has for centuries been divided between those who believe that the universe is a coherent whole, having large numbers of sub-systems all co-operating to achieve some greater result in accordance with a pre-determined plan. At the other extreme, there are the 'atomists' who place their faith in a world that is nothing more than atoms in a void with no overall long-term plan. These ideologies fall within the opposing camps of holism and reductionism, respectively.

Chaos theory, in fact, demonstrates that both viewpoints are valid, dependent upon the level of analysis. All systems have different properties and varying degrees of unpredictability and determinism that alter in line with the viewpoint: classical or quantum. Once the dynamics of complex systems are examined, it becomes clear that awareness of their initial condition will not help prediction of the final outcomes: determinism. For example, the input of raw materials, energy and people into the factory system will not guarantee the output of goods in the right quantity or quality.

Orderly determinism with perfect knowledge of outcomes was the foundation of traditional or classical science as propounded by such people as Isaac Newton. Unfortunately, at a certain level, systems fail to comply with the Newtonian viewpoint because they are:

- Non-linear. There is synergy; the whole is worth more than the sum of the parts.
- Large in numbers of components. Complex systems are more than just complicated versions of simple systems. They have identities of their own and their many elements have high degrees of freedom.
- Open. Complex systems are open to environmental influence and the driving forces contained therein and produce a 'rich' behavior. Chapter 1 is devoted to such examples.
- Unpredictable. Complexity appears abruptly with little warning and does not slowly evolve. It is aperiodic.

All systems, whether they are work systems or weather systems, have chaotic elements, and even the simplest displays a mixture of chaos and order to varying degrees. In the past, scientists have ignored the elements of chaos as merely background 'noise'; a random element that had no part of the system under study, not appreciating that it did, in fact, constitute *the* system and without it, the system would cease to exist.

Closely associated with chaos is the butterfly effect or more technically: 'sensitive dependence on initial conditions'. The concept means that with a complex, non-linear system, infinitely small changes in the starting conditions of a system will result in dramatically different outputs for that system in the future. If we cannot take into account the action of a butterfly flapping its wings in Argentina in our weather predictions, then we will fail to predict a thunderstorm in Norfolk two weeks from now because of this dynamic.

Small errors in the quality of inputs to a complex system can lead to dramatic and unforeseen consequences[10]. Changes and uncertainties multiply, cascading upward through a chain of turbulent features, from dust devils and squalls to eddies the size of continents. Even if computerized sensors were to be placed a foot apart over the whole earth, and then rising at foot high intervals into the atmosphere, it would still not be possible to predict with certainty the weather in New York in six hours' time. The spaces between the sensors would still hide minute fluctuations; these small errors would continuously grow and magnify across the globe.

Complex systems contain order and disorder, form and chaos, complexity in apparent simplicity, simplicity in apparent complexity, and regular irregularity. What then of management and business?

Organizations are complex systems; they are unpredictable and indeterministic to varying degrees and contain many 'soft' elements. Strategies are often emergent. Controls need to be simultaneously loose–tight. Performance measurement and evaluation is notoriously difficult. Forecasting is fraught with error. Functions require a degree of differentiation in order to interact properly with a corresponding sub-set of the environment. Complexity and difference between departments thus needs integrative devices.

Uncertainty in the market, as we have discussed in Chapter 1, leads to increased transaction cost. Excessive hierarchy in the business structure brings confusion. Highly diversified companies have control predicaments. Organizational visions and mission statements rarely convert perfectly into practice.

Organizations are open systems with little consensus as to the meaning and significance of their own constituents. Complexity and unpredictability are unavoidable and, in fact, like noise, should not be ignored or removed as they are probably the very essence of the system wherein the potential lies for

---

[10] Perhaps one of the most regrettable examples of this was the loss of the space shuttle Challenger on January 28, 1986. A relatively small quality defect, coupled with a series of poor management decisions, led to an enormous consequential loss of lives and dollars.

competitive advantage. Order and chaos are reciprocal, with both elements present in any management situation.

A fascinating application of the principles of chaos and the use of information is to be found in Levy (1992). The search for artificial life provides a pertinent example, one highly applicable to organizations and their supply pipelines. Living systems are typified by the degree to which information can move freely or be retained. If the value (dynamical state) is low, this represents a regime in which information is frozen. It can easily be retained through time, but cannot move. If the value is very high, then information moves very freely and chaotically and is difficult to retain. On the other hand, there is a certain

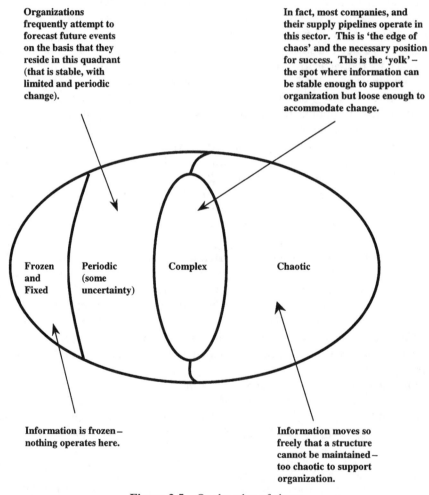

Organizations frequently attempt to forecast future events on the basis that they reside in this quadrant (that is stable, with limited and periodic change).

In fact, most companies, and their supply pipelines operate in this sector. This is 'the edge of chaos' and the necessary position for success. This is the 'yolk' – the spot where information can be stable enough to support organization but loose enough to accommodate change.

Frozen and Fixed

Periodic (some uncertainty)

Complex

Chaotic

Information is frozen – nothing operates here.

Information moves so freely that a structure cannot be maintained – too chaotic to support organization.

Figure 3.5   On the edge of chaos

area where information changes but not so rapidly that it loses all connection to where it had just been previously; it is this regime that supports the kind of complexity that is the mark of living systems.

The reader will no doubt be struck by the immediate comparison between the above and supply systems. Complexity is essential, but a proper degree of complexity that allows it to reside in that life sustaining spot between the barren, frozen void to the left, and the swirling maelstrom of chaos and confusion to the right that can never support structures. For optimal operation supply pipelines, and the companies that compose them, there is a need to operate

> on the edge of chaos ... at the edge of a phase transition between desert and cyclone. (Langton, 1992)

Figure 3.5 summarizes these contentions.

3.8   MANAGING CHANGE

Change is the very essence of business growth and, like death and taxes, is inevitable and unavoidable. For people and businesses alike change can be threatening and stressful. Uncertainty breeds accusation and recrimination as individuals struggle to make sense of the unfolding developments around them and come to terms with a new and challenging environment.

Change, however, is necessary. And it is not change in itself that we find daunting, but a fear of the unknown. Consequently we all have to learn to manage change. The first step is to understand the change process. Figure 3.6 is an adaptation from the work of Elisabeth Kübler-Ross. In her fascinating book, *On Death and Dying* (1970), she describes the psychological process patients undergo when confronted with the knowledge of a life-threatening illness. As the figure demonstrates, when faced with change, our reactions and emotions pass through the stages of denial and isolation then anger. A bargaining point is then reached where a trade-off is sought in mitigation of the full force of the change. However, with the dawning realization that escape is impossible, depression sets in and with it the lowest emotion level. From her study, however, Kübler-Ross noted that if the full change process ran its course, and patients worked through the stages, the final phase, acceptance, led to a higher order outcome: a steady state that marked growth, enrichment and development.

Many organizations still persist in viewing the future as stable and use past history as a basis for forthcoming assumptions: forecasting the future by extrapolating the events of the past. One only has to consider the momentous changes that have occurred world-wide in any 12-month period to appreciate

**Emotion
Level**

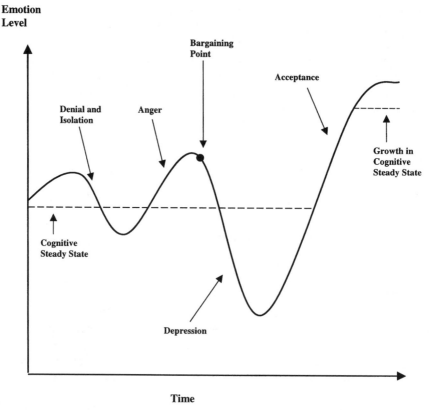

Figure 3.6   The process of change (adapted from Kübler-Ross, 1970)

their unpredictability. Is the past really a good basis upon which to view the future? As Godet (1982) points out, the future is in fact multiple and uncertain, it will not be a continuation of the past and can go in very different directions, as can be seen in Figure 3.7.

Unfortunately, what sold in the past will not always do so in the future, and certainly not in the same quantities. History in business counts for very little. Stability is a sham. Customers will change their tastes, often for all the wrong reasons, and the most sophisticated and expensive forecasting system will be of little assistance. The increased rate of adoption of new trends makes forecasting almost impossible. The only sure guide for any operation is, perhaps, activity at point-of-sale.

Organizations must manage change using the existing interconnections between environment, strategy, people, systems and structure: an ability to unfreeze, reconstitute and refreeze any situation and activity configuration. Such ability requires many attributes; for example, visionary leadership, a skilled and educated workforce, and constant communication, and there are

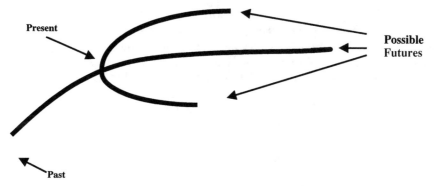

Figure 3.7   A multiple and uncertain future

numerous publications available that deal with the subject of change and its influence. The rest of this book will describe a very different type of change management; one that is proactive and intended to alter the organization in accordance with the new demands that we have discussed.

3.9   MANAGEMENT OF THE SUPPLY CHAIN VS. SUPPLY CHAIN MANAGEMENT (SCM)

The ideas collectively referred to as SCM have enjoyed a strong position in the thinking of management theorists for the past 20 years or so. And rightly so; they replaced the concentration of individual firms on purely internal measures of performance, and urged a broader view of business—one that took into account the total system in which a company operates. For the CEO and corporate strategists, SCM has proved to be a powerful tool for thinking about new ways of looking at business, including the need for operational simplification, cost reduction, distribution rationalization, and greater levels of customer service. True, gains have been made in the first three, but there is little evidence that service levels have improved.

This holistic point of view now has few detractors. However, we claim that the time has arrived to change and expand this paradigm. In recent years, there have been few insights, though the volume of writing on SCM has continued to grow. Further, there is a conspicuous absence of 'how-to' information; the kind needed more by the Chief Operations Officer (COO) or Operations Director and their managers, than corporate staffs. To emphasize this need, we chose to think in terms of 'managing the supply chain', with its hands-on connotation, rather than the loftier Supply Chain Management (the reader will note that we deliberately chose the former wording for the sub-title of this book).

Earlier we stressed the need to recognize the rapid growth of consumerism, and later we shall discuss at length the changes in consumer demand patterns that have led to levels of SKU complexity undreamed of when SCM was being formulated. These can have sharp negative impacts on both the firm and its supply and distribution systems unless recognized and dealt with. As with many other conceptual models, SCM avoids complexity; it is over simplistic. Any new paradigm must deal with this crucial element. We believe QR goes far to satisfy the operational manager.

We will examine QR in depth in later chapters. Here it is useful to compare a number of SCM dimensions with those of QR:

- QR recognizes that both *customers/consumers* and *products* are dynamic and place unique demands on the organization (this concept is more fully covered in the next section). SCM, on the other hand, ignores multiple SKUs and deals in one-dimensional widgets (one color, one size, one style) that rarely change. It hardly recognizes complexity, seasonality, short-seasons, volatility, markdown effects, buyer error (SKU mix) or what happens at the end of the season to all the unsold items. These are the very issues that are at the heart of the new consumer market.

- SCM concentrates upon making available to customers product volumes and assortments based on demand forecasts. QR, however, places less reliance on forecasts, preferring 'real-time' decision making closely linked to the demands of the market-place and utilizing optimal resource integration. It supplies customers with precision and flexibility according to actual demand. Supply and all other activities mirror this demand (both volume and mix).

- SCM is product and manufacturing driven. It arose in a mass production era when repetitive processes, unit cost pressures, the streamlined production line and the necessity of adopting new technologies were paramount. SCM can be viewed as the apex of Industrial Revolution thinking, focused heavily on manufacturing, but of declining use in a consumer driven world we now inhabit. There has been much fine writing of late about putting SCM in a strategic context—some of it purporting to close the loop by talking of meeting consumer wishes—and there are some valuable insights. But, virtually all of these improvements are manufacturing or distribution related and merely pay lip service to genuine consumer demand.

- The QR approach manages the supply chain, rather than the other way around, from innovation to delivery, with emphasis on the belief that all activity is market demand driven. It is based upon a strategic segmentation of products and customers, as well as flexibility, response and customization in order to maximize value.

- QR denotes service levels—a cornerstone. Multiple SKUs, seasonality, volatility, product velocity, complexity and markdowns are new measures of performance agreed between enterprises and subject to financial scoring. These are rarely dealt with in the SCM cost and efficiency thinking.

- Many of the SCM techniques are tailored to large organizations with appropriate staff groups, but are of little use for SMEs—the fast moving, entrepreneurial companies that excel in rapidly changing environments.
- QR adopts a contingent approach. Unlike the scattergun of SCM, aiming to satisfy all needs, QR is selective and flexible.
- QR is a quantitative discipline. Management decisions are made on the basis of specific, measurable benefits to operations. Little reliance is placed on generalized, qualitative guidelines.
- The QR philosophy is underpinned by the primacy of data and its translation into useful information. Further, it takes advantage of each and every development in technology that can add to measurable performance improvements.

It is our contention that QR is the new paradigm for examining and responding to the *Information and Consumerism Revolutions*, in which the wants of the final consumer are paramount and drive all industrial activity, and where the supply chain must be proactively managed.

As a summary of these points, Table 3.1 shows how QR relates to SCM concepts. It should help position QR in broad management terms and provide a bridge to what follows.

Table 3.1   QR and Supply Chain Management

QR	SCM and Traditional
Mass customization Diversity in products and processes	Mass production Homogeneity and superficial differentiation
Identification of unique customer/ consumer and product demands	One-dimensional product approach
Tailoring of enterprise resources to match each individual demand profile	Ignores complexity, seasonality and volatility
Demand driven system in which all activity is linked to demand. Management of the supply chain for flexibility, response, diversity and added value in the *Information and Consumerism Revolution*	Product and manufacturing driven system—the apex of the *Industrial Revolution*
'Real-time' decision making linked to actual demand data	Availability of product mix and volume based on forecasts
Flexibility in products, mix, volume, delivery. Service levels and product velocity act as new performance measures jointly agreed and scored in the pipeline	Rigidity in operations with long batch runs and a production to stock. Cost, efficiency and gross margin the imperative for 'lean' operations

(continues)

Table 3.1   *Continued*

QR	SCM and Traditional
Unique brands as symbols and images	Little real difference behind a promotional facade of choice
A philosophy developed and tailored with the ability of the SME in mind	Generally only effective in large organizations with high staff levels
Contingent upon circumstances and industry	Offered as a universal panacea
Quantitative and measurable	Often generalized, qualitative guidelines
Primacy of data and information	Secondary consideration after logistics and operations improvements
Small batch flexible production of a variety of product types (lots or batch size of one)	Mass production of homogeneous products. Uniformity and standardization
Mutual network complexity. Large number of horizontal and vertical negotiations and transactions. Virtuality, fractals and holographic 'pools' as metaphors	Principally an endogenous focus and little external integration on a vertical level. Chains and streams the dominant metaphor
Logistically distinct businesses and customization of supply channels	Universal logistics approach and uniform supply
Time as a critical source of competitive advantage that is closely linked to customer requirements	Gains in manufacturing time often dissipated by slow sales, marketing and distribution operations
Minimal pre-season retailer inventory. Thereafter, use of fast re-estimation and re-order procedures based upon consumer demand	Large initial retailer inventory based and subsequent replenishment all based on sales forecasts
Flow-through 'tailored' logistics and consolidation centers	Stocking points and little value added from lengthy storage and handling of products
Primacy of individual customer data/information flows along supply chain and electronic platforms	Data/information capture and interrogation does not differentiate between elements of customer base (e.g. product rather than customer sales forecasting)
Fast-cycle product development linked to customer needs	Little innovation with only superficial change when absolutely necessary
Individual customers integrated into design and development process	Any product development applies to whole customer base
In-store style testing and feedback before launch of new products	Big-bang launch and 'fingers crossed that we've got it right'

3.10   THE ROLE OF QUICK RESPONSE

There has been much confusion regarding the true role of QR. Definitions and descriptions of components have varied depending upon application (retail, manufacturer, supplier) and industry. As we saw in the last section, the development of a discipline can suffer from continual disjointed and fragmentary growth—some form of consolidation is needed; this we now provide.

QR has received many definitions in the trade, popular and academic press. For our purposes QR can be neatly defined as:

A state of responsiveness and flexibility in which an organization seeks to provide a highly diverse range of products and services to a customer/consumer in the exact quantity, variety and quality, and at the right time, place and price as dictated by real-time customer/consumer demand. QR provides the ability to make demand information driven decisions at the last possible moment in time ensuring that diversity of offering is maximized and lead-times, expenditure, cost and inventory minimized. QR places an emphasis upon flexibility and product velocity in order to meet the changing requirements of a highly competitive, volatile and dynamic marketplace. QR encompasses a strategy, structure, culture and set of operational procedures aimed at integrating enterprises in a mutual network through rapid information transfer and profitable exchange of activity.

3.10.1   Quick Response as a Strategy

From the definition it is clear that QR possesses a number of important strategic components:

The Alignment of Organizational Activity to Demand

This is a fundamental principle of QR. All activities within an enterprise should be paced to demand and customer behavior. Products and services are produced and delivered in the variety and volume that matches demand. The activity within a company moves to the beat of this drum. Oscillation and swings of demand are closely followed: too little or too much leads to waste and inefficiency. Whether it is marketing, purchasing, new product development or operations, all endeavors follow the market tempo—the realization of this alignment necessitates a change in culture. Consequently, it is important that senior management recognizes and understands these demand patterns. Resources need to be deployed that can undertake this vital externally focused role.

Linkages between Demand and Supply

Given the importance of the alignment activity, a strategic understanding of the drivers of demand and its synchronized connection with supply is imperative for QR. Under SCM, much attention has, quite rightly, been placed upon improvements in supply. However, increasingly these are at the expense of true demand understanding. Demand is the target—no matter how sophisticated the supply weaponry, it is ineffectual if the target is not understood. Only when the value and benefits sought by the customer/consumer are appreciated in all their complexity can a strategy to supply them be developed. This involves detailed assessment of supply and demand processes and sub-processes by customer or customer grouping. Together with the supply of a tangible product or service will be a myriad of other dimensions peculiar to the customer/consumer. This will include varying information content, time frames, physical arrangement for logistics, service support, marketing campaigns, information systems, etc.

Demand Relationships

QR recognizes that both *customers/consumers* and *products* are dynamic and place unique demands on the organization. Identical products, cans of beans for example, will have unique product flows depending upon customer/consumer buying behavior and QR needs (whether a supermarket, wholesaler, corner store, or catering company). Similarly, product attributes will vary: volume and flow characteristics, demand patterns, seasonality, promotional strategy, cyclical needs, hygiene factors (e.g. freshness), information content, credit terms and customer incentives, repeat purchase patterns, etc. These attributes can be aligned with the QR product categories of 'basic', 'seasonal', 'short season' and 'ultra-short season'. These different customer/consumer and product behaviors will customize and tailor QR channels in line with requirements. Once this assessment is done, it is possible to apply specific QR components or systems that can be tied into the unique supply stream.

Resource Configuration

Conventional strategy (forget the fads) looks long-term for some form of advantage by configuration of activities and resources to the environment of operation; a strategic fit between the strengths and weaknesses to the opportunities and threats. In the QR world, this strategic architecture is inter-organizational—strategy and strategic thinking are at a network level encompassing many external interconnections. In addition, within this configuration must fit the mapping of customer/consumer values and perceived benefits in order to underpin the link between demand and activity (as above). For QR, the only enduring competitive advantage comes from changing the rules of the game.

Time

The use of time and time compression have been discussed earlier (see Chapter 2, section 2.1.2). Time as a strategic weapon is vital to QR operation, but like any weapon its effectiveness depends upon the circumstances of its use. Strategies of time compression have gained much popularity of late. Unfortunately, as with many such movements, the application has been widespread but often ill considered. A time strategy is subtle and, above all else, must be well thought out. Mere slashing of time for the sake of it misses the point. As with demand, time based competition requires careful assessment as to where best it can serve customers/consumers. Fast and accurate adaptation to market change is perhaps the most important element of the QR time strategy. The adroitness and dexterity to move to satisfy unplanned demand or previously unrecognized market niches, requires any organization to be strategically configured for such a response. However, this architecture will only be effective if the operational environment is understood and the opportunities for time compression assessed. Accuracy and flexibility will reduce time delays and postponement strategies enable products and services, indeed all activity, to be tailored to known and exact needs rather than those forecast. It should also be remembered that the use of time for advantage will be inter-organizational; gains made internally will be rapidly lost if not carried through by network partners.

Primacy of Information

The use of data and information is the foundation of QR—every business is an information business. Here, we are not dealing with Information Technology (IT), but a strategy for Information Systems (IS). Technology is merely the vehicle used to carry vital data resources. As demonstrated in Figure 2.2 (d), in the QR context, the consumer dictates the activity of satellite retailers, manufacturers and service providers. The link between demands and successful, accurate and flexible supply is data and the resulting information. For operation in the 21st century the prime strategic consideration will be the use of information as a resource. Timely and accurate flows will enable fast and accurate responses without waste and cost. Strategic information systems can be categorized into four broad classifications: those that link the organization to its external networks (suppliers, customer/consumers); those that help to integrate the internal network value adding processes; those that enhance the information content of products and services; and, those that provide senior management with support (EIS and MIS). At a strategic level, the organization must conduct a full analysis of its internal and external data and information needs. Thereafter, it must decide which information systems best support these needs, see Figure 3.8; only then can the technological requirements be considered as part of a distinct IT strategy. Thus, we have distinct IS and IT strategies that are driven by the overall business needs (business strategy).

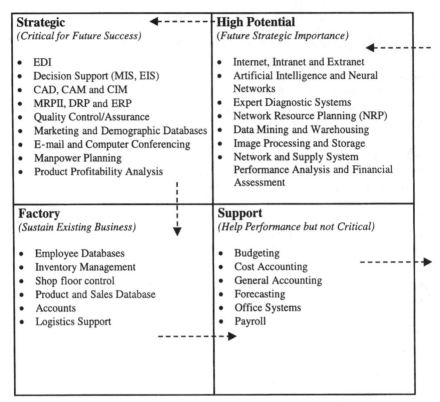

Figure 3.8   Business information system contribution (adapted from Ward et al., 1990)

Alliances

Perhaps one of the most significant developments in management and business thinking has been externalization: the recognition that performance relies increasingly upon a series of alliances and relationships with other enterprises in the environment as the most effective way to deal with constantly changing market conditions. Competition is now between mutual networks rather than individual firms. The co-ordination and relationships between these various entities is a matter for strategic consideration. Section 3.3 of this chapter has devoted time to the general partnership approach now being taken. From a QR perspective, the web of relationships and mutual networks upon which the organization depends requires a professional management approach, and increasingly firms are devoting staff and other resources to this task. The use of outsourcing, the concept of virtuality, and a focus on core value adding processes have heightened this pressure for proper external organization and management with commercial partners. This requires a greater understanding of organizational behavior and communication beyond traditional boundaries, particularly power and culture, in order to appreciate properly the huge number of strategically significant relationships necessary to the modern firm in the next century.

3.10.2   Quick Response for Operations

Throughout this book we have placed a great deal of emphasis upon the increasing complexity and dynamism in the modern business environment. To deal with this we have stressed that organizations must be prepared to customize their goods and services by individual customer/consumer groups and product attributes into distinct businesses.

Mass Customization—National Bicycle Company

In the mid-1980s the National Bicycle Company of Japan faced immense competition from other manufacturers in a market that was steadily declining: the fight for market share was becoming more intense. Cost efficiency drives and new product introductions were having less and less impact and cheaper imports flooding the market. A new approach was needed. A paradigm shift in the bicycle market. They decided to move into a market niche: customization. But not customization on an individual scale—mass customization. But how could this be done without long lead-times, huge component stock and high unit prices? Postponement was the answer. Traditionally bicycles had been built for stock and stored by retailer or manufacturer. National Bicycle decided to postpone frame welding, painting and assembly until individual tailored orders were known—these were faxed by retailers. Customers were individually measured by height and weight for each individual product (just like buying a tailored suit), and could choose from a wide variety of design elements (18 models, six handle stem extensions, 199 color patterns, three toe clip configurations, six brake systems, frame dimensions in 10mm adjustments, three handle bar widths, two pedal types, two tire types, two different name positions and five choices of script for the customer's name on the frame—a total of 11 231 862 variations). Lead times were kept to two weeks in Japan (three for export) and prices only 15% above the best mass produced cycle.

Today similar advances are being seen in a wide range of sectors, perhaps the most prominent being Levi's 'personalized pair' system of buying jeans, the Benetton 'knit now dye later' system for fashion clothing, prescription glasses produced in one hour, custom-made pizzas in 15 minutes and full five-course meals delivered to your door.

QR is not a universal panacea however; its processes, components and systems cannot and will not be applicable to each and every industry or business. It is, like its outcomes, flexible and contingent upon spatio-temporal considerations. This is the very strength of its philosophy. Therefore, the tactics of its application will be contingent and depend on the circumstances.

We can, however, offer some generalizations in Table 3.2.

Table 3.2   Generic QR systems, procedures and components

Electronic Data Interchange (EDI)	A vital technological component enabling linkages between firms in a mutual operational network. Notice that EDI now extends beyond the initial interconnection between supplier and retailer to an entire web. The advances in computing power[11] and reduction in cost make this possible.
Bar-coded merchandise	Enabling the unique identification and tracking of all components and finished goods throughout a mutual network.
PoS data sharing with customers	Essential for a flexible and responsive supply. Without these data large parts of the network are disabled and can only meet demand using forward inventory builds and forecasting.
Shared planning	The partners within the web, especially those closest, must be prepared to share a degree of strategic and operational planning. To act autonomously will reduce effectiveness.
Electronic reorder	The ordering and reordering of goods are performed electronically to increase speed and accuracy.
Continual and automatic replenishment	Once the right systems are in place, certain merchandise ('basics' with little volatility) can be replenished to sale. This demand information will also drive production schedules.
Universal Product Codes (UPC)	For identification and tracking of bar-codes, these must be unique to individual SKUs. Any duplication will cause inefficiencies. In addition these UPCs must be common throughout the whole mutual network.
Sales captured at item level	In conjunction with bar-coding and UPCs, it is of course necessary to capture sales activity by individual item or SKU rather than box/crate or container.
Store ready deliveries	Time can be reduced in the delivery cycle, if goods are ready to be placed on shelf once delivered. Price ticketing and packaging must be completed to retailer specification (each retailer may have specific needs). It is also essential to avoid packing and repacking at DC or warehouse (in fact direct store deliveries will become more common).

(continues)

---

[11] In 1965, the co-founder of the Intel Corporation prophesized that the capacity of the microprocessor would double every 18 months. This became known as Moore's Law.

Table 3.2 *Continued*

Container shipping codes	Just as each SKU has a unique identification code, so will containers. These will show the contents and destination.
Electronic purchase order and invoicing	Rapid transmission of data using EDI will include orders, invoices, advance ship notices, etc.
Shared inventory management systems	In the operational network a number of Information Systems will be shared. Details of inventory (both raw material, work-in-process and finished goods) residing at all supply points (retailer, assembly, raw material, etc.) should be open to access by any partner in the web. Without it some of the parties will be blind and operate to the detriment of the whole.
Small batch orders	The QR approach requires that all activity matches demand. Consequently, production batch sizes, to replicate orders, are in small and flexible lots. Amounts larger than demand will cause inventory cost and likely waste.
Sharing product information with trading partners	This encompasses more than just inventory holding. Promotions, new developments, availability, pricing, costing, logistics, etc. will all require an open-book culture between enterprises.
Modular or cellular manufacturing	As we will discuss in the next chapter, modular or cellular manufacturing will offer a far higher degree of response, speed and flexibility. Despite initial cost outlay, this form of production organization has proved to be, when compared to the traditional line, superior in most departments.
Joint product planning	Product development and modification can no longer be done in isolation. Customers, consumers and providers must all share in the process. As members of a network their input is vital and consideration of their needs paramount.
Consumer demographic information system	Through the use of PoS data and developments such as loyalty cards, more data than ever is being collected on consumer preferences. Third party firms now provide data collection, storage and analysis services. In short, consumer data mining is now big business. However, to date, much of this has been jealously guarded. We contend that firms operating in a mutual network must be prepared to share their demographic data and information for all to benefit.
Demand relationships	Customers/consumers, products and product flows are all unique. At an operational level QR recognizes that within a mutual network there will be a number of distinct businesses that are defined by product or customer rather than legal status. Therefore, each enterprise in the mutual network will need to assess and delineate these important flows (which are of course dynamic and liable to change).

3.10.3   The Quick Response Culture

The culture of an organization will both contribute to strategic direction and greatly influence its implementation. It should be aligned, as far as possible, to the desired strategic response. But, what is culture? Organizational culture is the deeper level *basic assumptions and beliefs* that are shared by members, that operate unconsciously and define in a basic taken-for-granted fashion the organization's view of itself and its environment (Schein, 1985). The culture is rooted in organizational, group, and individual experience over time. It is shaped by stories, symbols, power, organization, control, leadership, rituals, routines, and the overall paradigm that these comprise. In other words, culture is defined as:

> The psychological manifestation of incompletely shared and understood meanings of the environment, social relationships, patterns of behavior, norms of conduct, etc.

We believe that culture should be viewed as something the organization *is* rather than something an organization *has*. The latter signifies that it is something that is imported into an enterprise from the broader society or something created by management that can be changed by them. The former typifies an emergence from social interactions as the product of negotiated and shared symbols and meanings, and empowerment, through a sense of shared values, that can to a degree be manipulated.

It is clear that this ephemeral concept will have a significant bearing upon the effectiveness of the organization, especially through its dealings with the external environment.

What then of the QR culture. Whatever euphemism you care to use, 'downsized', 'flattened', 'outsourced' or 'rightsized', organizations of the 1990s are smaller, with fewer people doing more and feeling less secure. With this has come the increasing realization that customers and products or services are no longer homogeneous, there is huge variety and diversity. The QR organization has to replicate this and cannot rely on a deep-seated, ingrained and rigid set of assumptions and beliefs suitable for limited product/customer groups. Although, for many at this time a difficult concept to comprehend, the QR culture is by necessity diverse and flexible in the extreme: a multi-culture.

The successful use of QR strategies and operations will rely totally upon the cultural adaptation of the firm and its mutual network. To encourage this, attention must be paid to the following main elements:

- Structure. A vast array of organizational structures exists. The simple structure, the traditional functional structure, the multi-divisional structure, holding company structure, matrix structure, product or market based structures, process or horizontal structures, etc. The QR firm of the next century will increasingly rely on a transient network or virtual arrangement both internally and externally. Work groups and indeed whole organizations will form synergistic facilities dedicated to customer groupings or particular product processes. These will, however, be highly flexible and able to dissolve and reconvene as demand flows change. This type of agile allegiance will necessitate individuals being committed to particular parts of a network and often working physically within suppliers or customers premises.

- Externality. The ethos and philosophy of the QR organization is externally focused. Traditional boundaries are fleeting. Networks, alliances and working groups form and disband in-line with demand. This new constitution requires a change in thinking and approach. Individuals will rely upon leadership, communication and education to provide and assist the necessary external viewpoint.
- Information. In a similar manner, information must be comprehended as inter-organizational. In the past, information has often been jealously guarded, especially at the interface between firms. Futuristically, data and information can no longer be viewed as the sole property of a single enterprise. Once again, it is the culture of the web and the complete dependence on other firms in symbiotic relationships that must be instilled.
- Knowledge. With information comes knowledge and knowledge sharing at the point of need and use through a networked pattern of communication. A broad knowledge development, access, retrieval, sharing and use must be encouraged for the flexibility needed in the QR organization.
- Control systems and leadership styles. The traditional command and control hierarchy of large bureaucratic systems has dissolved into a decentralized process of efficiency and economic control. The QR approach takes this a step further by placing an emphasis upon open network co-ordination, cross-functional and cross-organizational processes and external systems integration. Leadership styles must reflect the need for an outward focus and recognition of the degree to which the new environment shapes and influences all activity.
- Management. Commitment to continual change and building a capacity for change. The management of the organization reflects the various requirements of the various markets served. The primary task of the management of the enterprise as a whole is relating the total system to its environment and network through the regulation of boundary interchanges, rather than internal regulation. Management that takes the environment as given and concentrates on organizing internally in the most efficient way is pursuing a dangerous course.

3.11 COMMENTS

The last three chapters have reviewed the new and growing environmental demands and some of the latest management thinking, tools, techniques and strategies. There is no shortage of theories for improvement. There are lots of phrases, words and terms in the literature, but little prescriptive direction. Wisdom exists, but what are lacking are the practical steps necessary for improvement.

The remainder of the book will draw upon these lessons and detail a different concept. In contrast to many of the other offerings in this field, an attempt will be made to explain the ideas with a methodology for implementation that is firmly based upon quantifiable and pragmatic management thinking, and sound Industrial Engineering.

The following chapters will attempt to explain how to organize for the future; how to build flexibility and responsiveness into all unique and core activities. This will be achieved through the theory and methodologies of Quick Response (QR). These ideas are applicable to many industries, whether they are retailing, manufacturing or consumer services. Examples will, in the main, be given from the immensely complicated textile and clothing industry for two reasons: first, QR was developed there, and second, this is possibly one of the most demanding and dynamic industries in existence—success there is hard won indeed!

PART II
QUICK RESPONSE WITHIN THE ORGANIZATION

There is nothing new about Quick Response; its forerunner was practiced more than 400 years ago, though in a different environment:

> In the early years of Elizabeth (1538), Exeter gained the third place among the ports of the kingdom for its exports of cloth ... . The organization of the trade is well known (Westcote's account): How the farmer sent his wool to the market; it was bought by the comber or spinner, who the next week brought in the spun yarn, which the weaver bought and the next week brought back as cloth. It was then sold to the clothier, who after fulling and sometimes dyeing it, transported it to London or exported it.
>
> AL Rowse (1950)

4
QUICK RESPONSE: ORIGINS, STATUS AND OUTLOOK

In this chapter, we take a brief look at the origins of QR, and the findings of the groups involved in its development. This is followed by an examination of the circumstances that slowed its adoption. Some of these were cultural; why should adversarial relationships suddenly change, while others had to do with technology and the ways in which industry segments communicate. There was also a lack of strategic vision; a failure to see that it is the profitability of the pipeline as a whole that is important—not the individual stages. Technology was moving at a rapid pace in the mid-1980s, but its use was limited to the larger companies, there was little standardization of electronic documents and formats, and the systems being used were, in large part, incompatible.

The third part of the chapter gives an overview of the current and future positions of QR among manufacturers and retailers. It includes the results of recent industry surveys, which make it clear that the future of QR is heavily dependent on progress made by many SMEs (Small to Medium-sized Enterprises).

4.1 ORIGINS

Early in 1984, a textile industry sponsored research program was undertaken in the USA[1]. Its mission was to develop procedures that would make the domestic industry more competitive with imports. These had surged over the preceding decade and had led to massive reductions in employment.

Table 4.1 below shows the pipeline inventories and Work in Process (WIP) in weeks for the various sectors as developed in the 1980s. For those with only

---

[1] Those interested in the historical development of QR are referred to what we believe are its earliest publications: American Apparel Manufacturers Association (1987) *Getting started in Quick Response*, Arlington, VA, USA; Gunston R and Harding P (1987) *QR: US and UK Experiences*, Textile Outlook International (10), 43–51; Kurt Salmon Associates (1988) *Quick Response Implementation—Action Steps for Retailers, Manufacturers and Suppliers*, KSA, Atlanta, GA, USA; and *Quick Response in Apparel Manufacturing*, Hunter NA (1990).

Table 4.1   Apparel pipeline inventories and work in process (weeks)

		Inventory	WIP
Fiber			
Raw material		1.6	
WIP			0.9
Finished fiber @ fiber		4.6	
Fiber @ textile		1.0	
	Total	8.1	0.9
Fabric			
WIP—Greige			3.9
Greige goods @ greige		1.2	
Greige goods @ finish		1.4	
Finishing			1.2
Finished fabric @ textile		7.4	
Fabric @ apparel		6.8	
	Total	16.8	5.1
Apparel			
WIP			5.0
Finished apparel @ apparel		12.0	
Ship to retail		2.7	
Apparel @ retail distribution center		6.3	
Apparel @ store		10.0	
	Total	31.0	5.0
Total		55.0	11.0

a sketchy knowledge of the textile/apparel industry, it should be read in conjunction with Figure 4.1, which shows, sequentially, the various components of the pipeline.

The time components in Table 4.1 added to a total of 66 weeks, though only 11 weeks were taken up with processing; the balance of over one-year was storage time. For knit goods, the pipeline is shorter—six to seven months —because of processes that are shorter, and more flexible. An interesting statistic was developed at the time of the original QR investigations: an individual fiber spends only about 20 minutes actually being processed during this 6–15 month period (Harding of Kurt Salmon Associates, personal communication).

Table 4.1 and Figure 4.1 also demonstrate the duplication of inventories. Product is held by a supplier as finished goods and additional stocks are held by the customer as raw material; the linkages between the various steps in the pipeline are interfaced (on both sides) by duplications of stockholding. These duplications of inventories reflect, in part, the one-time separation of the textile and manufacturing industries referred to in Chapter 2 of this book, and the lack of communication between the major players in the supply pipeline.

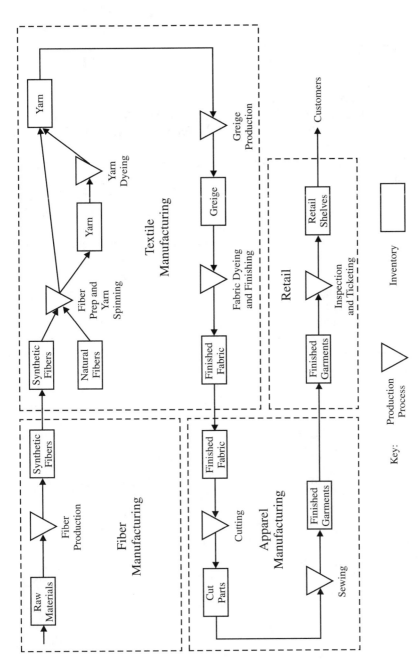

Figure 4.1 Steps in the apparel pipeline

Table 4.2   Revenue losses in the apparel pipeline (% retail sales)

	Fiber and textile	Apparel	Retail	Total
Forced markdowns	0.6%	4.0%	10.0%	14.6%
Stockouts	0.1	0.4	3.5	4.0
Inventory @				
15% carrying cost	1.0	2.5	2.9	6.4
Total	1.7%	6.9%	16.4%	25.0%

The type of pipeline analysis conducted in the 1980s is only now being seen in other industries, e.g. food, under the banner of 'Supply Chain Mapping' and ECR. Nevertheless, an understanding of the fuller picture that it brings is vital for successful implementation of QR and SCM.

The information obtained early in the study, and summarized in Table 4.1, had a double impact: it awoke the industry to the fact that massive cost reduction possibilities were to hand, ensuring that data and other inputs were readily available, and it pointed directly to the methodologies that were to become QR.

Table 4.2 above shows the revenue losses, expressed as a percent of retail sales for the pipeline. One item is the cost of carrying the inventories displayed in Table 4.1. The biggest item is forced markdowns—mainly at retail—with the total losses amounting to over 14% of retail sales. Here we differentiate between promotional markdowns, e.g. special sales, and the marking down that occurs out of necessity when a season ends and the goods must be moved to make way for new merchandise—forced markdowns.

Manufacturers are not immune to markdowns. They are carrying a great deal of inventory and at any time can be asked by the retailer to contribute to store markdowns. Further, if they are left with unshipped goods at the end of a season, they must get rid of their stocks at greatly reduced prices—called 'eating it'. This is one of the major drawbacks in the current trend toward adoption of Vendor Managed Inventory (VMI) systems.

Vendor Managed Inventory—Coats Viyella plc

Coats Viyella plc are an international group of companies operating in world-wide textile and precision engineering markets. With an annual turnover of £2.3 billion and a diverse product portfolio in 60 countries they are justly proud of their high levels of customer service.

In one particular market, their thread division, they offer a unique service to customers: Vendor Managed Inventory (VMI). Much has been written on the subject of VMI, but we have found that there are different forms of VMI, some more beneficial than others.

Coats operate what we term 'true VMI'. They supply numerous types of thread to clothing manufacturers. These are stored on site and

continues

only paid for when moved from the storage area to the production line. Thus, for the manufacturer, he is only paying for what is used. Coats work closely with manufacturers in order to keep them supplied in line with production schedules—full and frank information sharing is the bedrock of this agreement. They take full responsibility for the thread supplies leaving the manufacturer to concentrate on other aspects. Coats even employ staff to work on the customer's site advising line operators how best to use the raw material supplied. Consequently, they form a unique partnership with manufacturers and manage their inventory from raw material to finished goods stage.

We believe that often firms adopt VMI strategies as a precursor to full QR implementation. However, some forms of VMI are less pure. For example, a number of retailers in the food and grocery industry are intent upon imposing greater responsibility for stock management upon their suppliers—often right up to time of sale. However, they neglect to supply one essential ingredient: information. The vendor is thus 'myopic' and increasingly forced to react to demand without being told what it is!

The second category of losses is that due to stockouts. These occur when a potential customer cannot find the SKU he or she wants, be it size, color or style. The values shown in Table 4.2 were estimates obtained from retailers, but in all honesty, there was little basis for the entries as few retailers had any means of measuring this kind of lost sale. We will show later that more sophisticated values are now available, but even so, they remain estimates.

The most important finding in the 1984 study was that if the pipeline is condensed to about one-third of its traditional length, something very interesting happens. Not only is the design process able to reflect more accurate style information, but it is possible for the retailer to re-assess the demand for the apparel line while the season is under way and receive small, frequent reorders from the vendor, provided reorder lead-times are short enough—of the order of 2–4 weeks (Harding, 1985; Frazier, 1986). The effect on sales forecast errors of shortening the design process is shown in Figure 4.2. Here the central horizontal axis shows the number of months ahead of the season that style and color predictions are made and the upper and lower curves show estimates of the forecast error. Twelve-month lead-times are common and yet significant improvements are available if these times can be reduced. Discussion of what defines a forecast error is a topic reserved for Chapter 6.

Quick Response in Apparel Manufacturing (Hunter, 1990) gives the results of the above studies and an historical coverage of QR, together with other analyses, including the economics of Traditional vs. QR manufacturing for a variety of men's and women's clothing, and comparisons with off-shore pro-

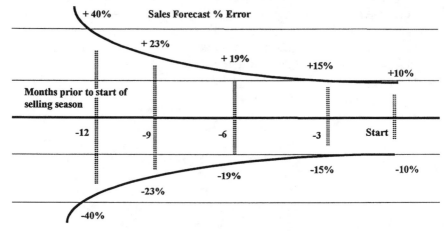

Figure 4.2   Lead-time effect on sales forecast error

duction economics. The analyses also examined the logistics costs associated with greatly shortened order lead-times, e.g. express direct shipping vs. the usual 'cost first' routes.

The same book describes the next phase of the research, a series of full-scale pipeline trials involving textile mills, manufacturers and retailers. The trials confirmed the research findings; inventory turns increased sharply, as did sales volumes, but they suffered from very high set-up and monitoring costs, and trial times of 12–18 months.

There were three trials carried to completion. The garments involved and some of the results obtained are shown below:

(1) Basic slack
   - Unit sales increased 31%
   - Inventory turns increased from 3.7 to 4.8
   - Average items out of stock decreased from 29% to 17%
(2) Men's suit
   - Sales increased 59%
   - Inventory turns increased from 1.1 to 2.1
   - Gross margin increased 82%
(3) Seasonal blouse
   - Sales increased 47%
   - Inventory turns increased from 6.2 to 8.5
   - Return on inventory increased 37%.

In general, the industry was impressed by the work but did little to follow up on it. In retrospect, few were ready for fundamental changes in procedures or partnerships, the costs of change were very large, and the technology required was in its infancy. There were also comments that undue attention had been paid to the merchandise involved in the trials, thus inflating the improvements shown above.

4.2 THE QUICK RESPONSE APPROACH

As discussed, QR has its origins in the textile and clothing industry of North America in the early 1980s. It was not long, however, before its utility in other sectors was recognized. The growing complexity and volatility of demand forced many industries to adopt an approach that recognized the heterogeneity of products and demand as well as their underlying turbulence and intricacy.

We now consider the wider viewpoints of QR; the various definitions that have sprung from numerous industry applications. Thereafter QR essential elements are provided that build on those in Chapter 3.

4.2.1. Definitions

We have already offered our preferred, generic QR definition in Section 3.10 of Chapter 3. However, in considering its origins and development, the reader should be aware that there are others from diverse sources. For completeness some of these are now provided.

A mode of operation in which a manufacturing or service industry strives to provide products and services to its customers in the precise quantities, varieties and within the time-frames that those customers require. (Gunston and Harding, 1987)

... integrated relationships between suppliers and customers; better flow of information; [and] flexible technology in manufacturing. (Braithwaite, 1990)

... (a) a strategy that uses Universal-Product Codes (UPC) for inventory control and electronic information sharing among textile mills, apparel manufacturers and retailers', and (b) 'a business philosophy that incorporates a just-in-time approach to manufacturing. (Sullivan, 1992)

... common among all of the QR definitions [are]: a) communication of information between trading partners, b) reduction in time ... , and c) responsiveness to consumer's demands. (Kincade, 1995)

A state of responsiveness in which a manufacturer seeks to provide a product to a customer in the precise quantity, quality, and timeframe required. In doing so, lead times and expenditures for labor, materials and inventories are minimized; flexibility is emphasized in order to meet the changing requirements of a competitive marketplace. (The Textile Apparel Linkage Council, 1988)

A new business strategy to optimize the flow of information and merchandise between channel members to maximize consumer satisfaction. (Ko, 1993)

QR is a co-operative arrangement of feedback and response. It is aimed at maximizing profitability of the pipeline and is driven by comprehensive and rapid information transfer between sectors, from retail point-of-sale back up-stream, utilizing frank and open dialogue between supplier and customer, thus relying upon high levels of mutual trust. It is a move toward creating value-adding partnerships. (Lowson, 1995).

QR depends upon integration of all parts: fiber, textile (spinning, knitting, weaving), clothing manufacture, and retail, into a consumer responsive whole giving highest standards of product quality at all stages. This allows significant reductions in safety stocks and product specification testing times. It calls for the use of up-to-date hard and soft technologies to minimize work in progress, maximize customer responsiveness, and to off-set the added costs of increased diversity in the system. (Hunter, 1990)

QR is a customer service strategy, (a pull system) that uses technology to make possible an industry pipeline so flexible and efficient that, ideally, retailers can continually replenish, with accurate speed of response, what is sold, and have the merchandise in store on time and in the right quantities, colors, sizes and styles. This ability is essential in an industry that is highly labor intensive, faces huge fashion volatility, and subject to massive import penetration. (Lowson, 1995)

QR is a company-wide commitment to quality, empowerment, customer service, continuous improvement and change. QR provides the ability to make information driven decisions at the last possible moment in time, prior to the need to execute the decisions by a flexible, empowered work-force. (Lowson and Hunter, 1996)

Enhanced responsiveness through greatly increased flexibility and continuous short-cycle innovation aimed at creating new markets for both new and mature products that are of a world class quality and service. (Authors)

QR uses many elements. Its underlying strength is its flexibility and adherence to a contingent philosophy. Unlike other approaches, QR believes that a host of techniques are required (a tool-kit) and that the emphasis used in any situation will vary.

4.2.2.   Quick Response Elements

It may be useful at this point to summarize the main elements of QR. These are given below in the form of a quasi definition and apply to any supply system:

- QR is a strategy, culture and operational philosophy together with a set of procedures aimed at reducing the cost of operating a supply pipeline while satisfying the requirements of the ultimate consumer.

- QR depends on the integration of all the parts—raw materials, primary processing, manufacturing and retailing—into one consumer-responsive whole.
- QR requires the highest standards of product quality at all stages to allow significant reductions in safety stocks and specification-testing times.
- QR demands frank and open dialogue between supplier and customer and relies on high levels of trust. Only with such trust are Value Adding Partnerships (VAPs) possible.
- QR is driven by comprehensive and rapid information transfer between the pipeline sectors, from retail point-of-sale back up-stream.
- QR calls for the use of up-to-date hard and soft technologies to minimize work in process, offset the added costs of increased product diversity and to maximize responsiveness to the customer.
- QR employs as its principal elements:
  — the pulling back of open-to-buy dates.
  — sharp reductions in pre-season deliveries of merchandise to the retailer.
  — point-of-sale tracking at retail.
  — flexible merchandise planning.
  — frequent buyer reorders.
  — pre-ticketing and drop-shipping of products.
  — standardized bar-coding of goods.
  — electronic transmission of orders, invoices, etc. (EDI).
  — highly engineered manufacturing, including such elements as computerized marker making, laser cutting, modular manufacturing and automated sub-assembly sewing.
  — Computer Assisted Design and Manufacture (CAD/CAM).
  — flexible short-run process operations.
  — Just-In-Time (JIT) shipping.
  — rapid development of samples or prototypes.

Undoubtedly, the early proponents of QR were naive. We now realize that their expectation levels were far too high. Two related examples will suffice to illustrate this claim:

- Changes in management practices and corporate culture are notoriously slow to occur and frequently require the ascension of a new generation of leaders.
- It was assumed that the often adversarial relationships between sectors would change readily, giving way to 'partnerships'. One of the problems with the latter assumption is that the major part of the increase in profits accruing from QR goes to the retailer, while up-stream participants take on most of the cost burden. Without some sharing of the benefits as well as the costs, amicable partnerships are unlikely to develop.

In fact, very few changes occurred in the pipeline for the next 10–12 years. US Department of Commerce data show that while the retail sector showed respectable gains in productivity (4–5%/year), the up-stream components achieved only 1–2%/year. A more specifically QR related index—Retail Inventory to Sales (I/S) ratios—has shown no improvement, hovering around 2.5 over the same period.

In the next chapter we will examine a number of industry sectors in more detail in order to try to discover which of them would benefit most from the application of QR. One of the most important indicators is the seasonality of the goods being moved. Figure 4.3 shows the Sales/month, and the I/S ratios for department stores as recently as 1997. The sharp increase in Sales during the holiday period, and the equally sharp drop in I/S ratios represent a

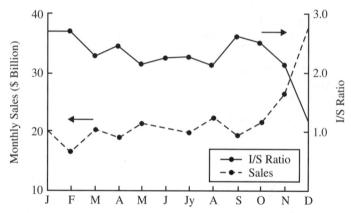

Figure 4.3   Monthly sales and Inventory/Sales ratios: US department stores—1997

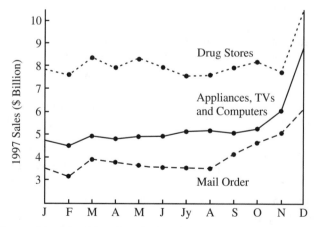

Figure 4.4   Monthly sales of miscellaneous merchandise—1997

nightmare for both retailers and customers as stock-outs and lost sales increase markedly. This pattern of holiday sales increase does not apply to all merchandise (see Chapter 5), but it is widespread. Figure 4.4 shows 1997 monthly sales patterns for several other industry sectors.

We now come to the heart of the problem of why QR was slow to be adopted—delays in using information technology.

4.3. INFORMATION TECHNOLOGY

The rapid and accurate acquisition, handling and transmission of information is central to QR. In 1985, bar-coding was common among supermarkets and food producers, but it was not clear that Universal Product Code (UPC) symbology could be extended to the more complicated apparel business. As it turned out, adoption by the larger retailers was fairly rapid, accompanied by bar-code scanners in the distribution centers and at point of sale. One problem remained; that of the accuracy of the bar-codes. Some retailers have estimated that up to 70% of Electronic Data Interchange (EDI) transactions, including bar-codes, contain wrong or incomplete information, making sales tracking, inventory holding and re-estimations/reorders error prone.

This lack of faith in the manufacturers' UPC numbers or item marks resulted in some retailers maintaining their own internal numbering schemes to associate the vendors' bar-codes with their own internal number or mark. This mapping of data-sets involves duplication of data, and is prone to errors; so much so that those retailers importing merchandise from the EU have considered discarding the European Article Numbering (EAN) system because of the inaccuracy of vendors' encoding and the lack of integrity checks on the creation and assignment of EAN numbers.

Considering that accurate UPC marking is a requirement for a true QR environment, little progress has been made towards having vendors comply with industry standards. Late in 1994, a number of major retailers in the USA implemented penalties for non-compliance. These include Dillards, Dayton Hudson, and Federated Department Stores; most recently, Sears (Canada) has joined the group. We believe this to be a necessity for the health of the industry, and preferable to opting out of UPC (or EAN) standards. There are approximately 1100 manufacturers in the USA now transmitting UPCs to the price sales catalogue—less than 7% of the market. We have a long way to go (Hunter and Valentino, 1995).

The storage and manipulation of inventory and sales data afforded more problems. In 1985, IBM dominated apparel pipeline computing with its mainframe and mini computers—mainly 34s and 36s. The cost of large computers and their software was, of course, prohibitive for any but the largest companies. Microcomputers had been introduced four years previously but, with their limited memory and speed, they were not considered suitable for enterprise data handling. For small companies, computing really only became feasible with the appearance of low cost 386 and 486 machines.

Another group of problems centers on information transmission: EDI. In 1985, the Value Added Networks (VANS) included General Electric's GEIS, the IBM Network, Ordernet (now Sterling Software), and British Telecom, concentrating on the grocery and food businesses. These networks acted as middlemen between those sending information and those receiving it, thus providing an 'added value' of in-house translation since there were no standardized documents for the retail-related industries. Standardized formats for orders and invoices for the general merchandise and retail industries were developed early in 1987 by the Voluntary Industry Communications Standards (VICS) committee when it set about the task of establishing EDI formats for the apparel industry (Kurt Salmon Associates, 1989).

It is no surprise, then, that it was the end of the decade before all the pieces were in place for QR even to become possible.

4.3.1   Universal Product Code/European Article Number Compliance

The requirement that there be a unique item number for each different product is essential if a global, consumer-driven POS-controlled system is to be established. The standards for full compliance with this concept have been developed in the USA and Canada by the Voluntary Industry Committee and published by the Uniform Code Council as the 'Data Communication Guidelines for Retail and General Merchandise'. In the case of apparel, the manufacturers must indicate their style number, National Retail Federation (NRF) color number and NRF size number. Together, these are associated with one unique 1-digit number represented by UPC/A symbology; i.e. a bar-code. It should be noted that the retail and general merchandise industry is the only segment with published standards for product identification. Such standards do not exist for groceries, over-the-counter drugs, health and beauty care products, prescription drugs and hardware.

The National Retail Federation is an organization that represents retail interests in the USA and Canada. Its color system currently recognizes 1000 color groups and the Federation has developed various size tables that are category-specific. Thus, a manufacturer must assign an NRF color number to the specific product within the category, size his product, and find the related mappings when comparing many manufacturers' sizing differences.

In countries other than the USA and Canada, a 13-digit EAN symbology is used. The UPC number becomes an EAN number by adding a '0' in front of the UPC number. This is possible since the USA and Canada share the same country code value of '00'. However, problems are now emerging. In countries other than the USA and Canada, there are no reference color or size tables, but manufacturers in Europe seeking to publish their product catalogues on various price/sales catalogues in the USA and Canada must assign NRF size and color values to their products. A US or Canadian manufacturer can create a compliant VICS 832 price/sales catalogue document and transmit it as an EDIFACT or an ANSI document. However, an 832 which is being generated globally according to EAN standards and which is sent to the USA and Canada for posting will be rejected since the global standards do not comply with the NRF standards.

The standardization of size and color reference tables which transcend geographical and country boundaries must become a priority if we are to succeed in creating a Quick Response environment that supports co-ordinated, demand-activated manufacturing responses. The lack or absence of data-compatibility standards among countries that produce apparel and general merchandise products will hinder the so-called 'co-ordinated responses' that retail communities are seeking in order to meet their customers' (the consumers) needs. Given the recent requirement of many US and Canadian retailers for their domestic suppliers to become UPC compliant, it may be safely assumed that similar pressures on overseas suppliers will be heightened. To this end, the value-added networks are now considering the business requirement of these suppliers, though they will need the assistance of the appropriate industry or trade groups to set up the necessary standards.

4.3.2   Electronic Data Interchange Standards

In addition to bar-codes, information that can be conveyed electronically includes orders, invoices, shipping notices and a variety of other documents.

It has been said—with some basis—that the only thing standard about EDI standards is the lack of a standard. Retailers and manufacturers use sub-sets of the existing standards; a retailer or trading partner feeling free to select from the available document those data elements that are applicable to their own operational needs. To give just two examples, among retailers in the USA and Canada, there is no single template for the Advanced Ship Notice (856), and the three networks that have a price sales catalogue (GEIS, Sterling, Quick Response Services), support different data elements within the 832 document and have different templates or requirements for the structure of the (832) document.

The likelihood that there will be 'universal documents' in the near future is small indeed; all participants in the EDI process, including the VANS, must make the effort towards greater levels of consistency.

4.3.3   Value Added Networks

The role of the Value Added Networks (VANS) has changed significantly since the inception of QR in 1985. Then, they were perceived as being only the telecommunication gateway for the trafficking of EDI documents among multiple trading partners. These third party networks provided 'added value' by offering retailers and manufacturers alike the ability to 'translate documents' among various versions and computing platforms and transmit them more quickly than the traditional physical forms of delivery. Speed of delivery collapsed order-fulfilment cycle time and this was perceived by many as the meaning of quick response.

In a strict sense, EDI is a sub-set of QR. The true benefits of an EDI environment are reached when there is application-to-application integration (APP to APP). An example of this would be when orders are electronically received by a manufacturer and the orders are automatically processed by the internal host system of the supplier without human intervention. Such a system would eliminate certain 'non-added value processes' and thus decrease labor costs to the manufacturer. In the event that the environment did not reflect APP to APP, the benefits to the retailer would only be to speed up delivery of the documents while the labor costs of the manufacturer would increase. An example of this is to be found in the majority of those smaller manufacturers new to EDI. An order is received, downloaded and then manually re-entered into the internal control network. This not only costs time and effort, but also increases the chance of errors occurring. Clearly, there is a need for software to link the external and internal systems. Such linkages are mandatory if the manufacturer is to streamline operational procedures so as to minimize inventories or make optimal use of contractors. Indications are that such software is becoming increasingly available.

4.4.   THE CURRENT POSITION

In 1984, when the data in Tables 4.1 and 4.2 were gathered, retail sales of apparel in the USA amounted to $100 billion. Today, the value is at least 50% greater. However, little has changed in most areas, and, while current UK estimates differ somewhat as to detail, they still put the overall pipeline losses at 24% of sales. Retail markdowns are believed to be on the increase as short season goods gain in market share, and eat into marketers' profits. Raw material stocks are smaller than previously, but the persistence of large minimum orders and long lead-times still penalize the manufacturer.

One improvement stands out. This is the reduction in inventories. In the early 1980s, inventories represented about 24% of the US gross domestic product. By 1995, they had dropped to less than 15%. These numbers, as a minimum, reflect the improvements in pipeline management.

In general, the vendors have improved their manufacturing methods. Increasingly, companies are converting from the classic 'straight line' assembly to more flexible modular systems which make for shorter order lead-times. Such changes are neither easy nor swift to execute; it can take two to three years to convert a plant to modular, or cellular, production, but the benefits in terms of customer responsiveness are highly significant. Thanks to industry

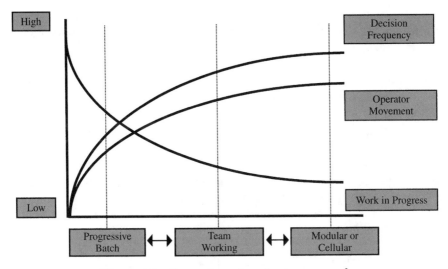

Figure 4.5   Comparison of production systems[2]

sources, it is possible to summarize the effects of these production systems. Figure 4.5 compares three systems, Progressive Batch (the classic system), Modular/Cellular (the most flexible and responsive) and Team Working (an increasingly popular system that is relatively easy to implement), in terms of three key attributes. Table 4.3 expands this information to include other measures of performance.

Despite the problems discussed above, all pipeline sectors have accepted that the entire system must be consumer driven via PoS information and there

Table 4.3   Production system characteristics

Attribute	Batch	Team Working	Modular/Cellular
Amount of work in progress	High	Low	None
Operator movement	None	Simple pattern	Complex pattern
Multi-skill training	None	Medium	High
Batch size (guideline)	12–48+	2–24	1
Product turn time	Days/weeks	Hours	Minutes
Remuneration system	Piecework rate	Group incentive plus production bonus	Group incentive and skill bonus

---

[2] We are grateful to [TC][2] for their help and advice in preparing Figure 4.5 and Table 4.3.

is now a well-defined movement towards one important aspect of QR; the major retailers have assumed leadership in its implementation. As mentioned earlier, with many of these organizations, suppliers are now on notice that EDI is, or will be in the near future, a condition of doing business. The result is a scramble among small and medium-sized vendors (SMEs) to acquire technology. The large manufacturers are, for the most part, already equipped.

4.4.1   Retail Industry Survey

Ko and Kincade (1997) recently surveyed retailers as to their adoption of the technologies underlying QR. The data in Table 4.4 summarize their findings.

The main points are easy to spot. SMEs lag far behind the larger chains and discount houses and for some technologies progress is small or nil. Bar-coding and PoS tracking is well advanced among the large stores, but achieving smaller lot sizes or inventory reductions lags. Overall, however, progress is good and the tools are in place for full QR adoption.

The driving force behind this movement among the larger retailers is the vision of inventory reductions, particularly of basic goods. These are year-round items or those with long shelf lives, relatively unaffected by fashion. However, once EDI is in place, garments of every seasonality will be affected. Led by Wal-Mart, there is a growing realization among retailers that replenishment of basic or long season goods could well become the responsibility of vendors once they have been supplied with accurate PoS data. The consequences for the manufacturer of assuming greater inventory responsibility will be examined later in the book.

Table 4.4   Usage of QR technologies: Retail stores

Technology	Specialty chain	Department store	Discount	Small individual
Automatic replenishment	63	56	56	4
Bar-codes on each merchandise	81	81	86	17
Electronic data interchange	69	63	67	0
Electronic purchase reorder	75	62	67	0
Inventory management systems	69	54	64	33
Product planning with customer	63	25	36	13
Reduction in inventory size	25	33	50	17
Sales captured at the item level	88	87	94	38
Scanning merchandise at point of sale	94	87	89	17
Sharing product information with trading partners	63	58	53	17
Small lot orders	13	12	11	13

The interaction between EDI and both Seasonal (12–20 weeks of shelf life) and Short Season or Fashion merchandise (10 weeks or less) is more complex. In addition to orders, invoices and advance shipping notices, full implementation of QR for seasonal goods will require re-estimation/reorder procedures to ensure the correct volume and mix of SKUs on the shelf, both during the season, to maximize customer service, and at the end of the season, to minimize the markdown effect. These are some way away from being developed commercially, though the software has already been prototyped.

QR impacts fashion goods to a lesser extent than either basics or seasonal merchandise. Though shorter pipelines improve the forecasting and order accuracy of styles and colors, there is insufficient time in the selling season to correct design or buying errors. In the early days of QR, it was hoped that the domestic time contraction and postponement of activities would help counteract off-shore cost advantages. The jury is still out on this aspect of the business. Off-shore suppliers have responded well to US retailers' insistence on shorter lead-times. An example of this is the 500-hour rule imposed by The Limited, a large specialty chain. Given the fabric and the pattern, Far East suppliers are to have goods on the shelf three weeks after order, with the aid of air transportation. However, for this important and growing class of merchandise, there is mounting evidence that competitive advantage involves more than just lead-times and Gross Margins. In later chapters, we will look at the importance of a variety of retail performance measures and demonstrate the case for QR with seasons as short as eight weeks.

4.4.2 Manufacturer Surveys

A survey of UK manufacturers has recently been completed that throws light on the readiness of manufacturing SMEs for QR adoption (Lowson, 1998a), as well as the problems they face and possible solutions open to them. The findings agree well with those of a smaller survey carried out in Canada (Hunter, 1996).

The UK survey covered 64 companies broken down into the groups shown in Table 4.5. Their customer groups are shown in Table 4.6.

Table 4.5 Types of manufacturer business

Manufacturer	Percentage
CMT	14
Contractor	19
Captive supplier	15
Independent manufacturer	27
Independent manufacturer and marketer	25

Table 4.6   Types of vendor customer

	Large multiple retailer	Department store	Specialty store	Discount/ warehouse club	Independent retailer	Non-store retailing
CMT	4	8				1
Contractor	1	1	4		4	8
Captive supplier	6	7	2		4	
Independent manufacturer	5	6	8	2	5	10
Independent manufacturer and marketer	8	9	8	1	8	7
Total	24	31	22	3	21	26
	18.9%	24.4%	17.3%	2.4%	16.5%	20.5%

Because there is no generally agreed upon definition of the descriptors used in this section of the chapter, the following notes are offered:

- CMT—Cut, Make and Trim. A customer, usually a retailer, supplies the fabric, and the design. The manufacturer makes up the garment according to instructions. Usually tied to a retailer, and leads a precarious existence when sales do not go according to plan.
- Contractor. Works to rigid customer specification but is free to source own cloth and accessories. Some room for diversity if sufficiently flexible.
- Captive/captured supplier. A wholly dedicated extension of the customer, usually a multiple/chain.
- Independent. Production driven by 'own' or 'private label' design. Many outlets.
- Independent manufacturer/marketer. As above but has own brand.
- Multiple retailer. A 'chain' in North America.

Clearly there is a great deal of overlap among these definitions, and that is reflected in the breakdowns of manufacturer/retailer relationships shown in Table 4.6. Several of the manufacturers interviewed had multiple customer bases.

The companies interviewed were questioned as to the QR methodologies used in their operations and the results are displayed in Table 4.7. A respectable number (39%) were using elements of modular or cellular manufacturing, 45% could accommodate small batch orders, and 78% bar-coded their merchandise (often at the retailers' insistence and not to aid their own operations).

The sharing of product information with trading partners was found among over a quarter of the respondents, though only 17% admitted to joint product planning with their customers. In terms of EDI, 39% claimed it existed with their suppliers, but only 14% of the manufacturers exchanged information electronically with their customers; though 27% indicated that purchase orders and invoices were handled through EDI. The most disappointing statistics were in

Table 4.7 QR methodologies in use by manufacturers

QR methodologies	CMT	Contractor	Captive supplier	Independent manufacturer	CMT Independent manufacturer and marketer	Total (%)
Electronic data interchange (with customers)			6	1	2	14.0
Electronic data interchange (with suppliers)		2	6	10	7	39.0
Bar-codes on merchandise	6	14	10	6	14	78.1
Electronic reorder						0.0
PoS data sharing with customers/suppliers		1	2		4	10.9
Re-estimation and reorder procedures			2			3.1
Continual and automatic replenishment			2			3.1
Universal product codes			4		2	9.3
Store ready deliveries	2	1	4	2	2	17.1
Container shipping codes		1	4	1	2	12.5
Electronic purchase order and invoicing		4	8	5		26.5
Shared inventory management systems		1	2		1	6.2
Small batch orders	1	5	6	5	12	45.3
Sharing product information with trading partners	2	4	8	1	2	26.5
Sales captured at item level			2	1	2	7.8
Modular or cellular manufacturing		1	6	10	8	39.0
Product planning with customer	1		8	1	1	17.1

the fields of automatic replenishment (3%), the use of re-estimation/reorder procedures (3%), and PoS data sharing (11%).

Despite the above results, which are certainly believable, over half of the interviewees were judged to be capable of development into QR operations. Some had no interest in the 'hassle' of conversion, and others were prisoners of their own cultural stasis. Certainly, it is difficult for even the most willing of manufacturers to go far without the assistance and support of suppliers and customers.

The problems facing SMEs, expressed in qualitative terms, are summarized in Table 4.8. Table 4.9 suggests solutions to these problems that complement the overall up-grading steps outlined in Chapter 6.

There are few surprises here. However, over half the respondents recognized that improvements are mandatory for future success and were willing to make the changes needed, but not in isolation; co-operation from suppliers and customers alike is the trigger that is needed.

The QR status of, and potential for, manufacturing SMEs are extremely important subjects. The SMEs produce a majority of the garments found on retail shelves, and an even larger proportion of fashion goods. Unless they can be converted to 'agile and responsive' suppliers, the larger retailers will continue to source off-shore, with all the concomitant impacts on employment generally, and on female/second-earner employment in particular. Most of this

Table 4.8   Major SME problems/roadblocks

Limited or no supply chain linkages (up- and down-stream)
Lack of flexibility to cope with greater diversity
Customer demand blindness (volume and mix) without PoS data
Poor data/information provision from supply pipeline
Over-reliance upon forecasting (own or partner)
Finished goods inventory burden
Raw material inventory burden
Retailer pressure for enhanced response
Limited financial investment
Shortage of skilled operators
High labor turnover
Poor training provision
Restrictive remuneration systems
Limited management skills
Dependency on single customer groups
Dependency on single season
Lack of product focus in high quality niche markets
Limited technological adequacy or integration (internal and external)
Poor CAD/CAM capabilities
Inadequate management information systems
Out-of-date work systems and practices
High levels of waste
Long supplier lead-times and high minimum order quantities

Table 4.9   Problem solving elements for SMEs

Better utilization of skill resources
Closer integration with suppliers and customers
Improved supply channel information flows
Enhanced flexibility and responsiveness through system changes
Network development for capacity sharing
Improved quality levels
QR strategies for flexibility and diversity
Greater opportunities for diversity
Sourcing analysis and understanding
Training needs assessment and implementation
Skills level improvement
Replacement of piecework rate remuneration system
PoS information (direct and processed)
Shortened product development times

class of producer operate on limited capital budgets and do not have sophisticated systems capabilities. Some way of training and encouragement would seem to be in urgent need.

The environments in which small manufacturers exist, together with the industry competitive pressures, have been described in both general management and industry specific terms in Lowson (1998b).

4.5.   THE FUTURE OF QUICK RESPONSE

Here we take a look at both the short- and long-term futures of QR.

4.5.1   Short Term

Over the next 2–3 years, the most pressing task for the industry will be to extend the use of EDI to all manufacturers as well as the smaller retail outlets and to forge better links with up-stream components of the supply chain.

The role of the VANS may be the most pivotal in resolving the QR supply chain's problems, as they have the technical expertise to effect change among suppliers. The retail community has, in many respects, already relegated to the VANS the task of implementing EDI solutions among their trading partners. Also, the competitive environment among the VANS has intensified, as the trafficking of electronic documents has become a price-commodity business. Certainly, they are able to provide the independent brokerage service that will facilitate the full release and sharing of PoS data in the pipeline; something that is essential for QR, in North America and in Europe.

The technologies among the VANS, although slightly different, offer similar speeds of delivery in real time terms. Since the documents are non-proprietary in nature, no one VAN provides a particular benefit. Product differentiation among the VANS in the near future will be the delivery of 'quality information products', as contrasted with speed of delivery; the VAN that provides the most accurate information to its trading partners will have the strategic advantage. To accomplish this objective, which the VANS will need to maintain or gain a share of the market, will require more 'ownership' of the supply pipeline. They will have to provide computer software solutions that add value to their information products by increasing the accuracy of the data as they are sequentially or concurrently processed, as well as permitting additional data processing and systems integration.

In order for the VANS to implement these value added applications and satisfy their retail customers' needs for quality information products, they will have to change their present training approach regarding software and solutions to an educational approach. The former stresses how something, be it a product or a process, works, while an educational approach is more concerned with why the product or process exists and how it facilitates or enables improvement or innovation.

Currently, Sterling Software's Network Division is the only VAN that provides educational courses for manufacturers. Sterling started 'COMMERCE: Institute' in 1991 to provide educational courses in supply pipeline business issues. Many of these courses deal with topics that offer no software or network solutions. What they do offer are alternatives and a vision of altered business practices that can lead to operational benefits. A strong case can be made for the retailers to tie into this aspect of the VANS' operations by mandating that their suppliers receive this kind of instruction, and awarding some form of certification to those manufacturers who comply.

In all respects, the VANS, through their value added applications, will need to champion ownership in the supply channel if the new co-ordinating technologies are not to open the door to a different kind of competitor who will fuse computers and telecommunications. Further, their job will not be complete until they streamline the interconnections, one to another. By this we mean that if a manufacturer deals with retailers using different VANS, it should not be *his* job to sort out to whom he should send what. Already, some progress is being made in this area.

Alongside the wider use of EDI must come improvements in the quality of the information being transmitted. UPC errors can be reduced or eliminated through use of such software packages as the Bar-Code Director, now being offered by the major VANS.

The reductions just beginning in retail inventories have led to a host of problems in both the short and the long term. We mention only one: that of balancing low retail inventories against desired customer service levels (the complement of stockouts) and supplier and Distribution Center (DC) leadtimes. This aspect of QR is not well understood, but progress is being made and it is, potentially, a major contributor to retail profits.

At this point, we should introduce the idea of an information field that will become increasingly important as QR develops: accurate color description. Currently, the color attributed to his merchandise by the manufacturer in the USA and Canada follows the standards set by the National Retail Federation. These can only be described as arbitrary or pre-Newtonian. There is little excuse for not adopting a more modern and accurate nomenclature such as the CIE (Commission International de l'Eclairage) system, which specifies color using three co-ordinates, and which would call for no change in standards or formats. Textile producers and the better dye houses routinely measure the color of their fabrics and could supply CIE co-ordinates. The reason often offered for not doing so (or supplying only partial information) is the claim of a need for security. This argument is indefensible—any commission dye house can match a shade in 24 hours.

4.5.2   Long Term

Having taken so long even to get started, it may seem presumptuous to guess how far QR will progress over the next five-plus years. The QR paradigm has become better understood, however, and a number of initiatives have already been taken.

The retailer, once he has worked out how to balance lead-times, stockouts and vendor lead-times, will start to examine the end-of-season markdown mix of seasonal goods, with its attendant margin loss, and install procedures for re-estimation of demand and the appropriate reorders. The problems associated with fashion merchandise, while similar, are more complex and call for sophisticated analyses of fashion and color trends. These techniques have yet to be developed; though some ideas are proposed later in the book.

While short seasons are, almost by definition, impossible to forecast, we believe that certain underlying trends can be projected, but these projections will require extensive historical databases, and these are not yet being accumulated.

Successful manufacturers will be those making use of PoS data, who can anticipate seasonal demands, estimate shifts from buyer projections and keep inventories to a minimum, while keeping their up-stream suppliers informed of their own requirements.

This kind of juggling act will require sophisticated software and innovative management. It will also call for flexible and rapid production techniques. It is in these areas that manufacturers can add real value to their merchandise and tie themselves more closely to their customers. This is the surest way to increase competitiveness—increasing the switching cost for the retailer.

It is certain that computing costs and speeds will continue to improve and we will soon be at the point where a new aspect of many businesses becomes possible on a broad scale. This will be a wider use of CAD, extended to include interactive designing of products with the customer—the retail buyer. At present, far too much time and effort is spent in making samples or prototypes and carrying them round to buying offices.

Time can be greatly reduced if the CAD images are reviewed electronically and modified as to color, style, etc. before any assembly is done. A second step will be inclusion of designs in the price-sales catalogue, thus allowing sales preference data series to be established, and the possibility of true color and style forecasting to open up.

So far, we have made little mention of the up-stream producers. This is not an oversight, but reflects our belief that the prime imperative for the pipeline is to broaden and focus the UPC/EDI aspects of the business. Given reliable PoS data and the manufacturer/retailer systems to make use of them, the industry will be in a position to tie into the very sophisticated up-stream systems capable of supporting demand-activated manufacturing.

Until this happens, we believe the most important role these large and disciplined enterprises can play is to partner the VANS in their attempts to broaden acceptance of and compliance with EDI standards. However, there is another aspect to such teamwork: developing a financial infrastructure that will allow the small manufacturer to invest in the software services needed to participate fully in the EDI process. We noted earlier the size discrepancy between the large majority of manufacturers and both their suppliers and their customers. The EDI ante poses problems for many small companies and some underwriting mechanism would do much to speed up the adoption of EDI. First and second tier suppliers, manufacturing companies, VANS and retailers alike have a financial stake in the health of the whole industries (including SMEs)—without it they have no customers.

However, in the past couple of years, there has been an interesting development. *Bobbin Magazine*, March 1997, examined the effect of e-mail, and faxes on the EDI scene. It seems that the smaller manufacturer is side-stepping the VANS and using cheap and easy to handle ways of communicating with customers—at least initially. Further, there is evidence that the retailer is encouraging and responding to this initiative. E-mail and faxes have no pre-set formats or protocols, but they are cheap, easy to use and increasingly popular. Further, waiting in the wings is probable use of web sites on the Internet by both vendor (for product catalogs) and customer (retail tenders). Many industries may well follow the example of automotive manufacturers and explore the use of EDI over 'intranets' and 'extranets' (the former are internal company web sites while the latter are Internet-like co-operative networks controlled by manufacturers and their suppliers). The use of the internet for electronic commerce is likely to increase with the development of secure data transfer tools and encryption technology[3]. This aspect of QR development must be monitored closely – its effect could be of major importance, though there remain serious questions of confidentiality of material.

---

[3] For example, DOE National Laboratories in the USA as part of the DAMA project under the AMTEX Partnerships have recently begun testing an application called TEXNET, which will soon be commercially available.

4.6   COMMENTS

Unlike so many management fads, QR is not a 'one minute wonder', it has steadily evolved over the last decade. However, this maturation and progression has been far from smooth: as so often happens, disparate standards and ill-considered systems development has led to expense and incompatibility along the entire supply pipeline.

As our research has shown, QR strategies, structures and processes have developed but are piecemeal and incomplete. Unifying industry initiatives are required (possibly from independent and objective third parties) in order that the next stage of growth can take place. It is this next step that will prove the most crucial, especially for manufacturers: the open sharing of PoS data along the entire supply system.

Having examined some of the methods by which QR has become an inter-industry approach, we now turn to some of its most useful applications. In Chapter 5 we look more closely at some of the industrial sectors that show promise for QR strategies and operations.

5

QUICK RESPONSE
APPLICATIONS

In this chapter we first examine the breakdown of markets in which consumers spend their money, their relative sizes and the degrees of importance for the buying public and for QR. There follow sections about each major market. These are speculative to the extent that they explore how QR may well be, or should be, used in the future. This in fact builds toward what we term the QR Domain (see Chapter 11, Section 11.10), the customization of products and customers by their various behaviors and attributes. For some of these markets the authors readily admit their lack of expertise, but basic failings of the present systems are not difficult to see, and possible improvements can readily be anticipated. The chapter closes with consulting studies of two markets—swimwear, and the important jeans market. Here the emphasis is on techniques for the application of QR.

When examining consumer markets, the databases used are important. We use two; the US Department of Commerce (DoC) records and those of either the UK or the combined EU data. DoC information is used, in the main, because it has a long and consistent history, it is concerned with a highly homogeneous market, it is voluminous, it is readily available on the Web, and is in the process of being expanded to cover all three North American markets—the USA, Canada and Mexico—the NAFTA countries. However UK and EU data are of interest because they exhibit different spending patterns, and have different ways of using economic entities.

5.1 THE CONSUMER MARKETS

A breakdown of US retail sales into their major components is shown in Table 5.1. As is usual, sales are broken down initially into Durable and Non-Durable, then into the major groupings, each with its market share.

A few comments are in order. The automotive industry dominates consumer

Table 5.1   Retail sales 1997 (DoC data)

	$US billions		% Sales	
Total retail	2566			
Durable	1058		41	
Furniture group		147		5.7
Building material		150		5.8
Automotive		626		24.4
Other		135		5.3
Non-durable	1508		59	
General merchandise		331		12.9
Food group*		430		16.8
Apparel		118		4.6
Gasoline		159		6.2
Eating/drinking		236		9.2
Mail order		49		1.9
Drug stores		98		3.8
Other		87		3.6

* Mainly grocers (including supermarkets).

spending in the USA—24.4% plus 6.2% for gasoline, for a total of almost 31%. The next in importance is the food industry (17%), which may be combined with sales of 'Eating & Drinking Establishments' to total 26%. General merchandise, Building materials and Apparel stores follow, though it should be realized that the General merchandise category contains a majority of Apparel sales.

In what follows, we will try to make some of these categories more specific, and will look at those major characteristics that make them suitable for QR reform.

5.2   AUTOMOTIVE

In Chapter 2 we touched on industry initiatives in the automotive sector and in Chapter 4 examined its supply structure. Here we suggest how QR can be used to build on developments such as Just-in-Time, Lean Production, Concurrent or Simultaneous Engineering, Supplier Collaboration, Cellular Manufacturing, Set-up Time Reduction, Continuous Improvement and Supply Chain Management. We contend that despite the global development of many 'leading-edge' practices, the automotive sector still fails to properly satisfy consumer demand in the vital areas of truly customized products, sales, service, pricing and support. In truth, despite its rhetoric, the industry remains ostensibly a production driven push system entering an era when satisfaction of new demands will heavily rely on speed, flexibility and responsiveness.

The customer is increasingly the focus of attention in most industries. Food, textiles and clothing, electronics and 'white goods' have revolutionized their approach confirming the customer as king. Grocery retailing provides micro marketing by store and family, as even basic goods are supplied with high quality and at a low price. The clothing industry adds speed of response and flexibility to highly individual and diversified design offerings and copes with a shorter and shorter shelf life. Personal computers are increasingly assembled to order and customized to demand with short lead-times. The proliferation and diversity of electrical goods is astounding. A new book can be purchased via the Internet from Amazon (based in Seattle) on a Monday and arrive in the UK by Wednesday. In short, these industries have recognized the critical success factors of the future. In the automotive industry, however, power resides some distance from the end-consumer and purchasers of automobiles remain largely dissatisfied and skeptical. Inadequate requirement assessment, suspicious sales techniques, inability to 'haggle' and compare product offering, lack of after sales service, lengthy lead-times, a dearth of supply pipeline information and supply chain planning, and most of all, the 'any color as long as it's black' view of new product development and customization, has increased the depth of the problem.

These outdated practices are exacerbated by a push distribution system relying totally on sales forecasts and using huge stockpiles of finished goods inventory as a buffer against uncertainty (despite the JIT claims of its supporters). The whole system philosophy is one of selling high volumes of what is manufactured rather than producing what is demanded—in all its complexity. There has been a total failure to integrate the needs of the consumer into the system and an over-emphasis upon cost reduction and the 'lean enterprise', at the expense of improvements in marketing, selling and distribution functions.

The automotive industry prides itself on the close links and partnerships between large manufacturers and their first, second or even third tier suppliers. However, it is the next stage that is problematical—integration of the independent dealers and end-consumers into the supply system[1]. In using QR strategies, structures and procedures, the whole supply channel will need to be welded into a cohesive whole. The first step is developing a QR strategy (see Section 3.10.1 of Chapter 3). This entails:

- *The alignment of organizational activity to demand.* A comprehensive understanding of the pace of the market and demand flows so that manufacturing and dealership activity is closely linked to consumer behavior.
- *Linkages between demand and supply.* Understanding the demand target.

---

[1] A number of enterprising manufacturers, such as Jaguar, Rover, Hyundi and Daewoo, have bypassed the traditional structure and established their own retail network.

What value and benefits are sought by consumers. This is of prime importance for the automotive industry who have, until now, sought to dictate these terms to the buying public.

- *Demand relationships.* Appreciation of the complexity and dynamism of both *customers/consumers* and *products* and their interactions and dependencies. Once the unique customer behaviors and product attributes are recognized, the automotive sector can move toward greater vehicle customization and shorter selling seasons with an increased diversity of range.
- *Resource configuration.* Creating an inter-organizational strategic architecture that builds on the close links between vehicle manufacturers and their suppliers and extends this to the rest of the supply pipeline. Once demand and demand relationships are better understood, collaborative initiatives can be developed that will introduce replenishment and reorder/re-estimation procedures. This will also necessitate closer integration of global operations and increasing the flexibility and co-ordination of product scheduling.
- *Time.* Reduce time delays in the order to delivery cycle. Compressing the time between design and development and offer for sale so that customized vehicles can be created as closely as possible to the point of sale and the exact demand profile.
- *Primacy of information.* The link between demand and successful, accurate and flexible supply are data and the resulting information. For the automotive sector, the challenge will be to integrate dealership networks and consumer requirements into the existing systems.

The specific QR tactics and operational approaches necessary (covered in Chapters 3 and 4) can then be implemented depending upon individual customer or product needs.

The automotive industry will not remain immune from the new demands we have discussed earlier. It will come under increasing pressure to provide the value that replicates true demand patterns. It will require the use of Quick Response, in whatever guise it prefers to use, if it is to offer the customer the diversity of range and customized products that are increasingly being demanded in every other commercial sector. Mere tinkering at the edges of cost reduction and leaner operations will not provide the radical reform that is long overdue.

5.3   FURNITURE AND ACCESSORIES

Early in the book, we stated that QR is not a universal cure for all that ails business. Here we give an example of a major industry some of whose characteristics prevent the application of QR in all of its major segments.

5.3.1   Furniture

The furniture industry is huge—$147 billion per year in the USA, though this figure includes sales at retail of not only household furniture, but goods for offices and public buildings, as well as appliances, TVs and computers. The retail data for the Furniture Group are broken down into: furniture and home furnishings, $72 billion; appliances, TVs and home computers, $64 billion; other, $11 billion. In the UK, the total furniture market is worth £7.26 billion (1997), with living room £2.1 billion, bedroom £1.9 billion, kitchen £1.5 billion and dining room £0.6 billion, being the major categories.

A more useful breakdown is that of manufacturers' shipments of the classes of products we are considering here. Table 5.2 gives this information. The first six items listed have been summed to give a total for Household goods, the part of the market on which we wish to concentrate. This accounts for slightly less than half of the total category. An important breakdown is that between wood furniture and upholstered furniture, the former being the larger.

A third way of looking at the industry is shown in Figure 5.1 where monthly retail Sales and Inventory/Sales ratios are plotted for 1996 — again DoC data are used. This graph is similar to that given for department stores in Figure 4.3. Although not as pronounced, both show a peak in sales and an accompanying fall-off in Inventories during the holiday season. However, it is doubtful that household furniture per se is responsible; the peak in sales is heavily weighted towards such items as radios, TVs, appliances and the like. From the QR point of view, the I/S ratios are relatively high and offer a way of reducing the cost of doing business.

Table 5.2   Manufacturers' shipments: Furniture and Fixtures 1996 (DoC data)

	$ billion	% shipments	% household
Wood household*	9.6	18	40
Upholstery household*	7.8	15	32
Metal household*	2.2	5	9
Mattresses and convertibles*	4.0	7	16
TV and radio cabinets*	0.5	1	2
Furniture (excluding wood/metal)*	0.5	1	1
Office wood	2.4	5	
Office (excluding wood)	6.1	13	
Public buildings	7.2	6	
Hospitals, restaurant, bars, etc.	3.1	6	
Partitions, fixtures	7.2	16	
Blinds, shades	2.2	4	
Total SIC 25	53.9	100	
* Household goods total	24.58	46	

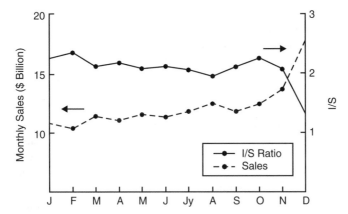

Figure 5.1   Monthly sales vs. Inventory/Sales ratios: Furniture group

Furniture is traditionally divided into upholstered goods (where the wooden frames are covered in stuffing and fabric) and case goods that are made of exposed wood or wood-like materials. This group includes such items as bookcases, radio and TV cabinets, as well as tables and chairs. A third group would include metal and plastic lawn chairs and tables, etc.

The furniture market is highly competitive and influenced to a large degree by fashion considerations—new styles are introduced annually or semi-annually. From the manufacturers' viewpoint the most important window on product preference comes when the markets are held once or twice a year in major cities. At these, all the major producers exhibit their lines and the different kinds of buyer start to place their orders. Based on these preferences, the production schedule is basically sewn up and manufacture starts.

Furniture retailing includes single-unit, full service stores, furniture chains, department stores, chains, warehouse showrooms, rental firms, mail-order and telephone retailers, catalogs and manufacturer-owned outlets, among others. The ability to handle a supply chain which is so long compared to the life cycle of the product is key to successful retailing. For example, everyone has experienced the frustrating situation where a particular style of upholstered sofa is selected, the salesperson asks which fabric is best, the choice is made, and then a delivery date is set for, say, six weeks in the future. And yet, this is reasonable—it is expensive to carry full yardage in a very wide range of very expensive fabrics. Add the production time and the delivery date becomes rational. Wood furniture, particularly the simpler items, is much more conducive to 'off the floor' sales.

Four to six months in advance of a selling season, 'demand forecasts' are used to determine which products and how many of each item should be manufactured. Manufacture is then planned in considerable detail. Two to three months in advance of assembly, the production schedule is finalized, giving a set of due dates for parts and sub-assemblies to arrive at the assembly line for each end-item at the right time.

Manufacturers typically kiln dry their own stock and then machine it into useful lengths and widths. Stock for upholstered items is left unfinished (for the most part) and assembled into frames for covering as needed (see Figure 5.2). The wood for case goods typically goes through many treatments designed to provide color and a high gloss. Machining set-up times are long and expensive, so that relatively long runs of a particular style are important (see Figure 5.3). Also, because finished goods are both bulky and come at a high cost (relative to apparel, for example), it is important to keep inventories to a minimum; one of the reasons the procurement and production decisions are made well in advance of the introduction date.

The primary mechanism for the introduction of new products has been major markets held semi-annually. At these, all the main producers exhibit their lines and the different buyers start to place their orders. Traditionally, the majority of orders sold to retailers occurred at market; however over the last decade or so, as with most industries, the trend has shifted to smaller retail inventories and on-demand orders to the manufacturer.

Upholstered goods are typically made to sold orders except for quick-ship programs or promotionally priced products that are produced in a limited number of frame styles and fabric choices and inventoried. Case goods are typically made to stock inventories based upon forecasts of retail demand. The trend is towards smaller and smaller lot sizes of items in a 'cutting' (production run of a given suite of case goods furniture).

The manufacturer must constantly access demand forecasts to determine which suites and how many of each item carried in the suite should be manufactured. Operations are then planned in considerable detail. Two to three months in advance of assembly, the production schedule is finalized, giving a set of due dates for parts and sub-assemblies to arrive at the assembly line for each end-item at the right time.

A key impediment to QR is the long lead-time to kiln dry lumber of the correct species and thickness to feed the rough mill where lumber is dimensioned prior to machining. The time to kiln dry to the appropriate moisture content can range from a few days to as much as three months depending upon species and thickness. While traditionally manufacturing maintained their own drying facilities, mills and other brokers have begun to provide dried and dried/dimensioned lumber. This allows manufacturers to purchase the stock they need at a price and reduce manufacturing lead-times considerably. New tools are being developed that allow manufacturers to schedule their drying resources efficiently and optimize the mix of in-house and out-sourced dried lumber.

Despite the above, there are market segments that are growing and compatible with QR. We refer, in the first place to the 'assemble yourself', functional, teen and young adult market, which is characterized by budget limitations, and

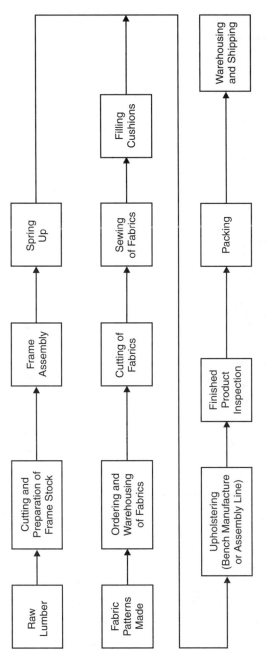

Figure 5.2 Manufacturing flow for upholstered furniture

122

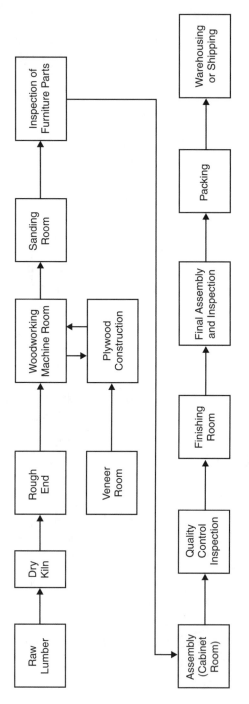

Figure 5.3   Manufacturing flow for case goods

a low concern with fashion as opposed to 'living style'. The exemplar here is IKEA, whose easy-to-live-with furniture at reasonable cost, limited choice, 'pick it up at the back door' philosophy has been so successful. This kind of marketing is tailor made for QR. PoS data can be used to make intelligent reorders on plants that are flexible, and use atypical raw materials such as particle board.

The second, smaller, inter-related market, is that inspired by the Japanese futon—raw wood, limited range of functional fabrics, adaptable bed-cum-couch furniture, all immediately available.

The furniture industry is well aware of its limited ability to satisfy immediacy of consumer demand. New assembly techniques, improved scheduling procedures, new joining technologies, CAD/CAM design and computerized cutting of wooden parts and fabrics are high on the research priority lists. Also, such furniture vendors as Sears have made excellent progress toward cutting sharply into customer order lead-times by limiting the numbers of styles and fabrics, paying close attention to PoS information, and working closely with their suppliers. Their progress augurs well for the industry. The same is true for the office furniture segment, not discussed above. Designs are simple, as is construction, and the passing up-stream of PoS information would allow minimum inventory levels to be maintained.

5.3.2 Sheets and Towels

Although this category is really a part of the Textile group, we find it convenient to include it here. While not as important as 'hard' furniture, several billion dollars a year are spent on such homewares as bed sheets, pillow cases, towels, mattress pads, table linen and mattress covers, and the first three of these cry out for QR management.

Sooner or later everyone encounters stockout situations when buying bed linen—it is difficult to find matching sets of anything, order lead-times are long and unreliable, and products change so quickly that there is little or no opportunity for replacement purchases (contrast this with crockery where many lines are held as open stock). Our estimate of % Service level is 65% or less.

This situation is a consequence of the rapid expansion of colors, print designs, fabric types, bed sizes, fitted vs. plain sheets, and the plethora of such accessories as bed skirts and pillow shams. Design changes are frequent and there is a trend toward pre-packaged 'sets'. Further complications arise because home owners have discovered that sheets make excellent window treatments for children's rooms and basements—a factor that leads to skimming off of carefully arranged combinations on the retail floor. In a word, fashion has turned a stable, traditional industry on its head.

Yet the supply chain for these products is short by most standards. Two groups of people are involved for the most part—a small number of broad-woven fabric mills who do their own finishing (including dyeing or printing, sewing and packaging), and a large number of two broad classes of retailer. These last are the Department store and Chains, and the Specialty stores that are steadily gaining market share. For table linen, the supply chain may split the fabric manufacture and cut/sew operations with a small, specialty house performing the latter.

The linen (or towel) manufacturer is dealing with a fairly small number of fabrics and has recently introduced the idea of weaving with the width of the sheet across the loom. This allows cutting of single through queen sizes from the same roll, thus saving on loom changes.

Dyeing and printing are usually in-house, and industrial engineering techniques have reduced reorder times to acceptable levels. What is missing is information from the retailer. PoS data can easily be accumulated and passed to the manufacturer together with store inventory information. In this way the manufacturer can plan his production and inventories in ways that will drastically reduce both stock-outs, and consumer frustration.

A simple study of a domestic table linen manufacturer supplying a national discount chain was performed using the Sourcing Simulator software described in Chapter 8. The product is offered in six colors and six sizes. As is the general trend, retailers are extremely concerned with reducing their inventory commitment and have been actively pushing more and more of the responsibility on to the manufacturers. The current practice is for the retailer to communicate to the manufacturer a plan of the next few months of anticipated demand along with weekly call-outs for shipments. Due to forecast errors and other factors the call-outs often bear little resemblance to the plan. In order to keep the business the manufacturer is forced to carry large inventories to buffer against the uncertainty in orders to provide the required very high service level. The level of finished goods inventory at the manufacturer is defined by a Model stock (reorder point) of over 50 000 units.

In the study we looked at the impact of sharing PoS data with the manufacturer. Specifically, how much could they reduce their inventory burden through a closer partnership and sharing of detailed PoS and promotional planning data. The manufacturing lead-time from receipt of order until delivery to the retailer is two weeks. Using PoS data the manufacturer can determine the needs of the retailer and move from a Model stock to a '(K_s) Target Weeks of Supply' as described in Section 5.9 of this chapter. Figure 5.4 show the impact of this information on three measures: Gross Margin, GMROI (Gross Margin Return On Inventory) and Stockouts. (GMROI can be thought of as the Gross Margin generated per dollar investment in inventory.) Each is plotted vs. the value obtained using the Model stock policy. For Gross Margin, the values have been scaled such that Gross Margin for the Model stock policy is $1.

For the Model stock policy there is so much inventory in the system that stockouts are virtually nil. Figure 5.4 shows that using about five or six weeks of 'Target Supply' yields virtually the same level Gross Margin and Stockouts as did Model stock, however with much less inventory investment (about a

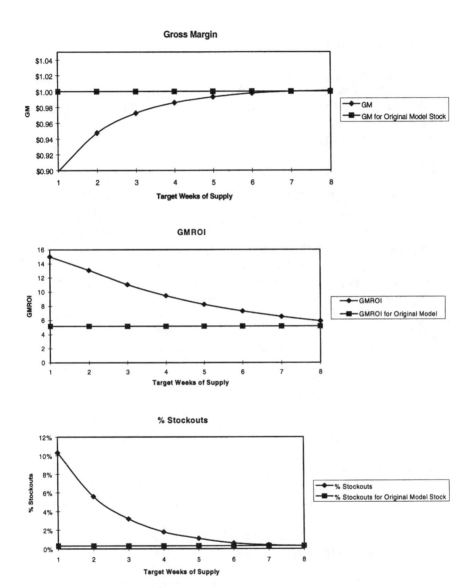

Figure 5.4   Impact of known PoS data on Gross Margin, GMROI (Gross Margin Return On Inventory) and Stockouts

40% reduction in finished goods inventory). This is reflected by the GMROI almost doubling.

5.4   FOOD AND GROCERIES

The food industry is probably the most complex of all those supplying the general public. Textiles/Apparel may have the longest supply chain and, perhaps, the greatest number of SKUs on display at any one time, and be affected most by fashion or short seasons, but for sheer variety, nothing comes close to food marketing.

Speed of Replenishment—A leading UK Food Retailer

A leading UK food producer has refined a short shelf life ordering process. The system covers fresh produce and provisions, meat, poultry and dairy products. Many of these goods have very short shelf lives and little or no stocks can be held. Lead-times have been cut to less than 48 hours. The store will generate orders on the morning of Day 1 and send them to suppliers electronically by midday. The supplier will deliver to the retailer's depot on Day 2 for shelf stocking overnight and sale by opening of Day 3. Increasingly the time involved in this process is being further cut by direct store deliveries from vendors.

Here we will consider mainly supermarkets and grocery stores. Fruit and vegetable stores, and meat and fish markets have their own characteristics, many of which are the same as those to be found in large markets. Food and drinking establishments, too, will be ignored, even though they account for a large percentage of consumer spending. One reason for not considering this group is that they are really part of the Service group of industries, with different imperatives and pressures. Also, they enjoy very different gross margins: 64–65% vs. the 22–24% that is normal for the grocery business—one of the lowest for retail establishments. They are, thus, less of a factor in food distribution than might be supposed from their annual sales given in Table 5.1.

Figure 5.5 shows two key aspects of food retailing. It shows monthly retail sales by food group stores for 1997, together with monthly Inventory/Sales ratios. As may be expected, sales are roughly level throughout the year except for a modest increase during the holiday season. The I/S ratios will come as a surprise to many people. They are far lower than for any other retailing group at about 0.85, or inventories of roughly 25 days, sales.

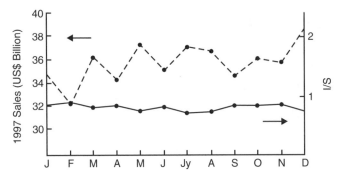

Figure 5.5 Monthly sales and Inventory/Sales ratios: Grocery stores—1997 (DoC data)

The low gross margins and inventory levels are indicative of the high levels of competition in the grocery business. They also reflect the nature of the product mixes offered to consumers. Some products, such as salad stuffs, bakery goods, and to a slightly less extent fresh fruits and vegetables, have shelf lives measured in days—they are perishable. Others, such as meat and fish, can be classed as 'sell by…' merchandise. Those with a longer shelf life may be classed as 'best sold by…', and include frozen vegetables and prepared frozen meals. But they all have limited shelf lives; far shorter than most consumer goods.

Another aspect of food retailing is the diversity of products competing for limited shelf space. This is largely a result of more and more couples, each holding down jobs, and thus having less time to prepare interesting and varied meals. Canned and bottled goods are present in an ever increasing variety, as are frozen or chilled pre-cooked meals. An added complication stems from information on exotic cuisines, and the desire to enjoy new and different foods prompted by the media. Moreover, customers increasingly expect to find assortments and varieties in the produce department, regardless of whether or not they are 'in season'.

Extremes of Diversity

- In 1997, almost 250 different, bottled salad dressings were shipped in the USA. By July 1998, 80 new varieties were available.
- Boned, skinless chicken breasts are now sold, packed in an increasing variety of different marinades, and sold alone or as brochettes.
- Pre-washed and cut salad mixes in plastic bags are now available in possibly a dozen mixes.

continues

- Canned soups, fish and preserves from around the world are now on-shelf alongside the classic offerings.
- Dozens of different bread types and other baked goods are on offer.
- These developments are all newer than five years old.

Table 5.3 is adapted from the much more exhaustive DoC reports on Manufacturers' Shipments to the food industry. Missing is information on fresh produce, and on those products going into secondary production industries. The full list accounts for $58 billion, excluding fresh produce. The reason for including Table 5.3 is to demonstrate the very wide range of food products and to highlight the fact that most of them involve different up-stream manufacturers, distributors, brokers and delivery systems, each of whom is concerned with reorder lead-times from suppliers, his warehouse inventories,

Table 5.3   The Food Group: Manufacturers' Shipments—1996 (DoC data)

	$US billions
Fresh and frozen meat, sausages, etc.	65.7
Poultry and egg processing	30.0
Canned goods	23.2
Fruits and vegetables (not fresh)	12.7
Pickles, sauces and salad dressings	5.9
Frozen specialties	8.6
Flour and other grain mill products	7.4
Cereal breakfast foods	7.2
Prepared flour mixes, doughs and pasta	6.1
Dog and cat food	7.2
Bread, cake and related products	17.0
Cookies and crackers	9.2
Frozen bakery products	2.7
Candy, other confectionery products and gum	12.8
Chocolate and cocoa products	3.3
Nuts and seeds	2.5
Edible fats and oils, other	5.8
Malt beverages	18.2
Distilled and blended liquors	8.6
Bottled and canned soft drinks	29.6
Fresh or frozen prepared fish and seafoods	6.2
Roasted coffee	6.0
Potato chips and similar products	9.2
Food preparations, other	15.4
Total shipments	320.5

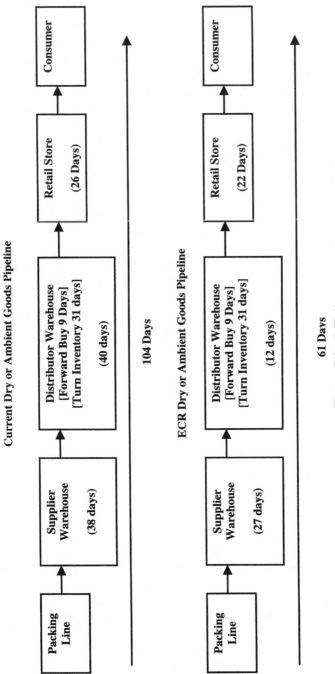

Figure 5.6 ECR improvements

and the speed with which he can get goods to his customer. The successful managing of relations with these myriad suppliers is crucial to the profitability of individual grocers, and the multi-store supermarket chains alike.

Several years ago the consulting firm of Kurt Salmon Associates (KSA), which had been a prime factor in the development of QR, did the food distribution and retailing industry a distinct service by providing a platform for industry groups in the exploration of the tools and alliances necessary for the efficient management of the industry in terms of customer service. This, they chose to label Efficient Consumer Response (ECR) (see also Chapter 2 for further details). In our view, this is QR under another name; the key elements are the same—partnership, the use of EDI, flexible production systems, efficient distribution systems, etc. Good progress in the implementation of their recommendations is now being reported (see Figure 5.6). However, we see the need for a shift in emphasis.

In the face of the explosion in product offerings discussed above, the supermarkets and grocery stores have been increasing floor and shelf space, but at a much slower rate. This implies that fewer items of each kind can find space on the shelf. Under these circumstances, it is paramount that the relative preferences of the consumer, e.g. for soup types or brands, be known quickly and accurately. Further, the PoS data underlying this information must be relayed quickly to the up-stream system members in order that their in-house inventories may be kept current and at acceptable levels. This process is not simply a matter of talking over the phone or having meetings with suppliers. New software of the types described later in this chapter and in other parts of the book will be needed to optimize the marketing, manufacture and distribution of food stuffs.

5.5   FOOTWEAR

Here we look at two aspects of the footwear industry, conventional shoes and boots, and industrial footwear.

5.5.1   Shoe Retailing

Earlier in the book we mentioned shoe retailing as an example of poor inventory control; specifically as to the poor in-store mix of product sizes. This is evident from the frequent 'sales' by Specialty stores in every mall. A look at the racks of shoes, etc. being offered at discount prices reveals that the articles are almost all either very small, very large, or in low demand widths—too narrow or too wide. Even early in a new season, it is not unusual to find popular sizes out of stock.

It must be remembered that the majority of shoes sold in Europe and North America are imported from low wage countries. Large orders are placed by the brand houses well ahead of new style/season dates. These products are then distributed to outlets that vary from Chains to small independent stores. At the end of a season, store inventories must be cleared to make place for alternative (e.g. winter boots vs. sandals) or new merchandise. In the case of Department stores or the large Chains, one would expect the product mixes to be better handled than in the case of Specialty stores, either owned by the branding houses or independent. However, the evidence is there that the mix of sizes required by the consumer is not well understood at the store or is not being recognized by the wholesaler or manufacturer.

Forecasting a Folly?—Clarks International

C & J Clark Limited are a UK-based international footwear retailer with a diverse range of brands including: Clarks, K, CICA, Bostonian, Hanover and Hush Puppies. With a turnover of £80m and sales of £684.3m, they manufacture 16.7 million pairs of shoes and resource or import 12.0 million.

Clarks' markets suffer from high levels of import penetration from low wage economies and for several years they have been forced to operate 'defensively' in a number of countries. In short, they have been struggling for some time.

The senior management team embarked on a review of their performance and discovered some stark realities:

- Average lead-time from design to shop was 15 months.
- They consistently failed to deliver from their own factories.
- They failed to get fully resourced products into the business when due.
- Availability of raw materials was poor.
- Stock levels were high.
- Overall, manufacturing sources were totally inflexible.
- The true costs of sourcing off-shore were not known.
- Demand forecasting was the principal driver of all activities.

It was clear that Clarks had to make changes. They certainly needed to concentrate on four core themes: availability, flexibility, reliability and speed. Changes were made and a group-wide initiative launched to re-engineer business processes from top to bottom.

Twelve months later performance was still poor. Despite attempts to introduce a Quick Response capability and culture, substantial problems with supply remained. The question is, why? The basic problem Clarks faced was an over-reliance upon detailed demand forecasts. QR

continues

can only operate using 'real-time' demand. Certainly, some short-term forecasts may be needed, but the bulk of operations for replenishment and reorder/re-estimation are tightly linked to demand data. Clarks possessed some of this data but failed to use it. Firstly, not all their retail outlets had the facility to produce PoS data. Secondly, the data from those that did were not used to drive activity (see Chapter 3, Section 3.10). Consequently, it was not only problematic to introduce QR, it was even more difficult to fully understand customer demand, choice, product availability and customer service.

Clarks are now taking steps to rectify some of these failings. Improvements are being made, but the jury is still out!

Under QR, frequent monitoring of sales from the onset of a season, using PoS data, would allow an accurate estimate of the optimal size mix. Further into the season, stockouts will distort this picture, and by the end of a season, the picture will be extremely distorted. Accurate knowledge of the true demand mix would allow more sophisticated ordering in the future at both the wholesaler and retail levels. This same monitoring would also allow two other characteristics to be examined—the differences in size mix between customer categories (e.g. Teens, Office Wear, Conservative), and the popularity of each style.

Knowledge of size preferences can be extremely profitable, and in Chapter 8 we take a closer look at this topic.

Now to push QR a little further. So long as a season's volume, style and size mixes are predetermined, all of the season's goods arrive pre-season, and there can be few, if any, revisions made, little can be done to change an unacceptable situation except to 'do better' next time around. The driving force behind importing is, of course, the lower costs of goods. In Chapter 9, however, we show that much of this advantage is not real. If QR reorder techniques are used with domestic suppliers for at least a part of a season's business, the low wage advantage disappears. Such a mixed off-shore/domestic sourcing strategy might work as follows. Place some part of the expected season's sales off-shore—say 40% to 60%—wait for the PoS information to appear and then place suitable reorders on a responsive domestic manufacturer. In this way, the on-shelf stocks are adjusted to reflect the consumers' size, style and color preferences. Service levels and Sales increase, Markdowns and 'Liquidation' decrease.

It may seem that the above comments apply mainly to manufacturers and large retail operations. This can, however, be changed, and the small Specialty store brought into the loop by means of one simple software development.

Virtually all stores now have a PC and an accounting package. All that is required is for some entrepreneurial software developer to design either an add-on to existing programs (e.g. Quicken) which would take inventory data, accept daily or weekly bar-coded sales information, apply a reorder cut-in level, and send reorder faxes—all automatically. The sales information could be handled via a scanner, or punched in after store hours. Both the SME and the wholesaler would benefit enormously.

5.5.2   Safety Boot and Shoe Manufacturing

We now turn to the problems of a typical SME manufacturer which were examined quite recently—a maker of top-end safety boots and shoes selling to a regional market. Almost 250 styles are produced each year for markets that include construction, linemen, forestry workers, foundries, etc. The large number of styles is partly accounted for by the different types of sole offered to customers, but is growing because of the increasing numbers of women in the workforce. Demand cyclicality is low, though some styles are mainly in demand during the winter, and style changes are infrequent.

There are about two dozen sizes, including half sizes. Most of the business is in sizes 7 through 10 1/2. Although not all styles are included, 12–15 colors of leather are used.

Production is complex, with many dozen operations involved in much of the product line. The production operation is modular and a Kanban system is used. Batches are small, usually 10–14 pairs in a mixture of sizes, though this can be reduced to one per batch if need be, and the order to shipment time for out-of-stock merchandise is approaching only two weeks (excellent considering the complexity of the manufacturing operations).

In-plant raw material stocks are no problem because the manufacturing operation is closely tied to a nearby tannery. The problems lie, as so often with this type of SME, with the distribution network and its very high service standards. Because of these, and the competitive nature of the business, finished goods inventories are high. Essentially, the manufacturer is 'blind' to the consumers' needs; little or nothing is known about individual purchases or distributor/retailer inventory levels or product mixes.

The substantial majority of sales are handled by distributors of safety equipment, the rest through independent, small retailers. Customers are of two kinds—walk-in tradesmen, and workers with 'chits' sent by companies. The former will choose another brand if their preferred boot is out of stock; the latter will put up with stockouts provided their requirements are met with little delay. The danger is that companies will change specifications if a supplier is deemed unsatisfactory.

Distributors are seen as key in this kind of situation. They normally record each transaction, up-date inventory, and use a max–min inventory control. However they do not usually reorder immediately; instead they will stack reorders for two or three weeks until they have a minimum order size. The manufacturer charges a premium for orders that are less than a minimum, a practice the distributor tries to avoid.

What to do? Bar-coding of merchandise is a necessary first step. The next is for the small order premium to be removed in exchange for PoS information, frequent reorders and distributor inventory data. Given this information, the manufacturer is in a position to control the finished goods inventory in a more cost-effective and service oriented manner. The reductions in the cost of carrying goods more than off-set any minimum order premium.

5.6   CATALOGS

The major catalog houses may well be the most advanced of QR practitioners. Certainly, they are the retailers who have to pay most attention to sales data.

The major difference between catalog houses and conventional stores can be summarized as follows:

- Less emphasis on short 'shelf-life' merchandise.
- High levels of vendor and customer loyalty.
- Fewer impulse purchases.
- Less reliance on sales promotions and marking down.
- Ability to track lost sales and back-orders, as well as color and size preferences, and second choices.
- More stringent quality standards and greater size consistency.
- High levels of service to customers, including both telephone assistance, and such things as inseaming and monogramming.
- Greater level of in-house product development.
- High shipping and handling cost.
- Long lead-time between order and receipt of goods.
- High cost of frequent catalog mailings.

Within this 'hands-off' world, however, catalog houses have developed techniques for running a business that are entirely compatible with QR teachings. For example, off-shore sourcing is done in smaller batches with several reorders per year based on how well goods are moving.

Catalog houses have also learned to co-operate closely with domestic vendors. Sales information is shared, and consumption patterns well understood. Based on this information, many vendors undertake to keep the catalog supplied with 'x weeks ahead' of inventory—very similar to the jeans study reported later in this chapter.

Mixed sourcing is also used with pre-season inventory supplied from cheaper, typically off-shore, suppliers and in-season replenishment supplied from a domestic QR vendor.

Among the performance measures used by the catalog houses are those that measure customer satisfaction—lost sales, out-of-stock levels and returns—as well as the usual financial measures.

5.7 MILITARY

Since the end of the Cold War, there has been an increase in the number of small-scale ethnic feuds, religious wars, coups d'etat, and similar confrontations rather than large-scale conflicts. The outlook is for more such activity in widely varying climates, and the ability of the Western powers to respond flexibly using rapid deployment to small-scale, special needs in a timely and cost effective manner is of growing importance. An example of the shortcomings of existing supply systems occurred in the Gulf War when the build-up of military personnel was hindered by a severe lack of equipment—principally, suitable uniforms.

The Importance of Managing the Supply Chain— The Canadian Navy

A report issued 16 June 1998 by HMCS *Toronto*, a Canadian navy frigate, listed a number of problems that arose when the ship, which was involved in NATO exercise off Norway, was reassigned to the Arabian Gulf on 10 February 1998 to help enforce an embargo against Iraq.

Among the serious operational problems reported (those that actually hindered their capability) was: the absence of short sleeved shirts essential in temperatures of 33° C with high humidity, a lack of appropriate medical supplies, a shortage of basic toiletries, and oil and grease supplies that broke down in the intense heat. These problems persisted during the whole of the southern engagement.

We believe that QR methodologies have much to offer in these types of situation, and some time ago developed a prototype model of a military supply system suitable for sewn as well as other necessary supplies. Here we give an outline of the thinking behind the model structure that would allow investigation of the interdependencies of textile production, garment manufacturing, distribution processes and inventory levels under uncertainty.

The prime purpose of the model is to estimate, for any scenario, and for any desired confidence level, the minimum pre-mobilization levels for fabric (or components) and garments (or assembled goods). In addition, the major

bottlenecks to streamlining the supply system are identifiable and their downside effects quantifiable.

We assume the following:

- A bar-coding system similar to that used by retailers will record the SKU
  issued to the service person.
- An EDI system is in place to allow rapid re-estimation and reorder on the
  manufacturer.

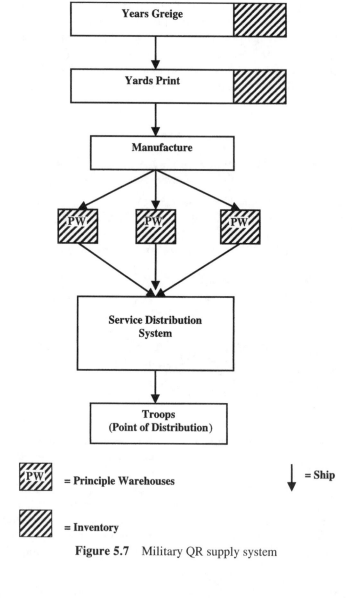

Figure 5.7   Military QR supply system

Figure 5.7 outlines the primary component (textile), secondary assembly (manufacturing) and distribution set-up. The top box represents the estimated yardage of greige fabric (or raw material) needed for a campaign. The shaded area shows the inventory on hand when the decision is made to mobilize at time T_o. The second box is similar to the first but represents finished fabric/components (i.e. material to go forward to manufacturing). After manufacture/assembly (note, no inventory), goods/uniforms go to principal warehouses that at T_o carry some inventory. The last boxes represent the service distribution system, though its various distribution levels are not shown. Arrows represent shipping.

Figure 5.8 shows the time frame for the initial decision to mobilize and subsequently deploy troops. If the total number of troops is N, then we assume that at time T_i, some fraction a_iN of the total number of troops will require uniforms (or equipment). We also assume that the different waves of troops will have different needs as to uniform size distributions—Z_i. Although the model would first use the discontinuous mobilization just described, there is no reason why a continuous scheme could not be investigated.

An important aspect of this type of model under consideration is its stochasticity. Shipping and process/manufacturing times would be treated as probability distributions, not fixed quantities. Also, lead-times, setting-up times, process times and rates, shipping times, and inventories would be treated as variables, as would the values of N, a_i and Z_i.

For a given scenario, the computer would simulate the issue of clothing or equipment to troops. The SKU data streams generated in this way would be used to re-estimate the size distribution required at the issue points, and to send reorders up-stream. It should be remembered that as the size distributions for the various 'waves' of troops and support personnel become better known, use could be made of large cartons containing the appropriate mixes of SKUs—known as Code 128 in North America.

The type of model described is not 'blue-sky'. The reader is referred to Part III of the book, and in particular Chapter 8, where modeling is explored in some detail.

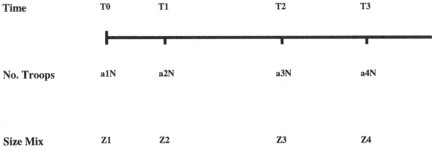

Time	T0	T1		T2	T3
No. Troops	a1N	a2N		a3N	a4N
Size Mix	Z1	Z2		Z3	Z4

Figure 5.8   Time frame—mobilization to deployment

5.8 SEASONAL GOODS

We opened this chapter with a promise to include two 'worked examples' of QR applications. An opportunity to validate the Sourcing Simulator tool (described in Chapter 8) was provided by a national retail chain that operates stores in several regions of the country. The product was a line of swimsuits offered in two styles: one-piece and bikini. Each style was sold in three colors and five sizes.

The swimsuit season is unusual. Starting around February, demand grows only slowly through April, and then quickens during May and June. Once July is reached, demand slackens and discounting starts. Based upon the previous years' sales, retail buyers produced a forecast of the total season demand, as well as the fraction of demand for each SKU. The weekly selling pattern for the new season was assumed to be the same as the previous year. Using the initial forecast, the manufacturer produced 75% of the forecast ahead of the season and half of the garments were shipped ahead of season. However, demand fell far short of the forecast; in fact, it came to only about 60% of expectations.

Table 5.4 presents a comparison of the initial buyer's plan for each style versus the actual total at the end of the season. The retailer agreed to provide data weekly through the selling season to allow the Sourcing Simulator to be run in parallel using these data for each region and in aggregate. Sales, inventories and replenishment receipt data for each style were provided for stores in five regions. Using the re-estimation procedures within the Sourcing Simulator, a new estimate of the total season demand and color distribution was calculated at the end of each week at the SKU level. Using the PoS data provided, the Sourcing Simulator was able to correct the error in demand and color mix as early as the end of the fourth week of the selling season.

Results are presented for one region separately for each style. The results for this region are representative of what was seen in each of the other regions, and also for all regions in aggregate. For both styles, the predicted sales volume was severely overestimated, and the color percentages and predicted

Table 5.4.   Predicted vs. actual sales by style and color

	Volume (units)	Color 1 (%)	Color 2 (%)	Color 3 (%)
Style 1				
Predicted	1339	33.3	33.3	33.3
Actual	822	30.5	36.3	33.2
Style 2				
Predicted	743	33.3	33.3	33.3
Actual	553	37.8	33.6	28.6

seasonality of demand were in error. Figures 5.9 (a) and 5.9 (b) show the difference in the presumed and actual seasonality patterns for each style.

For Style 1, the total volume was initially overestimated by 63%. By the end of the fourth week of the selling season, however, the re-estimation of the total season demand was within 0.4% of the actual total volume despite the actual seasonality being different than presumed. Because customer demand is greatest at the end of the selling season, this estimate was made after having seen only a total of about 5% of the demand for the entire season. As the season progressed, the total volume estimate stayed within 12% of the total actual volume as shown in Figure 5.10 (a).

The volume estimate over the course of the season for Style 2 was not as accurate as Style 1 in the early weeks of the season. This is explained by the difference in the seasonality pattern for the two styles. For Style 2, the demand

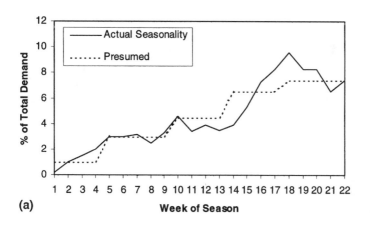

(a)

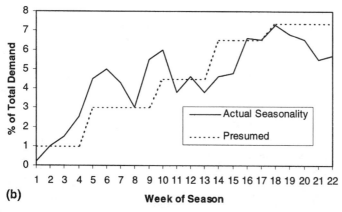

(b)

Figure 5.9 (a) and (b)   Presumed vs. actual seasonality: Styles 1 and 2

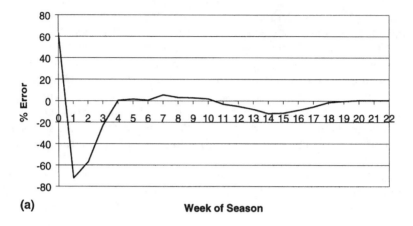

(a)   **Week of Season**

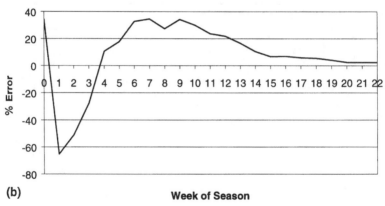

(b)   **Week of Season**

Figure 5.10 (a) and (b)   Volume error estimates: Styles 1 and 2

was more nearly constant over the season, with a larger percentage of the demand occurring in the earlier weeks than for Style 1. Until week 11, the fraction of demand occurring each week was greater than predicted. This caused inflation in the estimate of the overall season volume. Even with the difference in seasonality, however, the overall season volume estimate remained within 20% after week 12. By week 15, the total season volume estimate settled to within 7% of the actual total sales—Figure 5.10 (b).

The color percentages for Style 1 were not significantly in error at the start of the season, being incorrect by at most 3%. By the end of week 4, the estimated color percentages were within 1.5% of the actual for the season. After seeing just under 5% of the season's demand, the color error was cut in half.

For Style 2, where the color percentages in the buyer's plan were more significantly in error, the re-estimation procedure proved to be very accurate. In this case, at the start of the season, the largest color error was 4.7%. By the end of week 4, the largest color error was only 0.5%. The color mix re-estimates converged very quickly to the correct percentages for the season, despite the overall volume estimate not converging as quickly. Even when using a simple demand re-estimation algorithm, retailers can very quickly see how well the original buyer's plan is doing against actual customer demand.

Using this information, the retailer would have been able to see very quickly that they were in for a disastrous season, and if the supplier allowed replenishment based on PoS data, they would have been able to order less and avoid the huge excess inventory remaining at the end of the season. The season develops only slowly, giving ample time to tailor supply to demand. Had only 40% of expected demand been made pre-season, no-one would have had to 'eat' the excess.

5.9   BASIC APPAREL

Most of the work on QR reported in this book has to do with Seasonal or Short season goods sold through retail stores. Now, for the second 'worked example' of a QR application, we turn to Basic merchandise; i.e. goods sold year-round and for which style or color changes are infrequent and not far reaching. The number of SKUs involved varies widely depending upon the industry. For example in clothing, the number ranges from the few necessary for boys' tube socks or jockey shorts, to the several dozen needed for a line of youths' or men's slacks or jeans, where a wide range of waist/leg length combinations is required.

The class of retailer on which we based the work was also different. Specialty chains are characterized as having dozens to hundreds of stores scattered across a region or, indeed, the entire country. Typically, the stores are supplied from one or more distribution centers (DCs), with all major operations controlled from a head office. In the USA, centralized control presents a variety of problems. Very different climate conditions and distinct customer demographics lead to significant differences in store characteristics. Any distribution system must be able to cope with them. In the UK, this is less of a problem, although retailers are increasingly trying to target customers by region and even town—micro marketing.

Within the Specialty chain, there is usually wide variation in the size of stores—again a function of the customer base—and this presents a different kind of problem. Any store, no matter how small, must carry a full range of garments. Each SKU must be on display, and there should be several items of the more popular merchandise. When a line involves a large number of SKUs, this presentation stock (PS) can represent many weeks of sales. In the case of the larger stores, however, the PS may be the equivalent of only a few days' sales.

One other point should be made. Basics are carried year-round, but the sales intensity often varies markedly from one period to another. In the case of jeans, sales levels during two periods—back-to-school (August) and holiday (November/December)—can be at least three or four times the levels for the slower periods (Figure 5.11). Further, stockouts are more likely to occur during peak periods, leading to underestimates of true volume demand and size mix. Coping with such volatility and uncertainty are major features of the work.

5.9.1   Methodology

Weekly data provided by the sponsor gave aggregate seasonal selling patterns for the product lines of interest; while a sampling of data for individual stores allowed estimations of normal store-to-store variability and provided information relating to store size and geographic location. Other data streams showed weekly inventory levels by SKU for both stores and the DC.

We had originally envisaged a model in which each store would act independently with regard to replenishment orders placed on the DC, thus developing, over time, its unique seasonality and assortment patterns. Company policy and the volume of data required, however, precluded such a procedure, which meant that any aggregate model had to be robust enough to handle variability in seasonality between stores. As will be shown later, this turned out not to be a limiting feature.

The final version of the model was based on the behavior of 18 stores selected to cover a full range of sales volumes and geographic regions, together with one DC. Figure 5.11 shows the average week-to-week sales pattern for one of the garment styles investigated, together with the maximum and minimum percent of sales each week for the 18 stores calculated every fifth week. Clearly, the models had to be very robust to handle this level of variability.

The stores alone and the DC component were modeled, first separately, and then linked. Store size, PS, store and DC target inventories, order lead-times (both vendor to DC and DC to store) were made variables, as was the 'pick' frequency—the number of times per week a DC would meet orders outstanding. A 'ramping' feature was also developed to allow for unusual occurrences such as change in the general sales climate or a sales promotion. The model outputs were simple: % Lost sales at the store, % Stockouts at the DC, and Units of Inventory/Weeks supply at both the DC and the stores.

5.9.2   Store Model

The model simulates arrivals of customers (non-stationary Poisson process) to a set of retail stores for purchase of some style. Garments in the style are sold in a number of sizes. For each store, the average number of arrivals is based on

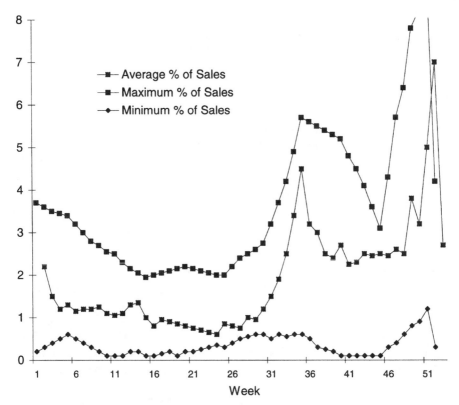

Figure 5.11   Seasonality of sales of jeans

the company-wide weekly seasonality and the customer's choice is randomly assigned based on an underlying, store specific, size preference. The initial size preference estimate is in error of the underlying size preference. This error level is an input. For the bulk of the experimentation, this was set at 25%. Also, the underlying size preference, which, too, is an input, changes (twists) each week. In other words, the distribution of demand by size changes from week to week, e.g. back-to-school sales are weighted more toward smaller sizes. For the experimentation reported here, this twist factor was set at 10%/week.

The basic question at the store level is how much inventory should be carried in order to minimize lost sales. The desired level of inventory is specified as the number of 'Weeks of Supply', K_s, required. It is important to recognize that an inventory of K_s weeks of supply is defined as the number of units expected to be sold over the next K_s weeks. This can be markedly different from week to week due to the seasonality of sales. The initial inventory level is set at $(K_s/52)\%$ of annual sales; i.e. if 10 weeks supply is desired, roughly 20% of estimated annual sales is placed on shelf.

A purchase reduces the inventory of the selected item if in stock, otherwise a lost sale is recorded. The model continuously re-estimates the underlying store size preference and store volume. The store makes reorders (replenishment requests) on the DC that arrive some lead-time (LT_s) later. The model issues reorders to attempt to maintain inventory to satisfy the next K_s weeks of demand, taking into account any modulation/amplification in demand due to factors other than normal seasonality, e.g. a sales promotion.

For purposes of re-estimating the 'true' demand for a given size (SKU), PoS data are used. If the size is in stock for an entire week, then it is assumed that no lost sales have occurred. (In reality, there may have been lost sales due to poorly positioned stock or stock in the back room and not on the shelf.) If, however, an item is stocked out at the end of the week, then it is assumed that the last item was purchased in the middle of the period and that half of the demand was 'lost'. A seasonalized average week's demand estimate is used for this purpose. Note that this procedure is used only to approximate more accurately the true store demand and is not reported in the 'Lost Sales' figure for the simulation run.

The reorder scheme for each SKU is based upon the idea that the store should carry inventory to meet the demand expected in the upcoming weeks. The value K_s defines the number of future weeks' demand to carry, on average. It is important to understand that 'average inventory' for a week is computed by averaging the beginning-of-week and the end-of-week inventories. This assumes a nearly linear depletion of stock—a commonly used approximation. In order to average K_s weeks of supply, the store should start the week with at least K_s weeks on hand.

The structure that has just been outlined leads to the order scheme for each SKU shown in Appendix I to this chapter.

5.9.3   Distribution Center Model

The stores make weekly reorders (replenishment requests) on the DC. These reorders are then received by the stores LT_s weeks later and added to the stores' inventory.

The DC operates with inventories of each SKU. The initial inventory level is $(K_{DC}/52)\%$ of annual sales where K_{DC} represents the target weeks of supply in the DC inventory. These inventories are drawn upon by reorders from the individual stores; thus, the aggregated store reorders are the 'customers' of the DC. The reorders generated from the store models are fed into the DC model.

Reorders reduce the DC inventory and stocked-out items are recorded. It should be noted that there is more than one way of handling DC stockouts: the shortfall can be included in the next store shipment (used here), or the store could explicitly include the shortfall in its next order on the DC if the stock is still needed. Also, a priority class system was used to determine which stores would receive how much stock when the inventory in the DC is not adequate to meet the aggregated stores' orders.

DC inventories are resupplied by weekly DC reorders on the vendor who is assumed to be a perfect supplier. The lead-time for DC reorders (LT_{DC}) is an input variable. The DC attempts to maintain a 'target' inventory in each SKU equivalent to K_{DC} weeks of supply. It is important to note that this target reflects the product line seasonality.

The model continuously re-estimates underlying size preference. A reorder volume adjustment factor is included to reflect modulation/amplification in demand due to factors other than normal seasonality.

Appendix II outlines the DC reorder algorithm for each SKU.

5.9.4   Results

Stores

The following results were obtained early in the study using a simple model that did not include presentation stock minima and assumed perfect supply from the DC.

The initial inventory 'placed on the shelf' was ($K_s/52$)% of annual sales for each of the stores representing the entire company. We ran five replications of two years' simulated sales for each store, and the average of % Lost sales, Sales units, and Inventory units were recorded. Figure 5.12 is typical of the results obtained. The smallest and largest 'stores' are recorded with two intermediate sized stores. The horizontal bands at the target 5% and 2.5% Lost sales levels suggested that the larger stores should be able to meet acceptable customer service levels with inventories well below the initial target of 10 weeks. When presentation stock is introduced, this leads to levels of 20 or so weeks of inventory for the smallest stores. Figure 5.12 indicates that as a result of carrying presentation stock, much lower inventories can be aimed at, company-wide.

Figure 5.12 also suggests that stores of such a size that the overall target inventory is close to the presentation stock, may be more prone to lost sales

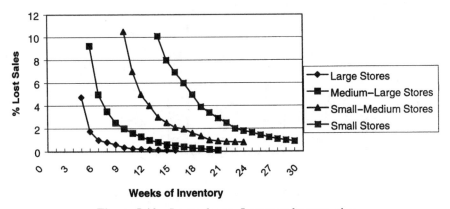

Figure 5.12   Lost sales vs. Inventory by store size

than larger or smaller stores. Further investigation showed this to be the case, but the effect was not large enough to matter at the low levels of % Lost sales being achieved.

The number of weeks of store inventory, K_s, can be calculated in several ways. For example, if 10 weeks is desired, the stock levels for each of the next 10 weeks can be read from the seasonality curve and summed. Alternatively, the sum of the values for the next five weeks can be multiplied by two, or a $3 * 3.3$ combination may be used. The different ways of arriving at a set number of weeks of stock have different % Lost sales and Inventory characteristics. Taking a small number of weeks and scaling up reduces the lost sales, but at the cost of increased inventory. Figure 5.13 shows this relationship.

Clearly, the larger the number of weeks summed, the more the back-to-school and holiday peaks are smoothed out, reducing the inventories carried during these periods of peak demand. As attention became centered on smaller store inventories, however, this aspect of inventory control decreased in importance.

Distribution Center

The DC model described above allowed us to explore the relationships between vendor/DC order lead-times (LT_{DC}), DC Target Inventory and % Stockouts, before linking the two models. As the Target Inventory decreases, the % Stockouts increases, though the effect is modified by shorter vendor lead-times. A number of runs showed that the inventory carried by the DC was actually greater than the Target Inventory, though this excess was modified by decreasing lead-times. Thus, in runs incorporating an eight-week lead-time and a Target Inventory of six weeks, the actual inventory carried was 7.3 weeks. This level was reduced to 6.6 weeks when the lead-time was shortened to four weeks.

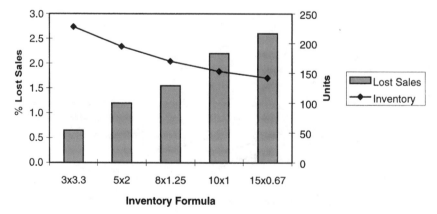

Figure 5.13   Inventory and Lost sales vs. 10-week formulae

Linked Models

Running the linked models proved to be very rewarding. The DC reorder algorithm worked so well that, at least for steady market conditions (see below), no more than four weeks of DC Target Inventory was needed to maintain very low levels of % Lost sales. Under these conditions, DC stockouts of no more than 2%—and usually less than 1%—were found, and at these levels, the % Lost sales in the stores were the same as with a perfect supply system. Reducing the DC inventories to target levels of three weeks' supply, however, lead to sharp increases in Stockouts and Lost sales.

Large Store Inventories

The results obtained from the models raised the possibility of carrying very low target inventories at the large stores. Stock levels of three or even two weeks appeared feasible, though one week stock gave unacceptable lost sales levels—at least so long as the store 'picked' its reorders once per week; i.e. reorders were placed and received once per week. To learn more about how low inventories could be allowed to fall, an additional procedure was added to the system— maintenance of presentation stock. When any SKU falls below its minimum presentation level, P_{SKU}, the difference is ordered immediately.

Before looking at the consequences of this addition, it is worth noting that the work on low inventories uncovered a flaw in the reorder algorithm used up to that point. As the target stock level was reduced, the actual stocks fell well below the target, though the effect was negligible for more normal inventories. For example, with a target stock of one week, the actual inventory dropped to 0.6–0.7 weeks. Accordingly, an adjustment allowance of one week's anticipated sales was incorporated. This step satisfactorily closed the gap between actual and target stocks.

Three garment styles were used in this phase of the work. They were selected because they covered the range of % Lost sales encountered. A high value was needed to show the effect of multiple picks, while a low value was chosen to show the effect on store inventory. The analyses were carried out using a 'worst case' DC scenario—four weeks of inventory and a vendor lead-time of 12 weeks.

When % Lost sales are very low, increasing the picks per week had, naturally, little impact; the inventory did increase by some 5–10% whether there were two or three picks per week. In the case where % Lost sales were high —between 3% and 4%—multiple picks had a significantly beneficial effect and store sales increased by up to 7%. Also, performance was better at the three pick than the two pick level.

Overall, the results indicated that if very low store target inventories are sought, then multiple picks per week could only be beneficial.

Variations in Seasonality

As mentioned earlier, at first we envisioned a store model that was based upon the seasonality of sales for the particular store. Due to the volume of data required, corporate policy precluded this approach. Instead, the modeling assumed a 'corporate average' seasonality of sales; i.e. the underlying re-estimation algorithm assumed customers arrived to all stores according to the corporate average seasonality. However, it was realized that certain stores do not closely follow this seasonality of sales. For example, a store may demonstrate a larger 'back-to-school' peak than the average.

Three large stores were targeted as being abnormal. The seasonality for each of these target markets vs. the corporate average for a large number of styles was investigated. The corporate seasonality of sales for a representative style is compared to those of the three target stores in Figure 5.14. Notice that the Store 1 seasonality is relatively flat compared to the corporate average, with the prime difference occurring at Christmas time where there is less of a peak, and Spring where sales are somewhat heavier. The Store 2 seasonality is very similar to the corporate average, with the prime difference occurring at Christmas time where there is a slightly higher peak, while Store 3 seasonality has a significantly higher 'back-to-school' peak and a somewhat lower Christmas peak than the corporate average.

A 'worst case' analysis was performed in which it was assumed that customers coming into all stores in the model followed the Target store seasonality while the re-estimation algorithm assumed they followed the corporate average. Poor performance would be mitigated if only one or two stores did not follow the corporate seasonality. However, as the results using Store 1's

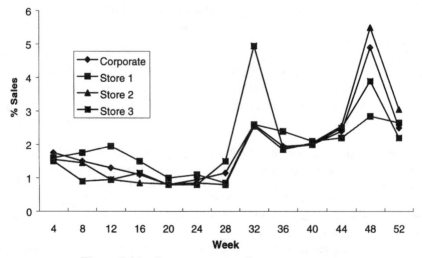

Figure 5.14   Corporate seasonality vs. target stores

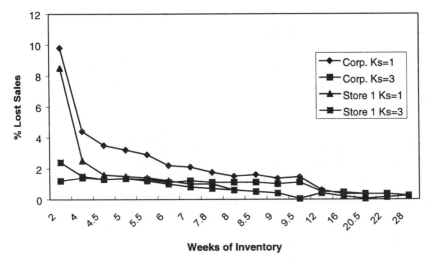

Figure 5.15 Lost Sales vs. weeks of Inventory (corporate average vs. Store 1 seasonality)

seasonality shown in Figure 5.15 indicate, even this scenario does not lead to poor lost sales performance.

The horizontal axis in Figure 5.15 is the average number of weeks carried in a store. This value may be larger than the target (K_s) because of the presentation stock requirement. Thus, smaller stores are well covered (>15 weeks supply) as to presentation stock. For the larger stores (those with few weeks of inventory), there is a significant difference in performance when the target inventory is a one week supply $(K_s = 1)$ versus a three week supply $(K_s = 3)$.

We believe this phase of the work is important because it provided a strong check on the robustness of the model. Had we been allowed to develop a system in which each store 'ran its own business', the work would not have been needed.

The News Boy Algorithm

So far, we have discussed a reordering approach based on carrying a specified number of weeks' supply in the retail store (K_s). If the store reorders weekly, carrying more than one week's supply is a buffer against the variability of demand. There is an alternative approach called the 'News Boy Policy' or 'News Vendor' (Morton, 1971), which explicitly considers this variability. The name comes from the dilemma faced by a street corner newspaper vendor who each day must decide how much stock to buy from his supplier. Purchasing too little leads to lost sales while purchasing too much results in inventory obsolescence. If demand is known with certainty this is a trivial problem; however, when there is variability, it is more complicated. Without going into the mathematics, the basic idea is to find the level such that the marginal cost of one more unit of inventory equals the marginal expected cost of lost sales.

The true cost of a lost sale is often quite difficult to estimate, however, an alternative is to determine a 'target service level', i.e. a fraction of the demand to satisfy. For example, a 95% target service level implies the inventory should be set such that 95% of the possible demand would be satisfied. However, this requires a good estimate of the distribution of demand over a specified coverage period.

Comparison of the K_s strategy vs. the News Boy approach has been carried out by Martin (1997) for the same styles as in the basics analysis presented above. A summary of the observations from this analysis follows.

(1) When ordering over a long planning horizon using fairly reliable demand estimates, a reorder strategy that orders using expected demand (such as the K_s strategy) works best since the actual demand over the horizon tends towards the expected demand.

(2) For shorter demand periods where orders are made more frequently and when the distribution of demand is fairly well understood, service level oriented strategies like the News Boy tend to be better.

(3) When the distribution of the demand is not well understood, ordering using expected levels of demand helps guard against excessive inventories or excessive stockouts. For example, consider two cases when the demand during a coverage period is normally distributed. In each case, the expected demand for a given SKU is, say, 100 units. However, in one case the variance is, say, 100, while for the other the variance is 10. A 95% service level for the first case is about 117 units and for the second case about 105 units. In this case, the difference is that 12 more units are required for the first case than the second. If we believed the demand was one case but in reality it was the other, then we would end up either over- (or under-) stocking by more than 10%. Compounded over a number of SKUs, the difference could lead to considerable excess Inventory (or Lost sales).

Theoretically, the News Boy algorithm is a better strategy, as demonstrated above, but it requires a greater degree of confidence in, and understanding (and thus a greater cost) of the underlying consumer demand.

These remarks about the merits of the News Boy approach to inventory management were related to Basic goods. The implications for short season fashion merchandise could be more important, and are discussed in Chapter 11.

5.10 COMMENTS

Since adopting the reorder procedures outlined here, and more fully in King and Hunter (1996b), the retailer in question has achieved very substantial reductions in inventories (of the order of 40%) while improving customer service levels. We continue to believe, however, that decentralization of the reorder process would yield still greater benefits as individual stores tailor inventories to their unique requirements. This is far from a trivial concept. We believe that the SME, whether manufacturer or retailer, needs all the help he can get.

An important result of the work was the realization that inventory control at the DC is crucial to any attempt to reduce store inventories. This calls for discipline on the parts of both the vendors and the retailer. Vendor to DC lead-times are important but less so than the assurance that the volume and mix of goods reordered will arrive as and when requested. All too frequently, buyers make last minute schedule changes that affect vendor and DC performance.

The two studies described in this chapter represent only a small part of the types of enterprise in the market. In the next section we take a look at several supply chains that almost scream out for a QR approach to solving their manufacturing or retailer related problems.

5
APPENDIX I

1. Compute the percentage of expected annual sales occurring over the next K_s weeks beyond the store order lead-time LT_s using the company-wide seasonality factors.
2. Compute the expected annual demand D, as the sum of the actual sales over the last 52 weeks plus a lost sales allowance for each week that ends with an SKU out of stock or use some other statistical approach such as exponential smoothing.
3. The Gross Requirement, GR, is simply the product of the estimated annual demand, the percentage of demand over the next K_s weeks, and the Sales Forecast Factor (SF), i.e.

$$GR = D * K_s * SF.$$

4. The presentation adjusted gross requirement, GP_{PA}, is the maximum of the gross requirement for this SKU and the minimum presentation requirement for the SKU, P_{SKU},

$$GR_{PA} = \text{MAX}(GR, P_{SKU}).$$

5. This quantity represents what is wanted on the shelf at the end of the current week. However, since demand will have occurred over this week and have reduced the on-hand inventory, the end-of-week inventory will be below target. Accordingly, in order to cover this week's demand, an estimate of this demand is added to cover the reduction in stock. This estimate is added to the GR_{PA}.
6. Subtract quantity on hand (shelf), I_{SKU}. (It is assumed that the previous reorder has already been received into inventory.) If the result is negative, then do not order any units of this SKU. Therefore, the reorder for this SKU, RO_{SKU}, is as follows:

$$RO_{SKU} = \text{MAX}(0, GR_{PA} - I_{SKU}).$$

A specified number of years of operation are simulated and replicated for statistical validity.

5
APPENDIX II

---

1. Determine the fraction of annual reorders (from stores) occurring over the next $LT_{DC} + K_{DC} + LT_s$ weeks using the seasonality curve. The idea is to generate a DC reorder on the vendor in anticipation of the stores' future orders. The stores' orders this week will include demand LT_s weeks into the future. The DC must take into account its own lead-time (LT_{DC}) and also try to maintain K_{DC} weeks of inventory.

2. The gross requirement, GR_{DC}, is an estimate of the DC demand occurring from now (when a reorder on the vendor is being calculated) until K_{DC} weeks after the reorder is received at the DC. The idea is to have enough stock in the DC inventory to cover K_{DC} weeks of demand after the reorder is received.

3. Next, on-hand inventory, I_{DC}, and any outstanding orders (I_{OO}) are netted out to yield the net requirement NR_{DC}, i.e.

$$NR_{DC} = GR_{DC} - I_{DC} - I_{OO}.$$

4. A reorder is issued for $\text{MAX}(0, NR_{DC})$.

6
QUICK RESPONSE IMPLEMENTATION

We now address questions relating to the implementation of QR, both within the organization, and between suppliers and customers. By now the reader has been exposed to the major components of QR management; this short chapter has the aim of pulling these together in more of a 'how-to' fashion. We have chosen to do this in terms of the major components of QR, rather than under 'retailer' 'manufacturer', etc. headings. There are two important reasons for this choice. First, we believe that for QR to work, anyone in a supply chain should have a firm grip on the operations of the business with which they interact. Second, as we have said earlier, the major strength of QR is its contingent philosophy: adaptation and flexibility of its components depending upon the individual circumstances.

6.1 GENERAL CONSIDERATIONS

We will assume that, for the most part, the larger companies are moving in the direction of, or have implemented, some of the QR disciplines. The smaller concerns, the manufacturing and retailing SMEs, are in the greatest need of assistance (see Chapter 4). They have limited resources, financial and managerial, and they must interact with larger suppliers and customers who are demanding new procedures, shorter order lead-times, smaller lots, or a greater degree of inventory management by the vendor.

A number of other important factors should be noted:

- A disproportionate share of the increased profits resulting from a pipeline shift to QR that accrue to the retailer. As yet there are no mechanisms in place that will correct this inequity. However, as we have discussed earlier, there is a growing interest in the idea of Added Value Assessment (AVA) in support of pipeline integration.

- There is a strong need for the retailer to keep to an absolute minimum changes in the orders and order schedules placed on suppliers—one of the most disruptive of factors.
- Increasingly it is becoming clear that the full co-operation of up-stream raw material and component manufacturers is mandatory for success with QR. And yet their needs—usually driven by cost factors—are frequently at odds with their customers. Small shipments, frequent deliveries, etc. add to their costs, and they see little immediate advantage in them.
- Many retail control, data storage and reporting procedures were developed when large, mainframe computers 'ruled the roost'. These tended to be inflexible and almost 'hard wired', making change difficult, though such database software programs as 'Oracle' are playing an increasingly important role.
- Frequently, internal procedures are at odds with the newly emerging industry standards for bar-codes, different reporting requirements, EDI formats, etc. Certainly QR practices require far more flexibility in computing, including interfacing workstations and PC networks.
- Whenever there is a radical shift in the way a company does business, the change in corporate mindset is at least as important as the change in procedures. Be it the adoption of a Quality Management program or the decision to go to QR, it is essential that the CEO leads off and then continues to devote attention to progress and to reward those members of the team who make the kind of progress that has been called for. It is only when the change in culture has been fully adopted at the shop floor level, and ideas flow back up-stream, that the process is complete.
- It goes without saying that the equipment needed to make the change to QR must be installed, and training must be stepped up in order to allow successive levels of supervision to learn new procedures. Further, it is recommended that as many members of the SME group as possible participate on national and international committees on protocol, UPC and design issues to make sure their voices are heard.

6.2 PARTNERSHIPS

It is essential to remember that QR requires the participation of pairs or triplets of pipeline members; primary and secondary producers, manufacturers and retailers. Much can be done in isolation, but it is essential that activities carried out between adjacent entities in the pipeline be undertaken on a 'partnership' basis.

'Partnership' is not an idle word, but a real and necessary concept. Granted, some groups must take the lead in pushing things forward, and the retailer has a prime role to play in the evolution of QR, but the most important feature of QR is communication between vendor and customer.

The '24-Hour Industry'—KLM Royal Dutch Airlines

We hear much of the '24-hour economy'. For KLM Royal Dutch Airlines the 24-hour industry is nothing new. Every second of the day one of their aircraft is flying to somewhere around the world. KLM have synchronized schedules over a world-wide network of more than 350 cities in more than 80 countries. To achieve this coverage on their own would require a huge operation at vast cost with all the problems of control found in many diversified international corporations. With safety and customer service such prominent and critical factors in this type of service industry, how do they achieve this vast coverage yet maintain localized integration? They think globally, but act locally through a number of strategic alliances and network agreements.

The current KLM fleet consists of 120 aircraft, but through their partnership agreements this is increased by 981 to 1101 that covers nearly every part of the globe. Some of the partners include: North America (Northwest Airlines); South Africa (Sun Air); India (Jet Airways); Norway (Braathens); Japan (Japan Air System); Australia (Ansett Australia); Africa (Kenya Airways); Dubai (Oman Air); Indonesia (Garuda); Cyprus (Cyprus Airways); China (Air China); Alaska (Alaska Airlines).

These are, however, more than just partnerships in name. KLM have deliberately sought close operating links that will allow the sharing of major resources such as facilities, staff and aircraft across the normal organizational boundaries, so offering customers a seamless service providing extra destinations, more frequent flights and smoother, quicker transfers. As Leo van Wijk, President and Chief Executive Officer of KLM, declared: ' ... we have worked hard with a number of prominent partners, who were once competitors, to build a long-term vision of an enduring, world-embracing airline alliance'.

Quality Management (QM) provides an excellent example of partnership planning, a concept that has proven to be both workable and profitable throughout the whole supply pipeline. In this, a company sits down with suppliers and customers in a series of meetings at which target quality standards are thoroughly discussed and analyzed. Time-tables are agreed on and measurement schemes set up. Successful QM programs are dependent on active participation by all levels of management working with the shop-floor labor force. In the case of QR, such meetings would be concerned with issues relating to information transfer, inventory holding, reorder lead-times, replenishment procedures, accuracy of bar-codes, EDI formats and the like.

Partnerships and alliances are an important strategic weapon. Firms are increasingly concentrating upon their core competencies and out-sourcing non-essential activities. However, strategic partnerships are more than this. They should combine the specific strengths and abilities of the partners and create a supply pipeline synergy that results in increased profitability, efficiency and market share for those involved, and also, most importantly, greater value for consumers. The ultimate strategic alliance should completely redefine and re-engineer the supply complex from concept to consumer. It should eliminate all duplication of processes, infrastructures and check points throughout the whole pipeline. The concept of the partnership sounds simple, indeed many are. The true competitive alliance is, however, a complex relationship requiring much effort, trust and an open sharing of information. Few have yet attained this advanced status.

6.3   BAR-CODES

Bar-coding of merchandise is essential. Without bar-codes, there is no feasible way that information on SKU volumes and mixes can be accumulated, ana-lyzed, and used to manage transactions and inventories. Equally important is that UPC compliance be strictly enforced—there must be a unique and unequivocal item number for each individual product. As noted in Chapter 4, the standards for full compliance have been developed in the USA and Canada and published by the Uniform Code Council as the 'Data Communication Guidelines for Retail and General Merchandise'. In the case of apparel, the manufacturer must indicate his style number and National Retail Federation (NRF) color number, as well as the NRF size number; though a great deal of work needs to be done on standards for both of these attributes. A similar, but less rigorous, system applies in Europe.

Even if there is not yet a call for manufacturers to bar-code, they should do it, because when the call does come, it will do so with little or no notice. Further, the bar-code demonstrates a willingness to interact with the customer on other matters and form semi-permanent linkages.

It is strongly urged that the printing of bar-coded tickets and hang tags be done in-house by the manufacturer, rather than an outside supplier, where mis-takes can occur and shipping and corrections can add to order lead-times. From the retailers' point of view, the low cost and other advantages of pre-ticketing by the manufacturer are now well understood. In the past two years or so, soft-ware designed to prevent bar-code errors has become available.

Last, it is important to realize that the present practice of many retailers to re-ticket merchandise at the store or DC is often associated with inaccurate manufacturer bar-codes. Not only is this time consuming, but it frequently leads to retailers applying their own, one-of-a-kind identification protocols. The result is chaos when it comes time to reorder goods.

A note for SMEs. Many of their customers are small retail operations without sophisticated computer abilities or PoS scanning. This is less and less a problem as the cost of computers is rapidly dropping and the availability of Internet (World Wide Web) applications is growing steadily. However, some level of sales data interchange can be achieved even more simply by modifying the bar-code tickets to include a 'tear-off' section. This can be used to inform the vendor of daily sales transactions—via fax, for example. The big point here is that a start is made on rapid communicating of consumer preferences.

6.4   ELECTRONIC DATA INTERCHANGE

EDI is the exchange of business documents such as purchase orders and confirmations, invoices, remittance advices, shipment releases, advanced shipment notices and planning schedules, on a computer-to-computer basis. Once this way of communicating has been adopted, there are very significant benefits to the company. There is no down-loading of transmissions such as e-mail or faxes, followed by re-entry into the company's internal business system, errors are minimized, time is saved, and fewer people are required. An important side benefit is that EDI provides an opportunity for forming strategic alliances with customers.

There are, however, two major points that must be recognized. The first is that because computers are involved, the messages or information must be in a language or structure that the computer understands—plain English will not do. The formats required for 'dialog' are now well established. The most commonly used in North America is ANSI ASC X.12, while in the UK TRADACOMS is most used. Over time, it is likely that the various standards will converge on the United Nations' standard, EDIFACT.

The second point is this. Most manufacturers deal with a variety of trading partners using a variety of needs, computer systems and software. To establish separate linkages with each partner would place a heavy burden on the vendor, particularly one that is an SME. Signing on with a Value Adding Network (VAN) is one solution. Another is the Internet that now offers similar secure facilities. Messages can be sent to any number of partners at any time. They are stored for retrieval by the partner, data security is tight, and documents can be converted to other formats and standards.

The EDI World institute, headquartered in Montreal, has published an excellent book for Small and Medium-sized Enterprises (SMEs). Entitled *The Why EDI Guide* (EDI World Institute, 1995), it includes the results of a survey of 149 companies in North America, Europe and Australia as to how they have benefited from the adoption of EDI. The survey covers a wide range of industries, including food processing, clothing, chemical products and metalwork.

The emphasis is on implementation of EDI, the times and resources required, the personnel involved, and the sequencing of different EDI documents. Additional features are reviews of the impact of EDI adoption on the financial, market and operating improvements enjoyed by the companies surveyed.

The *Guide* also covers in detail the adoption of EDI by 12 selected organizations; who did what, over how long a time period, and at what cost. Finally, there are excellent self-analysis tools and check lists to allow assessment of readiness for implementation and planning of the adoption.

6.5   POINT OF SALE TRACKING

The use of PoS systems has expanded dramatically in the past few years, supermarkets leading and department stores and other large retailers following. For the most part, small retailers, shoe stores and the like have not yet made much progress. This is to be regretted as they penalize themselves by recording only cash transactions, with little thought to automatic inventory adjustments, and the kinds of information obtainable from SKU data.

Financial software for small stores is now available which also tracks inventories, provided SKU information is made available. One way of handling this would be for the vendor to use the tear-off tickets with numerical SKU information mentioned above that could be entered into the PC at the end of the day. Certainly there is need for a simple software package that will estimate reorder quantities if and when required.

The larger stores have made some advances in the use of PoS data, particularly for inventory control, though the accuracy of bar-codes still leaves much to be desired. As we have seen earlier, the full power of PoS data lies in its conversion to estimated demand and reorder information, and there is still far to go.

Based on either original PoS data or on reorders, programs can be designed to instruct the manufacturer on optimal finished goods inventories and raw material requirements. These algorithms or 'calculations' are not complicated and follow common sense rules. The cost reductions associated with them are highly significant.

6.6   FLEXIBLE MANUFACTURING SYSTEMS

Short cycle, flexible manufacturing systems allow small numbers of any one SKU to be manufactured quickly with minimum order lead-times. The most popular, and well publicized of these is the modular system where a small number of cross-trained employees make the whole finished product. There are difficulties; breaking away from traditional straight-line systems is not easy and calls for patience in dealing with the shop workers. Also, though accounts vary, the consensus of opinion is that 2–3 years is required to complete a shop changeover. Frequently, companies have found it more convenient and productive to build the modules one by one, rather than attempting a wholesale, and possibly disruptive, change. Variations on the modular method have also been investigated (Mazziotti, 1995).

Modular, and 'team', manufacturing ran into a great deal of criticism in their early years because they gave the impression of requiring one or more of each type of machine—many of which remained idle for much of the time. There is something to this point of view, but not much, and the benefits far outweigh the costs. For simple products, the range of machines is small. In the case of more complex finished goods, those with more manufacturing steps, team manufacturing companies have found that machine types are kept to a minimum by preassembling as many components as possible in sub-modules.

An example of the operational improvements obtained by switching to modular manufacturing was given in Hunter (1990) and is summarized in the box.

Modular Manufacturing

A manufacturer of T-shirts in the USA converted two plants to a modular set-up and over a period of one year saw the following improvements:

- Manufacturing cycle time down from four days to one day.
- Productivity up 10–15%.
- Workmanship 'seconds' as low as 0.2%.
- Floor space reductions allowed 24% more direct labor to be added.
- Labor turn-over halved.
- Absenteeism of only $2\frac{1}{2}$ to 3%; a third of normal.

There is another aspect of flexible manufacturing systems that should not be forgotten. Increasingly, retailers are looking to their suppliers to hold greater percentages of their requirements—Vendor Managed Inventory. In order to hold finished goods inventories at a satisfactory level, manufacturers must be capable of very rapid production of small batches. Similarly, retailers can only hold smaller inventories of goods if they are assured of short reorder times and good vendor service levels, otherwise they will suffer item stockouts and lost business. In line with this thinking, manufacturers should become aware of what we believe is the next wave of retailing strategy—Mixed Sourcing. This will be explored in more detail in Chapter 9, but in brief, it means that the retailer takes advantage of very low off-shore costs for the early part of a season, and then switches to domestic production for the critical later part, allowing the benefits of re-estimation and reorder to swing into action.

Assembly is not the sole component of flexible manufacturing. CAD should be used for initial design and pattern generation. Patterns should be relayed directly to a high-speed robotic cutting device, e.g. a laser cutter, and low ply cutting is needed for very short runs. Products are now coming onto the market-place that help automate this process to significantly reduce the time to market. CAD systems are also having an important impact on the merchandise planning efficiencies of retail buyers. Later in the book we will explore the so-called 'buyer error' in more detail. For the moment it will suffice to say that the difference between what a buyer plans on selling and what the consumer actually wants is a function of how far ahead of a selling season the mix of styles, shapes, colors, flavors, sizes, etc. is decided on and firm orders placed with the manufacturer.

The Boston Consulting Group and Kurt Salmon Associates worked on this aspect of QR in its early years. The results varied depending on the type of merchandise, but a generalized relationship was developed (unpublished) which is shown in Figure 6.1 below. The placing of initial orders by the buyer can occur many months in advance of the selling season; the closer to the date, the lower the forecast error. Under QR, once a season starts, and the re-estimation/reorder process kicks in, the error becomes negligible.

In the USA, a strong training program is provided by [TC]² in Cary, North Carolina. In addition to seminars and traditional training sessions for first level and higher supervision, the organization has developed computer simulation software for manufacturers. These are 'shop-floor' models—unlike those of NCSU—showing how raw material and finished goods stocks accumulate at various points or machines in the manufacturing process. These models include an animated Process Simulator that allows quick design and analysis of production systems, an animated Modular Manufacturing Simulation System, and a Line Balancing Decision Trainer (see Chapter 4). [TC]² also operates a small manufacturing facility which produces, to order, merchandise for a retailer using state-of-the-art technology.

6.7 SEASONALITY

It is important at this point to consider the classes of manufacturer grouped by retail shelf life. We refer to these as 'Basic', 'Seasonal' and 'Fashion', but terms such as Year-Round, Winter/Summer, and Short Shelf Life would have the same connotation (for example, the grocery industry uses fresh, chilled, ambient and frozen). These groups of merchandise have different characteristics and QR requirements, but they share the same ambitions; i.e. the provision

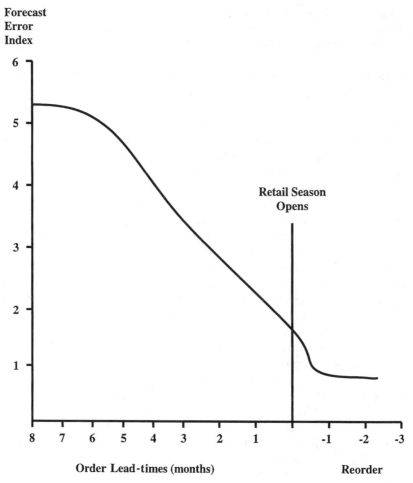

Figure 6.1   Order lead-time vs. forecast error (short season product)

of the goods demanded by the consumer at the right mix, time, place, price and volume.

6.7.1 Basics

The main elements here are a sound knowledge of the patterns of buying seasonality, an accurate understanding of size (or flavor, etc.) preference (perhaps by season), solid estimations of any DC stocking requirements, and the inclusion in store ordering procedures of minimum store display quantities. Except for those occasions when there is a style change or modification, or there is a sharp change in demand, the whole manufacturing/retailing system should operate smoothly, provided the vendor is fully conversant with sales volumes and SKU patterns (see Chapter 5). Given these, finished goods inventories can be kept to a tight minimum and vendor stocking of the shelves and management of the retailer's inventory becomes a real possibility.

Most of the above information comes from fairly trivial analyses of PoS data. Individual store data are extremely useful and it is our belief that each store, as part of or outside a chain, and no matter how small, should be given responsibility for its own stocking if such a procedure can be accommodated by the parent company's operational philosophy.

But, problems are growing. If the vendor and retailer do not share sales data openly, and (as noted above) if the retailer drives single-handedly toward his own inventory reduction, the manufacturer can face escalating finished goods inventories in his own plant. Worse, if there is little communication and the retailer adopts the growing belief that shelf stocking is the responsibility of his supplier, manufacturers' inventories can get out of hand. Short cycle manufacturing may not seem as important as for seasonal goods, but at least a part of the plant should be made flexible in order to control inventory costs.

6.7.2 Seasonal Goods

Here we come to the core of QR managed operations. The re-estimation/reorder algorithms we will describe later in the book produce the greatest benefits in terms of customer satisfaction, first price sell-through, and return on investment, among others. Further, these benefits apply to toys, games, some kinds of produce, pharmaceuticals, clothing and many others. It is debatable whether the raw, i.e. unprocessed, PoS data should be restricted to the retailer or shared directly with the manufacturer and component producer—assuming a formal reorder process. There are considerations that call for exclusive use by the retailer—privacy, etc.—but in general, we believe that PoS based information is most useful when it is shared by the supplying pipeline. Let it be clear, however, that the store must hold responsibility for the re-estimation/reorder process; data passed to the manufacturer/component producer are mainly for use in anticipating demand and controlling both raw material and finished goods inventories. However, without full knowledge of WIP and inventory holdings in down-stream operations, PoS data can have only limited usefulness to the up-stream manufacturer.

There are roadblocks to progress in this area. An example of these is the reluctance of the textile industry to share color specifications with their customers and the retailing industry. All this does is slow down the bar-code and allied identification processes, and little is concealed, as the dyeing industry is fully capable of shade matching in very short order. A similar example can be drawn from the food and grocery industry—the majority of retailers prove remarkably obdurate when it comes to PoS data provision to their supply base.

Now for an important point concerning the seasonal goods manufacturers. If the manufacturers are involved in producing multi-season lines, for example

164

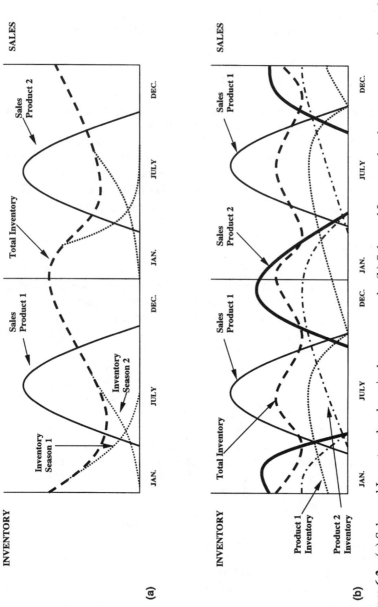

Figure 6.2 (a) Sales and Inventory levels—single season goods; (b) Sales and Inventory levels—contra-seasonal goods

they make, say, both Spring/Summer and Fall/Winter lines of clothing or food products, there is no problem; they can keep their machines busy and the application of QR principles merely makes them more responsive and keeps their inventories to a minimum. However, many SMEs make single season goods, e.g. lawn furniture, chocolate Easter eggs, or souvenir summer tops, such as T-shirts or sweatshirts. It is difficult to operate such plants in a QR environment. Traditionally, they spread out manufacture, and build finished goods inventories over a long period so as to keep the workforce steadily employed. Then they ship the goods in a very short space of time, maintaining operations by working on the following year's line. Getting reorders from those retailers' customers who are themselves small would only complicate matters.

One way of incorporating such manufacturers into the QR world is for them to diversify into what we called, in Figure 3.1, contra-seasonal goods. Through acquisition, merger or internal development, a workforce or combination of workforces can enjoy re-estimation/reorder procedures, while ensuring continuity of production with minimum finished goods inventories. In Figure 6.2(a) sales and inventory are shown over a two-year period for a manufacturer supplying a single season product. Note that pre-season inventory builds prevent adoption of a proper QR mode. In Figure 6.2(b), however, we see the effect of having two lines. The finished goods inventory is largely smoothed out at roughly the previous average level, but with far higher sales figures.

6.7.3   Short Season Merchandise

This is a relatively new area for research and speculation. When shelf lives shrink to 6–8 weeks (or less, as in the case of perishable foods), a different paradigm arises. One approach to this problem will be discussed in the final chapter, but much remains to be examined before new methods of buyer behavior can be defined.

The simple fact of the matter is that the whole field of short season demand/supply/marketing is undergoing almost constant change. At some point, reason must come back into the picture; poor demand forecasting, antiquated buying practices, markdown extravaganzas, etc. will have to be rationalized. As we have noted earlier, some European and Japanese companies appear to have a better handle on these problems than does the USA, which continues to deal at a distance with off-shore suppliers, rather than 'down the road' manufacturers.

One thing is clear: the manufacturer must not only streamline the design process, but also maintain very close contact with the customer and be prepared to make rapid changes in such things as style, shape, flavor and color (as well as volume). The technology required for interactive design is just recently available on a commercial scale, and we see it as a prime requisite for success, not only for the manufacturer/retailer team, but also as a way of combating imports.

6.8   BENCHMARKING

This is a phrase that has become popular in the past 2–3 years, and is really a part of forming and maintaining strategic partnerships. It means, simply, that any enterprise wanting to become responsive and flexible—as in QR—should track its progress towards meeting its goals. There is everything to recommend this procedure. In the late 1970s and early 1980s, the Quality Management (QM) movement used exactly these ideas. Anyone participating in a QM program will remember the seemingly trivial graphing of anything and everything followed by the pleasant shock of improvements in operations and profits. Progress toward full QR implementation requires the same emphasis on changing the corporate mind-set. Benchmarking is simply a way of recording where you used to be and the progress made since then. However, there is a movement toward the opposite: assess where the trade leaders are and gauge yourself against these 'world class' standards. There are problems with the latter. Industry leaders are unlikely to tell the world how they are doing. Further, their targets and achievements are constantly shifting; if they were not, they would not be leaders.

The two schools of thought are exemplified by two pronouncements; a recent seminar in the UK entitled 'Supply Chain Benchmarking' under the auspices of the Apparel & Textile Challenge, an industry group (ATC, 1996), and the findings of an apparel industry study group in the USA. The latter, the American Apparel Manufacturers Association (AAMA) QR Leadership Committee (1996), set out to establish performance measurements that would allow pipeline members to assess their progress over time toward meeting QR targets. The best course is probably a combination of the two approaches.

Table 6.1 shows some of the results presented in the UK. Three values are given for selected parts of the manufacturers' business; current level, international best practice, and a vision of where values should go.

In contrast, the AAMA work focuses on defining the things to be measured, with the emphasis being on how far the company has advanced from the start of benchmarking. The aspects of the business that are covered are shown in

Table 6.1   Benchmarking (ATC)

Attribute	Current	Best practice	Vision
Sample adoption ratios—%	36	55	68
Stock turns—manufacturing	4.0	5.2	7.3
Stock turns—retail	3.5	6.8	9.0
Order lead-times (days)	35	18	6
On-time delivery—%	81	96	100
Cost of distribution (% of sales)	5.0	1.8	1.0—1.5%

Table 6.2, and for each, there are major sub-divisions, each with definitions and, where appropriate, worked examples. Definitions are important as many of the terms in common use in the trade have different meanings for different companies.

Of course, not every company will wish to record all of the above; selectivity and understanding of those attributes that are of unique importance to each individual business and supply pipeline are important. But once decisions are made about the weaker parts of an operation, there will be no trouble in finding the appropriate attribute to measure. Indeed, we firmly believe that one of the strongest aids to the implementation and/or development of QR strategies, structures and procedures is the use of measurement to drive improvement.

Table 6.2   Benchmarking (AAMA)

Order management
- Order fulfillment cycle (days)
- Orders shipped complete—%
- Percentage of on-time shipments

Production
- Cycle time
- Quality
- Asset utilization
- Change over cost
- Throughput time
- Styles produced/accepted
- Work in process
- Conformance to plan—%
- Plant efficiency
- Turnover
- Cost conformance

Finished goods inventory management
- Inventory turns
- SKU planning frequency
- Forecast accuracy
- Plan-to-cut time

Distribution
- Shipping cycle time
- Floor ready shipments—%
- Automatic replenishment shipments—%
- Shipping accuracy
- Shipping cost per unit
- Inventory accuracy

Retail logistics
- Direct to store—%
- Vendor ship to shelf cycle time
- DC cross dock—%

Retail inventory management
- Replenishment cycle time
- Automatic replenishment orders—%
- Retail GMROI
- Retail inventory turns
- In-stock—%

Merchandising and Sales
- Product development cycle time
- Sell through—%
- Initial forecast accuracy
- Manufacturer GMROI

6.9 COMMENTS

This chapter has synthesized the major components of QR. It has a large number of important elements that are all essential, but with varying degrees of emphasis. Unlike the approaches of SCM, QR recognizes that the approach needed for successful adoption will vary from firm to firm (we believe that each is individual and unique), and from industry to industry. This is why we advocate that QR requires careful and considered implementation at strategic, operational and cultural levels.

In Part III of the book we examine how QR methodologies have been used in a number of supply pipeline settings. Various approaches are examined, including simulations and full trials. Most importantly, we begin to quantify some of the major benefits and costs that participants have experienced in these programs.

PART III
SUPPLY PIPELINE MODELING

The innovator has for enemies all those who have done well under the old conditions and lukewarm defenders in those who may do well under the new

Niccolò Machiavelli, *The Prince*

Knowing is not enough;
we must apply.
Willing is not enough;
we must do.

Goethe

7
SIMULATION STUDIES

This is a short chapter, but an important one from the point of view of understanding the rest of the book. Among what may be termed generalists, there is a low level of understanding of modeling (and especially, computer modeling), what it means, and how it is carried out. We hope the reader will bear with us as we spell out the basics of this discipline, and why we use it.

In Chapter 4, we referred to a series of trials undertaken in 1985–86 by a consortium of textile, manufacturing and retailing companies to demonstrate the viability and benefits of QR. These produced excellent results, but nothing much came of them. First, the trials were highly specific in that they were concerned with particular garments for specific sales periods. The usual comments then appeared:

> Of course, my lines are different; I don't deal with that retailer; With all that attention, I'm not surprised sales took off.

Second, they were extremely expensive (approximately \$250 000 per trial), and took a long time to organize and carry out (12–18 months). This is precisely the environment for which modeling is designed.

7.1 SIMULATION MODELS

There are many kinds of model, and they are used for different purposes. For example, models may be 'physical', such as flight simulators; 'mathematical', such as Newton's equation '*Force = Mass times Acceleration* $(F = ma)$'; or 'computer-based', such as simulations. Here, we are interested in models designed to answer questions about the behavior of a system of interest.

Typically, these questions concern how the system will behave under different conditions and situations. It is convenient to think of a model as a 'black box' that accepts inputs that reasonably describe the situation being modeled, churns them around according to certain rules of behavior based upon assumptions about the process (algorithms), and spits out the outputs (measures of performance) that describe what happened.

Many models are termed 'analytic'; that is, the 'black box' is able to generate 'exact' outputs according to a set of mathematical equations, given the assumptions of the model. However, because of complexity, few real-world problems can be represented in this way, and the only alternative is for the modeler to resort to simulation. Simulation models allow great flexibility in representing the real system, and generally require fewer simplifying assumptions than analytic models.

A simulation takes the form of a set of assumptions about the operation of the system, expressed as mathematical or logical relations between the objects of interest in the system. Simulation involves 'playing out' the model through time, to generate samples of the measures of performance. As a simple example, consider a pair of loaded dice. You could roll the dice several times over and record the outcome of each roll. From this you could get an understanding of the behavior of the dice. Obviously, the more you roll them, the more comfortable you would feel about your understanding of their behavior.

Of particular importance when modeling manufacturing plants, is the scheduling algorithm. Over time, many enterprises have learned to live with a particular scheduling process, e.g. the MAX/MIN, where, if stock levels fall below a pre-set level, new production is scheduled. When stocks exceed a 'max' level, production is stopped. However, when order lead-times are of importance, or small minimum order sizes are part of the company's policy, other scheduling rules may be preferable. Intelligent simulation allows such changes to be examined.

Another component of the model may well be capacity utilization. Most managers prefer to see equipment operating flat out, but in a QR environment, where the customers' needs are paramount, this may not provide the optimal response—activity is linked firmly to demand. Surplus equipment may be preferable, providing it is inherently flexible.

A simulation may be deterministic or stochastic. With a deterministic model, there is no source of variability and a given situation would 'play out' the same every time; i.e. the relationships between variables are fixed. Stochastic models, on the other hand, assume that there is some inherent 'random' behavior in the system such that a given situation does not always 'play out' the same.

As will be seen in the next chapter, consumers are viewed as an entirely stochastic element—their actions are not predictable and can only be described in terms of probabilities. For example, of the customers coming into a retail store, 50% might prefer a blue item, 30% beige and 20% a green one. Thus, for a given customer entering the store, we can only say probabilistically what he or she prefers. These probabilities can be replaced or modified at will to match different situations, or if the values of the output variables make no sense, or additional information becomes available.

In order to obtain useful and meaningful results, the model should be 'played out' several times in order to gain an understanding of the output of the system. The output can then be averaged and a histogram, showing the distribution of outcomes, can be generated. The power of this approach is that it becomes possible to make claims such as: *'In such and such a set of circumstances, there is a 95% chance of a particular outcome occurring'*.

It is important when developing a model to ask, *'What kinds of questions will I be asking of it?' 'Who will be using the answers?' 'In what way?'* In other words, at what level should the modeling take place? A model designed to throw light on the operations on a shop floor will be radically different from that designed to help a senior manager trying to cope with pressure from customers asking for shorter lead-times, a wider variety of products, or lower minimum order quantities. Similarly, there are other types of model better suited to the interactions among industry-wide variables. System Dynamics models are typical of these 'high level' tools. An example of such a model is the celebrated *The Dynamics of Growth in a Finite World* (Meadows et al., 1975). A more recent and focused example is the 'Items' simulation model developed under the Demand Activated Manufacturing Architecture (DAMA) project of the AMTEX Initiative (an industry/government research consortium).

It is a general rule of thumb that as much time should be taken over scoping the model and worrying over its purpose as is spent on the programming. Once a model is built, it can be used to analyze different policies, parameters or designs. Its major purpose is to analyze 'what if' questions. If built properly, the flexibility allows operators (retailers, manufacturers) to modify the model quickly and easily in ways that resemble their own companies.

In the final chapter, we will be concerned with 'management' level models geared to answer 'bottom line' type questions. We have in mind a kind of Interactive Management Information System (IMIS) process—broad questions with provision of rapid answers in the language of interest to senior executives.

Before going further, however, we wish to introduce a different type of model, one based on common sense and very little mathematical or programming skill. It should prove useful to those working in fields other than textile or apparel. The methodology is applicable to any pipeline situation—just change the names.

As noted above, in Chapter 4 we referred to a number of investigations carried out to show that QR has tangible benefits. The reader may wish to glance quickly at Table 4.1 and Figure 4.1 to refresh his or her memory about the structure of the industry and the traditional WIP and inventories. The question arises, 'Is it possible to get an approximate feel for the quantitative benefits to be gained, on a pipeline basis, by implementing QR?' In Chapters 8 and 10, we shall examine detailed stochastic simulation models of the individual components of the pipeline, and how they are strung together, but here we need a kind of 'quick and dirty' look at the entire system (Hewitt et al., 1991).

7.2   A SIMPLE PIPELINE MODEL

The model described below is not a simulation, nor is it stochastic. It is a textile supply chain model. We use it deliberately in preference to a generic, less complex supply channel. It is a common sense approach to estimating the impact of QR and is based on the supply of a generic seasonal good over a 20-week selling season. Traditionally, the retail order is placed on the manufacturer 26 weeks prior to the start of the sales season. The fabric order from the apparel manufacturer is placed one week after the receipt of the retail order. Fabric shipments are received 16, 20 and 24 weeks after the order was placed, and contain 50%, 40% and 10% of the total order, respectively. Similarly, apparel is provided to the retailer in two shipments, the first arriving one week prior to the season and containing 60% of the order, with the remainder arriving 10 weeks into the season. These and the other values shown in Table 7.1 are typical of traditional practice in seasonal goods production (Kurt Salmon Associates, 1988).

The actual pattern of sales observed during a season can vary depending on the particular good and season. For most garments there is a peak at some point in the season but, with no significant loss in generality, we use a steady rate of sales in this analysis.

7.2.1   Graphical Representation of Traditional Practice

The entire apparel production pipeline is shown in Figure 7.1 as a cumulative seasonal graph.

The horizontal axis represents weeks into the selling season, with negative values representing weeks prior to the start of the season.

The line on the far right of the graph represents the cumulative retail sales. The next line moving to the left is the cumulative apparel shipments, 60% arriving at week 1 and the remaining 40% at week 9. A vertical line traced through week 2 (line A) indicates that by week 2 under the constant demand scenario, 10% of the total seasonal quantity has been sold, while the retailer has

Table 7.1   Traditional and QR parameters

Parameter	Current practice	Quick Response
Apparel production	3 weeks	1 week
Fabric finishing	2 weeks	1 week
Greige production	3 weeks	1 week
Yarn production	2 weeks	1 week
Number of shipments to retail	2	6
Number of shipments to apparel	3	6
Greige transfers	3	Weekly
Yarn transfers	3	Weekly

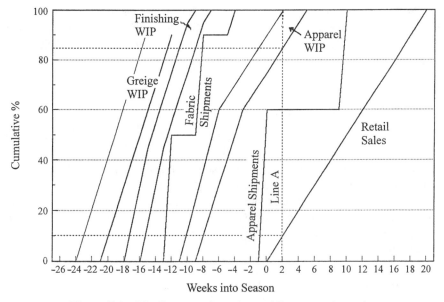

Figure 7.1   Pipeline manufacturing and Inventory dynamics

received 60%. The difference between these two is the current inventory held by the retailer (50% of the season's order).

Continuing to the left in Figure 7.1, the next two lines represent the completions and starts of apparel production, with the area in between the two being the work-in-process. Where line A intersects these lines is an indication of the state of the production pipeline two weeks into the retail season. This line intersects the apparel completion line at 85% and the apparel start line at 100%. In other words, all of the total apparel order has been committed to the production process.

The remaining lines to the left represent fabric shipments, fabric finishing and greige production, respectively. Thus, the diagram presents the seasonal production as being continuous throughout. This may not be the case for an individual product due to batching considerations, but is representative of the production of a distinct product line.

It is apparent from Figure 7.1 that regardless of the instant availability of PoS data from the retailer, the apparel manufacturer is too far along in the seasonal production plan to make any modifications based on actual sales data. Therefore, if in-season apparel reorders were the goal of the retailer, the clothing would have to be available in the inventory of the apparel manufacturer. In this case, the apparel manufacturer would be accepting all of the responsibility for carrying these extra goods together with the risk associated with the uncertainty of what will actually sell.

The final shipment of fabric is received by the apparel manufacturer five weeks before the retail season starts, so there can be no modification to the available fabric, either as to volume, or to color mix, in response to actual sales data.

In the following sections we will examine what happens as some of the operating assumptions are changed.

7.2.2   Reduced Apparel Production Time

The first modification is a reduction in the apparel processing time from three weeks to one week (see Table 7.1). The effect of this change is shown in Figure 7.2. As before, production is assumed to be more rapid early in the season, then it slows down after the initial shipment.

There are substantial improvements in the percentages of both apparel starts and completions committed to by week 2 of the selling season, but not enough for comfort if the buyer order is too far off the mark in terms of SKU mix or total volume.

7.2.3   Reduced Apparel and Fabric Inventories

Figures 7.1 and 7.2 show that a major problem for the apparel manufacturer, with respect to retail reorders, involves working around the large initial shipment to retail and the subsequent shipment 10 weeks later. Figure 7.3 shows the system under all of the traditional practice assumptions, except that the initial apparel shipment is reduced to 35% of the total seasonal order followed by five orders of 13% each, shipped every three weeks.

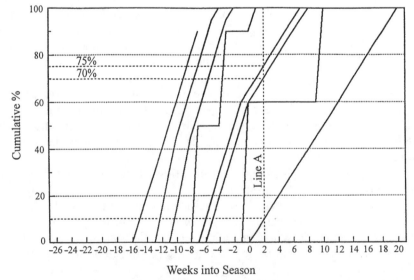

Figure 7.2   Reduced apparel production time

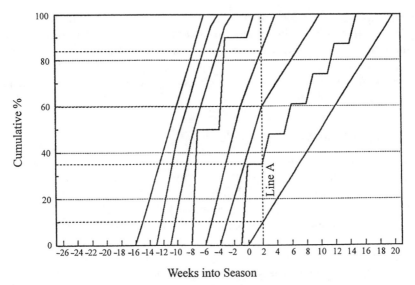

Figure 7.3   Reduced apparel inventory

Figure 7.4 shows the retail inventory under this scenario compared to the original two-shipment scheme.

We now include the reduced apparel production season and make similar improvements to the preceding production stages. This is the complete

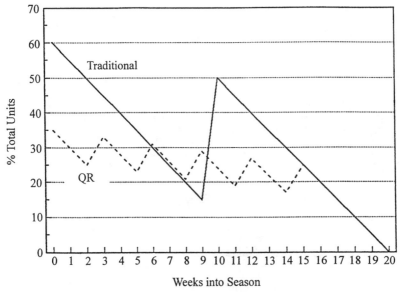

Figure 7.4   Comparison of retail inventories

implementation of the QR parameters from Table 7.1. The results are shown in Figure 7.5. In this case, the greige production starts 13 weeks prior to the start of the retail season, down from 23 weeks under the traditional practice. Less than 50% of the cumulative seasonal apparel production has been committed one week into the season, and, even more surprisingly, 15% of the greige production has yet to begin.

7.2.4   Short Season or Fashion Goods

Next, we turn to goods that sell in shorter seasons, which may amount to a third of all apparel. Hunter et al. (1992) have shown that it is necessary to make a larger initial shipment for the shorter season goods to compensate for the uncertainty in demand. Figures 7.6 (a) and (b) show the effect of implementation of the QR assumptions developed in the previous section for a 10-week retail season.

Here an initial retail shipment of 60% is used, with additional shipments made every two weeks. The state of the pipeline for this scenario two weeks into the selling season suggests that there is little opportunity to change the apparel production based on PoS data, but the more sophisticated models described later will show that down to an eight-week season, application of the

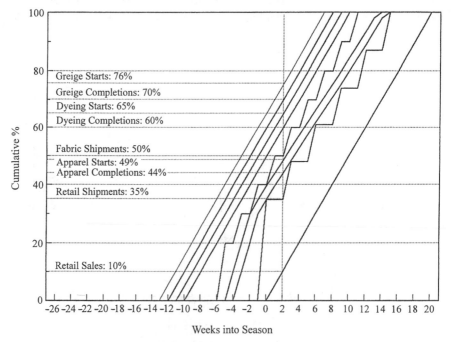

Figure 7.5   Full QR implementation

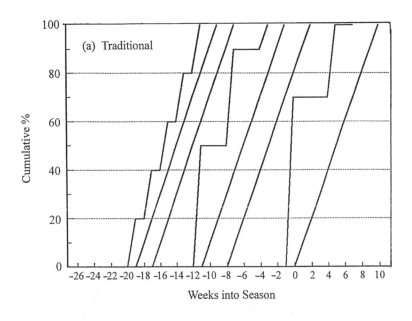

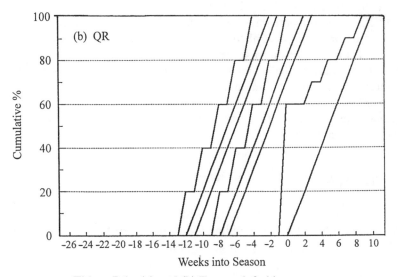

Figure 7.6   (a) and (b) Ten-week fashion season

Table 7.2   Comparison of model attributes

Model attribute	Improvement from Quick Response operations
Retail inventory	28.5% reduction
Apparel finished inventory	78.7% reduction
Apparel work in process	69.7% reduction
Apparel fabric inventory	66.0% reduction
Textile work in process (greige and finishing)	56.2% reduction
Initial order lead-time	13 weeks reduction

QR parameters—including weekly reorders and shipments—can give excellent results.

7.2.5   Results

This study was performed to determine the benefits achievable from the implementation of Quick Response practices for the pipeline as a whole, as well as to establish some limits on its effectiveness. The single product model used was necessarily simplified and idealized in order to portray the results. However, it allows display of the time phased relationships of the product throughout the pipeline more clearly than would be possible looking at actual production data for tens or hundreds of goods, and provided a solid basis for the construction of more detailed simulations.

Table 7.2 lists the performance changes observed in the single good model under the assumptions described in the earlier sections. The inventory values given in Table 7.2 are the time averages over the entire season. The results shown in the table are based on a 20-week selling season; they were substantially less for the shorter fashion goods season. Overall, they are in very good agreement with those shown in Chapters 8, 9 and 10.

Readers associated with other consumer goods industries may wish to construct similar models.

7.3   COMMENTS

Simulation and modeling have provided invaluable aids to business development, while at the same time avoiding the excessive costs often associated with pipeline trials. For QR, such approaches have graphically demonstrated how long standing, underlying operating assumptions, so often taken for granted and dictated as 'the way we do things around here', can be shaken and removed.

In the next chapter we begin to examine one particular simulation and modeling program: the Sourcing Simulator.

8
THE SOURCING SIMULATOR[1]

Again, we refer to the first industry trials carried out to validate the research findings that underpin Quick Response. The results of the trials were extremely encouraging, but were expensive and time consuming. The Sourcing Simulator modeling program was designed to simulate such trials for general consumer products, under a variety of conditions, but quickly and cheaply. It was the first of a number of research initiatives undertaken at North Carolina State University to explore and evaluate QR methodologies.

In designing it for people with limited computing capability, as well for ease of use, the program runs as a Windows application on a PC (under Windows-95/97 or Windows NT). There are two versions of the program. The first (Version 1.2), described in detail below, is primarily concerned with the retail end of the supply chain. The second (Version 2.0) incorporates a model of the manufacturing process (described in Chapter 10), along with a Neural Network Tool (described in Chapter 11) for characterizing the behavior of the system under different conditions. While both have their roots in the apparel industry, they are generic and can be applied to virtually any inventoried consumer product. Interest is currently being shown in this program by the soft drinks industry.

8.1 SOURCING SIMULATOR OUTLINE

Here we describe the analysis tool referred to above in terms of inputs, outputs and the 'engine' driving it. Sourcing Simulator was developed primarily to provide an instructional, hands-on tool for educators and retail buyers for exploring the impact of a wide variety of ordering, demand re-estimation, reordering and price markdown procedures, in both traditional and QR settings.

---

[1] The Sourcing Simulator © North Carolina State University is available through the Textile Clothing Technology Corporation, Cary, NC, USA (+1) 919 380-2156 (http://www.tc2.com).

It allows for analysis of seasonal or basic items. An important feature is that the user specifies the level of consumer forecast error to be experienced and in this way answer questions like:

> How well will I do with a given sourcing policy given my forecast—is this good or bad?

Obviously the user will not know exactly what level of forecast error they will actually encounter so the model allows the user to experiment over a range of possible errors and determine the robustness of a sourcing policy.

The Sourcing Simulator performs analyses from the retailer's perspective since, ultimately, any improvement in the supply system must benefit the retailer to justify the increased cost of doing business under QR operating practice. The Sourcing Simulator is focused on a single retail store. The reason is twofold. First, it reduces the input data requirements to allow rapid analysis. Second, our experience with related tools that allow analysis of more encompassing systems has been that perhaps 90% of the gain in understanding of the behavior of the system can be obtained with the simple model.

It is important to realize that the use of the tool is not limited to retailers since an understanding of the benefit at retail of an improved supply system should be of interest to the entire supply complex. The Sourcing Simulator is designed to analyze the benefit side of a cost/benefit analysis. It does not consider the costs of converting a traditional manufacturing system to a Quick Response supply system. These costs are case specific and difficult to quantify in any general way. This part of the analysis is left for traditional tools.

The objectives of the development may be summarized as follows:

- to evaluate the impact of a sourcing decision in terms of financial and non-financial measures including losses due to markdowns and lost sales
- to quantify the potential benefits of QR supply systems for Seasonal/Fashion or Basic merchandise
- to explore the limitations of QR benefits imposed by order lead-times and short selling seasons
- to provide a tool to evaluate the effectiveness of retail re-estimation, reorder and price markdown policies
- to provide a training system for retail buyers which could be expanded as a prototype paperless operating system
- to provide the 'hooks' to allow the system to be expanded to include manufacturing and other up-stream processes.

The Sourcing Simulator V1.2 has two components: a Seasonal Model and a Basics Model. Version 2.0 has a somewhat different interface.

8.2 DESCRIPTION OF THE SEASONAL MODEL

This model is used to analyze the performance of a line of merchandise in a retail store sold over a finite season. The product is offered in a range of styles, colors and sizes, resulting in a number of stock keeping units (SKUs). The product need not be offered in a range of each attribute. For example, if a product is only offered in four sizes, then the number of styles and colors is assumed to be one. The model tracks store inventory by SKU throughout a sales season (Figure 8.1).

The inventory is affected by the initial supply, replenishment stock that is received during the season, and consumer purchases. In-season replenishment stock, if any, is determined by arrangement with the vendor. The model tracks retail costs and revenues and other non-financial measures of performance (described below).

The buyer's plan (pre-season) determines the initial supply. Within the season, the buyer may employ one of several alternative techniques for re-estimating demand and incorporate the re-estimate in some scheme for issuing reorders on the vendor. The buyer may also employ price reductions (mark-downs) in order to stimulate sales. It should be noted that the model allows the user either to assume the retail buyer is able to predict the seasonality pattern with reasonable accuracy or not, as the case may be. Buyers are typically able to estimate such patterns because of past experience with similar items.

A major requirement of the model is that it should capture the random nature of consumer behavior in the store within a framework that allows investigation of buyer strategies for seasonal goods. Consumer arrivals at the store are modeled as a non-homogeneous Poisson process (see for example Winston, 1987), i.e. the time between arrivals is exponentially distributed with a given rate. This distribution is commonly used to model the arrival of individuals to a system when the population of potential customers is large but the

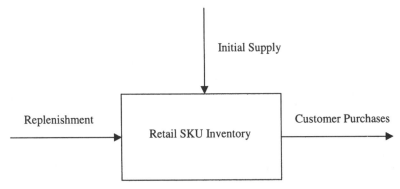

Figure 8.1 Simplified view of the model

probability of any one individual arriving during a period is relatively small. The rate of customer arrivals is determined for each week in the retail season from the specified volume for the season and the seasonal demand pattern.

The customer branching diagram, which models customer behavior, is shown in Figure 8.2. The customer is randomly assigned an SKU preference according to the underlying demand mix specification. If the assigned SKU is in stock, the customer will purchase it and leave. The stock for this SKU is then reduced by one. If the item is out of stock, a stockout is recorded, and the customer chooses an alternative item of another style and/or color in his or her size or leaves the store (implying a lost sale) with specific probabilities P1 and P2, respectively.

The initial supply, the demand re-estimation procedure, and the reorder scheme are specified as input to the model, as is the reorder lead-time, i.e. the time between placing the reorder and its appearance on the shelf in the store. Clearly, the reorder lead-time delimits the possible number of reorders, and, with re-estimation, the content of successive reorders reflects improved knowledge of the underlying demand.

A more complicated model of consumer behavior, including such things as multiple purchases by the same customer and 'browsing' has been developed (Nuttle et al., 1991); however, we have found that the results are not sensitive to the added complexity.

A common practice is to mark down prices for a specific period of promotional or end-of-season selling. In the model, price reductions of any magnitude can be initiated in any week. They can have two different effects on consumer behavior. First, the rate of customer arrivals to the store in period j, C'_j increases

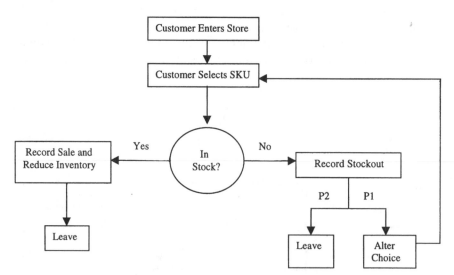

Figure 8.2   Customer branching diagram

in proportion to the price reduction—referred to as 'price elasticity'.

$$\text{Let } C'j = C'_j{}^*[1 + (E^*MDj)/100]$$

where,

Cj = Average number of customers in period j,

E = Elasticity value,

MD_j = Percentage of price markdown in period j.

Foxall (1981) suggested values of 26% and 74% for P1 and P2, respectively for grocery items, although users are free to select their own values. Subsequent empirical studies of a catalog operation confirmed these probabilities for a line of apparel (King and Zozom, 1997). In contrast, a recent study by Kurt Salmon Associates (1998) suggests that only 9% of customers would take an alternate color for an apparel item. Clearly, these values are dependent upon the type of product and diversity of the product line. However, relatively extensive experimentation suggests that the model outputs are not particularly sensitive to moderate variations in the P values; although it would be instructive to work with a retailer or marketing researcher to examine this area more fully, and we are currently doing so with a major catalog operation.

The model allows consideration of four types of relationships with the vendor: Traditional; Vendor Managed Inventory (VMI), Quick Response and News Boy. Under a traditional relationship with the vendor, the delivery of goods to the store is determined ahead of the selling season; no in-season adjustments are made. A VMI relationship models the case where the retailer desires rapid shipment of PoS based reorders but the vendor does not have a QR system. Therefore, the vendor tries to accommodate the retailer by carrying inventory based upon the pre-season plan and hoping there is a match between reorders and stock, i.e. little forecast error. Under this kind of relationship, the vendor gets stuck with excess stock of SKUs whose demand was overestimated and the retailer is unable to get more of the SKUs whose demand was underestimated. In effect the inventory burden is moved from the retailer to the vendor.

A re-estimation/reorder procedure is central when using a Quick Response vendor. Having received information from PoS data, the buyer can modify the original plan and begin to structure the on-shelf display of merchandise to reflect consumer preferences through replenishment orders on the vendor. The size and mix of the orders are flexible to allow the retailer to shape the stock inventories according to need. In this case, the manufacturer employs a rapid production system that allows shipments to match reorders within some specified lead-time.

There are a number of methods that can be used for re-estimation of demand, particularly those employing exponential smoothing. Analysis has shown that more sophisticated methods typically only lead to marginal improvements over the simple one presented below (Hall, 1991).

The estimate of a total season's demand for SKU n through period t, E_{nt}, is computed by adding the cumulative sales for SKU n through period t, S_{nt}, a lost sales allowance (estimate of cumulative lost sales) for that SKU, L_{nt}, and dividing by the fraction of demand that was expected to have occurred by time period t, F_t; i.e.

$$E_{nt} = (S_{nt} + L_{nt})/F_t$$

where: $F_t = \Sigma f_i$, f_i being the expected percent of consumer (demand) volume in period i, and the summation is from $i = 1$ to $i = t$, the current time period.

The lost sales allowance, L_{nt}, where

$$L_{nt} = \Sigma l_{ni}, \ l_{ni} \text{ being the lost sales allowance for SKU } n \text{ in period } i,$$

is clearly a fuzzy number because while sales are directly observable, lost sales are not (unless a catalog sales operation is being studied), though they are a part of the demand. However, good results have been obtained in trial runs by calculating L_{nt} as a fraction of actual sales of SKU n in week t, whenever SKU n is out of stock at the end of week t, and 0 otherwise. The re-estimation of demand is used in conjunction with a reorder procedure to restock the shelves. There are many possible procedures; the one used in the model is as follows. At the end of any week t in which a reorder is to be placed, the estimated remaining net requirement for each SKU n, NR_{nt}, is calculated by subtracting the sum of the sales (S_{nt}), lost sales allowance (L_{nt}), current on-hand inventory (I_{nt}) and on-order balance (O_{nt}) from the current estimate of the season's demand; i.e.

$$NR_{nt} = (1 - F_t)^* E_{nt} - (I_{nt} + O_{nt}).$$

The reorder quantity for each SKU n is then specified by dividing NR_{nt} by the number of reorders yet to be placed.

An alternative reordering strategy to the Quick Response approach just described is based on the so-called News Boy approach (Morton, 1971). Consider a street corner newspaper vendor. Each day he must decide how many newspapers to purchase. The goal is to find the balance between the cost of ordering too much (and being left with obsolete merchandise) and not ordering enough (and incurring lost sales). This can be adapted for retail goods by specifying a 'target service level'; i.e. percentage of customers who will find their first choice product. Details on the use of this approach for seasonal merchandise can be found in Reynolds (1995) and for basic goods in Martin (1997). We shall discuss it further in Chapter 11.

These, then, are the main structural elements of the Sourcing Simulator. The Input Variables for the model are described below. A summary of the types of output data is given in Section 8.2.8.

The user of the model plays the role of the retail store buyer and is responsible for specifying the characteristics of the product and the merchandising plan (buyer's plan). There are four groups of data associated with this information: Buyer's Plan, Costs, Markdowns and Premiums, and Sourcing Strategy. Since the Sourcing Simulator is a simulation model, the user has control over the actual consumer demand through a set of data that specifies its characteristics. In the Sourcing Simulator software, all these data are entered in a controlled, graphical environment using a set of file folders that are described below. Instead of describing each of these in detail, we chose to show the pertinent screens containing typical information.

8.2.1 Buyer's Plan

The Buyer's Plan folder (Figure 8.3) specifies the name of the product line, the number of styles, colors and sizes in the line, and the length of the selling season, as well as the pre-season estimate of total demand, the presumed seasonality of sales, and the portion of the demand in each style, color and size. The presumed seasonality is specified either by choosing from a list of common seasonality patterns or by entering the weekly values.

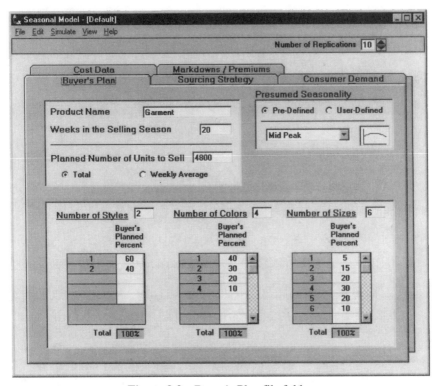

Figure 8.3   Buyer's Plan file folder

8.2.2   Costs

The Costs folder (Figure 8.4) allows the user to specify a set of financial data. This includes the wholesale cost of the product. The program allows for costs to be (1) the same for all SKUs in the line, (2) the same for all SKUs in a given style, (3) the same for all SKUs in a given color, (4) the same for all SKUs in a given size, or (5) different for each SKU. There is provision for two wholesale costs to be entered. The first is the cost for the initial shipment of goods, while the second represents the cost for in-season replenishment. These values can be the same or different as would be the case if the initial shipment were purchased at a lower cost off-shore while in-season replenishment was handled by a domestic, QR vendor at a higher price. Additional inputs are the planned offering price of the garment, the expected liquidation price for left-over stock, ordering, shipping, inventory carrying and handling costs, and program overhead cost. The latter is used to reflect the additional overhead costs including travel, people, etc. that the retailer incurs in dealing with certain vendors (particularly off-shore suppliers).

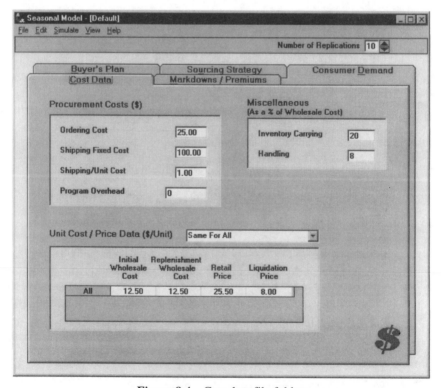

Figure 8.4   Cost data file folder

8.2.3   Markdowns and Premiums

The Markdowns and Premiums folder (Figure 8.5) is used to specify any planned markdown events. For each planned markdown, the following inputs are required:

- the week of occurrence
- the percentage price reduction
- the impact on the consumer, in terms of propensity to look for an alternative choice after a stockout, is specified.

The consumer price elasticity is also an input, i.e. the percentage increase in consumer demand for each percent decrease in the selling price. In addition, a performance-based markdown can be specified which is used to trigger markdowns earlier than anticipated if revenues fall below a specified fraction of (pre-season) anticipated levels. Finally, a price premium can be provided. This is used to reflect the practice of offering goods at the start of a season at a price above the target price point. The user inputs the percentage markup and the ending week for the premium.

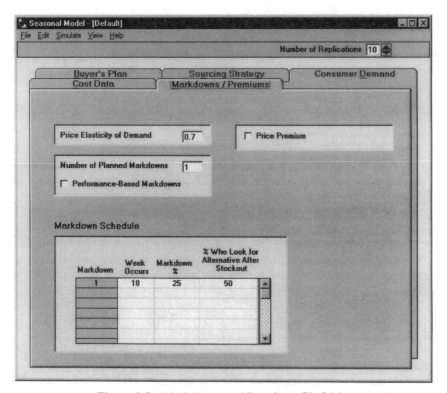

Figure 8.5   Markdowns and Premiums file folder

8.2.4   Sourcing Strategy

The Sourcing Strategy folder (Figure 8.6) is used to indicate the relationship with and characteristics of the vendor as well as the planned distribution of goods to the store. It includes:

- the type of vendor relationship (Traditional, VMI, Quick Response, or News Boy)
- the initial stocking of the store in terms of a percentage of the buyer's plan (a quantity that is influenced by the amount of merchandise needed to 'dress' the shelves)
- the minimum order quantities per SKU and/or per order
- the reliability of the vendor in terms of percentage of orders that come short and the range of the amount ordered but not received
- the replenishment schedule including the timing of orders and receipts as well as the size of each replenishment order.

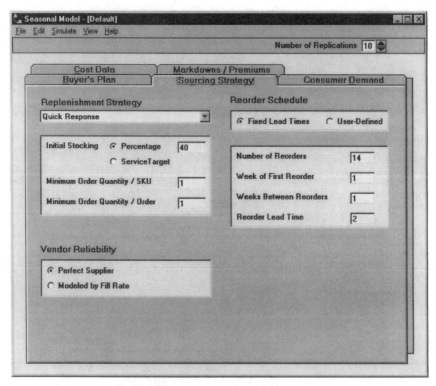

Figure 8.6   Sourcing Strategy file folder

8.2.5   Consumer Demand

No matter how carefully a demand forecast is made, it will contain errors. We classify forecast error in three ways: total volume, SKU mix and seasonality of sales. The total volume error is simply the percentage difference between the total forecast across all SKUs and the actual total demand. We describe the SKU mix error as having three components—color mix, style mix and size mix errors. For traditional, importing and, to some extent, domestic VMI operations, the buyer plan freezes the SKU mix. QR differs in that the SKU mix is checked against demand through the season and shelf stocks are adjusted to match the requirements of the consumer. Seasonality error allows the user to quantify the impact of assuming the wrong seasonality pattern, e.g. assuming a season which peaks mid-season when in fact it peaks early.

Since the Sourcing Simulator is a simulation model, it allows the user to specify what the actual demand for the product will be and, in effect, consider the impact of forecast error. The fifth file folder (Figure 8.7) allows the user to enter the following information. First, the total underlying consumer demand can be expressed either as a specific value or as a percentage error from the

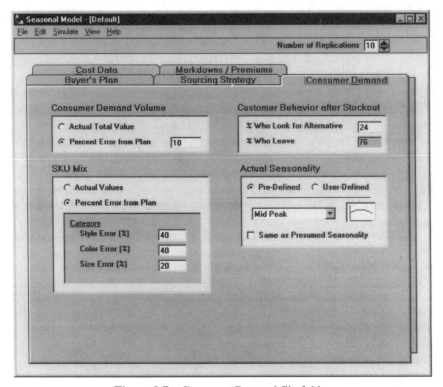

Figure 8.7   Consumer Demand file folder

planned volume specified in the Buyer's Plan folder. Second, the SKU mix, i.e. percentage of demand at the SKU level, can be entered as specific values or as an error from the planned mix specified in the Buyer's Plan folder. Third, the seasonality of actual demand; i.e. percentage of customer volume in each week of the season is specified. This can be the same as was specified under the Buyer's Plan or different to reflect an inaccurate estimate on the part of the buyer. Finally, the fraction of customers who look for another SKU in the line if their choice is out of stock.

8.2.6   Forecast Assortment Errors

In asking about the extent to which SKU mix errors hurt retail performance, some quantitative measure of error is required. We have used the following (King and Hunter, 1996a).

Suppose there are three levels of an attribute (color, size or style); call them A, B, and C. Further, suppose the expected or forecast mix of these levels is 10%, 35% and 40%, respectively. The demand percentages, however, turn out to be 10%, 30% and 30%, respectively. The attribute error is defined as the sum, across A–C, of the absolute differences between the expected and actual demand percentages. Thus, the difference for attribute A is $|10-10| = 0\%$, for B it is $|35-30| = 5\%$, and for C it is $|40-30| = 10\%$. Summing these values gives a total of $0 + 5 + 10 = 15\%$, the total error for that attribute.

It has been shown that the individual errors that comprise the total figure of 15% have little or no effect on retail performance; it is the total that matters (Nuttle et al., 1991). It should be remembered that the errors for each attribute are independent; for style/color/size, they may be 30%/30%/15%, etc. which, for convenience, we refer to as 30/30/15.

Table 8.1, below, will help to show what is meant by errors of different magnitudes. There, we give examples of 10%, 20%, 30% and 40% size errors for products sold in six sizes. These may help the reader make up their own mind as to what level of error is normal for an operation. For our part, we believe that a 30–40% error is not uncommon, depending on the line of merchandise under consideration.

8.2.7   Efficiency of Re-estimation Algorithm

With the meaning of 'error' defined, we can address a question that may have crossed the mind of the reader. Earlier we discussed the re-estimation algorithm, but said nothing about how quickly it homed in on the 'true' demand volume and attribute distributions, vs. the assumed 'plan'. The question is, then, 'How fast, and accurate is the re-estimation algorithm?' The answer is shown in Figure 8.8. In summary, the speed with which the QR re-estimation algorithm responds is extremely rapid.

Table 8.1   Examples of forecast and demand size distribution yielding 10% through 40% errors for six sizes

	Size						Total error (%)
	A (%)	B (%)	C (%)	D (%)	E (%)	F (%)	
Forecast	5	15	30	30	15	5	
Actual demand	3	17	28	32	14	6	
Difference	2	2	2	2	1	1	10
Forecast	5	15	30	30	15	5	
Actual demand	2	18	26	34	12	8	
Difference	3	3	4	4	3	3	20
Forecast	5	15	30	30	15	5	
Actual demand	2	10	25	40	20	3	
Difference	3	5	5	10	5	2	30
Forecast	5	15	30	30	15	5	
Actual demand	3	8	19	43	19	8	
Difference	2	7	11	13	4	3	40

In order to demonstrate this, the accuracy of the estimate of demand by color is used. For apparel products accurate color re-estimation is crucial if there is to be time for the mill or dye house to produce the correct color fabric needed to meet the actual demand. Figure 8.8 shows, for 0% volume error, the way in which the errors in the assumed distribution of three colors are corrected. The buyer plan forecast a color mix for colors 1, 2 and 3 of 45%, 30% and 25%, respectively. The real demand was for 30%, 60%, and 10%. Using the rule

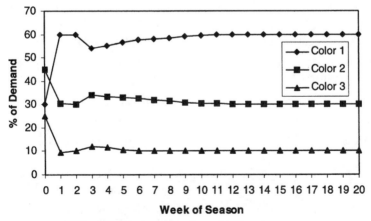

Figure 8.8   Re-estimation of 60% color error

spelled out above, this is equivalent to a 60% color error. A 60% error is judged to be far larger than would be met under most circumstances, but it is shown here because a 40% error proved to be correctable in only one week of sales. The vertical axis to the left shows the estimated color mix; that to the right, the demand color distribution. Aside from some uncertainty in the first couple of weeks, the re-estimation algorithm homes in on the consumer preference very quickly.

There is an interaction between the color error and the pre-season estimate of volume demand, but only when the volume is overestimated; underestimation of volume has little or no effect on the speed with which true color (or other attribute) demand is identified. The effect of overestimation of volume is to delay the identification of the color frequency by no more than one week.

The results above were obtained using a product line with two styles, three colors and four sizes, i.e. 24 SKUs. Further, sales were set at an average of 240 units per week, or 10 units/SKU/week. While this level of demand is realistic

Table 8.2 Model outputs

Weekly statistics	Seasonal statistics
Number of customer arrivals	Number of customers
End-of-week inventory	Initial inventory
Number of sales	In-season inventory receipts
Cumulative projected and actual $ sales	Average inventory
Inventory receipts	Inventory turns
Number of first stockouts	% of stock sold
Weekly and cumulative service level	% sell through (1st price)
Total number of stockouts	% liquidated
Number of lost sales	% lost sales, overall, prior to first reorder receipt and pre-markdown
Number of SKUs out of stock	Sales + liquidation revenue
Selling price	Cost of goods
Cumulative GMROI	Distribution costs
Cumulative gross margin	GMROI and GMROISL
Demand volume error	Average sales price
Color mix error	% service level: overall and pre-markdown
	% service level: overall, prior to first reorder receipt and pre-markdown
	% in-stock: overall, prior to first reorder receipt and pre-markdown

for a fairly large store, depending upon the product this may be far too big for an SME. Accordingly, we reduced the demand, by stages, down to an average of 1 unit/SKU/week. As might be expected, the re-estimation algorithm took longer to identify the true color demand, but surprisingly the extra time needed was only of the order of 1–2 weeks. This means that the methodology developed for the Sourcing Simulator is applicable to small specialty stores selling merchandise with a shelf life of, say, eight weeks.

8.2.8 Model Outputs

The output elements of the Sourcing Simulator are shown in Table 8.2. In the Sourcing Simulator, a table of the Seasonal Statistics listed in Table 8.2 is displayed that allows 'side by side' comparison of sourcing options. An example is shown in Figure 8.9 (for brevity, some of the outputs are not

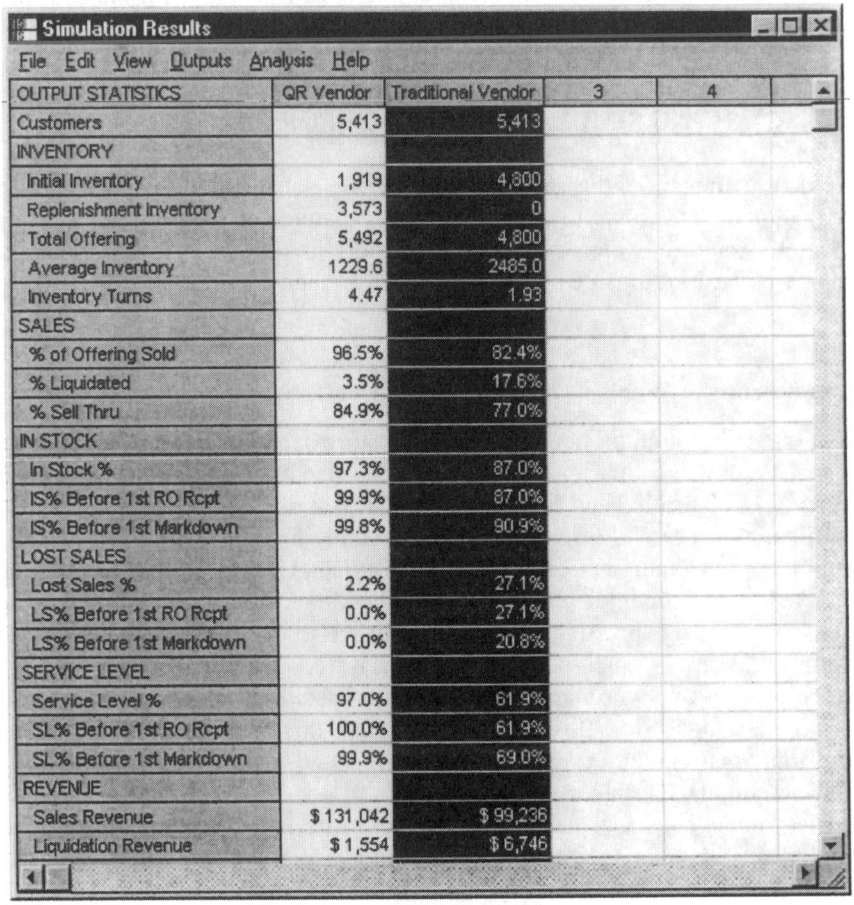

Simulation Results

File Edit View Outputs Analysis Help

OUTPUT STATISTICS	QR Vendor	Traditional Vendor	3	4
Customers	5,413	5,413		
INVENTORY				
Initial Inventory	1,919	4,800		
Replenishment Inventory	3,573	0		
Total Offering	5,492	4,800		
Average Inventory	1229.6	2485.0		
Inventory Turns	4.47	1.93		
SALES				
% of Offering Sold	96.5%	82.4%		
% Liquidated	3.5%	17.6%		
% Sell Thru	84.9%	77.0%		
IN STOCK				
In Stock %	97.3%	87.0%		
IS% Before 1st RO Rcpt	99.9%	87.0%		
IS% Before 1st Markdown	99.8%	90.9%		
LOST SALES				
Lost Sales %	2.2%	27.1%		
LS% Before 1st RO Rcpt	0.0%	27.1%		
LS% Before 1st Markdown	0.0%	20.8%		
SERVICE LEVEL				
Service Level %	97.0%	61.9%		
SL% Before 1st RO Rcpt	100.0%	61.9%		
SL% Before 1st Markdown	99.9%	69.0%		
REVENUE				
Sales Revenue	$ 131,042	$ 99,236		
Liquidation Revenue	$ 1,554	$ 6,746		

Figure 8.9 Example of tabular output

shown). The Weekly Statistics are displayed in graphs. Both can be tailored to fit the user's needs. In addition, a 'Break-Even Analysis' function is included to perform comparisons of the form 'How much more per item can I pay one vendor and still match the financial performance when using some other vendor?' This is discussed in Chapter 9.

8.3 THE BASICS MODEL

The Basics Model is similar to the Seasonal Model with a few exceptions. First, the product is sold year round; thus seasonal values become annual ones. Second, the re-estimation/reorder procedures and vendor relationships change. A description of one possible procedure is given in Chapter 5, together with some thoughts on alternative methods. Beyond these differences, the inputs for the Basics Model are essentially the same as those for the Seasonal Model.

8.4 SOURCING SIMULATOR RESULTS FOR SEASONAL GOODS

We now demonstrate the capabilities of the Seasonal Model of the Sourcing Simulator in two ways: to investigate the dynamics of a variety of retailing operations, and to explore the benefits afforded by QR in a range of settings. The quantification of QR benefits has always been a prime objective of this research.

8.4.1 Scope of Work

Retailing of apparel, particularly in a large store carrying many types of products and many lines in each type, is best described as frenetic. Personnel costs are closely controlled and it is simply not possible to review operations on a continuous basis. Thus, very few, if any, stores have a feeling for stockout patterns or customer service levels. Worse, financial data tend to be accumulated at the department level, where individual lines of merchandise are aggregated, thus hiding specific performance data. Also, retail merchandise buyers are often judged on such performance measures as post-season gross margin which leads them to primarily (if not solely) use wholesale costs as the basis for sourcing decisions. Based on our analyses, this often leads to the wrong decision when hidden costs such as lost sales and markdowns are taken into consideration (see Chapter 9).

The fundamental insight provided by this work is that a rapid supply (QR) vendor can overcome the consequences of forecast error and prove more attractive to a retailer, despite having higher unit cost. Analytic tools such as the Sourcing Simulator allow details of the retailing operation to be investigated and estimates of useful, and previously unknowable, performance indices to be generated.

In what follows, we consider a garment, e.g. a children's twill coverall/jumpsuit, having 24 SKUs—two styles, three colors and four sizes. We use a season of 20 weeks, though later we will use seasons of as few as eight weeks. The number of customers averages about 240 per week over the season. Here the customer intensity is greatest at mid-season, although other seasonal patterns have been examined. For example, when consumer purchases are concentrated in the early part of a season, the QR performance advantage is somewhat reduced vis-à-vis traditional.

Table 8.3 shows the other inputs used in the scenarios being described. Those inputs not specified in Table 8.3 may be assumed to be null unless explicitly stated.

One set of entries requires an explanation—the wholesale costs. The $2.00 difference between the cost of traditional goods and those for QR or VMI can be explained as: (a) the traditional is interchangeable with imports, or (b) the

Table 8.3   Inputs for test cases

Buyer's Plan			
Planned number of units to sell	4800		
Weeks in selling season	20		
Planned % demand			
	Style	Color	Size
1	60	45	10
2	40	30	25
3		25	35
4			30
Cost data			
Wholesale cost (initial and replenish)	$10.50 traditional		
	$12.50 QR/VMI		
Retail price	$25.50		
Liquidation price	$10		
Ordering cost	$25		
Shipping cost—fixed	$25		
Shipping cost—per item	$1		
Inventory carrying cost	20% of wholesale		
Handling cost	8% of wholesale		
Markdowns/premiums			
Price elasticity	0.7		
Markdowns	25% in week 18		
P3 value from Figure 8.3 after markdown	50%		
Consumer demand			
Seasonality	Mid-season peak		
P3 value from Figure 8.3 at first price	24%		

value of QR is recognized by the retailer, i.e. the retailer recognizes either the costs incurred by the vendor in carrying excess inventory and recompenses him, or the vendor's responsibility for disposing of unshipped goods. The $2.00 is somewhat arbitrary, but some differential is symbolic of 'fair' business practice.

8.4.2   Weekly Inventory and Stockout Patterns

The first scenario looks at traditional marketing vs. QR. By traditional, we mean that about 60–80% of the season's goods are delivered before opening day, with the other 20–40% dropped half way through the season. The word 'traditional' was used initially to describe domestic sourcing but, in fact, many imports either follow this procedure, or all of the merchandise is delivered ahead of the season.

This contrasts with QR where, say, 35–40% of goods are delivered initially, with the rest delivered weekly in about equal amounts based on the re-estimation/reorder procedures described in Chapter 6. For these experiments, 14 in-season reorders are made with a replenishment lead-time (receipt of order until arrival of new stock on the store shelf) of two weeks.

We also show, for comparison, the results for a 'modified traditional', a situation where traditional devolves into something similar to QR. This reflects the recently popular scenario in which a retailer demands rapid replenishment of garments based on PoS driven orders. However, the manufacturer attempts to do this by carrying inventory—largely made pre-season—based upon the initial buyer's plan. This way of supplying retailers we call Vendor Managed Inventory (VMI) and have referred to it earlier.

Here we consider the case where the retailer makes 14 weekly orders. The manufacturer ships within one week of receipt of order. We also assume that the manufacturer has the capacity to produce an extra 10% of the plan in-season.

Perhaps VMI is not the best description, though a better one has not yet been adopted. In the food industry, consumer products and in some apparel retailing and manufacturing companies, there is true VMI, i.e. the vendor assumes full responsibility for stocking the shelves or factory. In the situation being examined here, the manufacturer makes all, or most of the items, ahead of the season, and the retailer 'draws down', or 'calls off', weekly or bi-weekly quantities through frequent, small orders. This is not a good procedure so far as the manufacturer is concerned; payment is only for what is ordered and shipped, and carrying costs increase sharply. Also, as the season progresses, because of the SKU errors in the original buyer plan, fewer of the retailers' demands can be met, and the manufacturer will probably end up having to absorb the cost of the unsold goods.

The retailer benefits considerably from this form of VMI, but only in terms of store inventory carrying costs. There is no improvement in terms of customer service or in supply chain optimization—and it is here that future improvement is crucial for the benefit of the whole pipeline.

In the first set of runs, we consider the case where the retail buyer has a perfect estimate of the total demand volume but is wrong about the SKU mix; specifically a 40/40/20 error pattern as described earlier. Recall that such an error pattern has been accepted as very common among retailers with whom we have spoken.

Figure 8.10 shows, for traditional and QR marketing, the inventory held each week by the retailer. Clearly, QR is consistently lower. Later, we shall show the importance of low retail stock holdings, the number of inventory turns, and other financial measures of performance.

In Figure 8.11, we show how stockouts are delayed and held to a minimum by QR procedures until the very end of the season, whereas traditional marketing allows stockouts to climb steadily from week 6 through 9, fall again in week 10 (due to the arrival of the in-season drop), and then climb again through the end of the 20-week season. Note that around week 12 or so is typically the time that serious marking down occurs to get rid of what is, in fact, a 'white elephant' situation.

In Figure 8.12, we see the impact of stockouts on % Service level for both traditional and QR marketing. Recall that we define service level as the percentage of customers who find their first choice garment. QR is able to maintain very high service levels until the end-of-season markdown in week 18. Overall, traditional practices result in about a 71% service level for the season, while QR yields 96%. These values agree with industry experience.

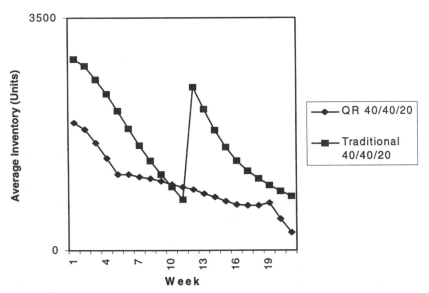

Figure 8.10   Average weekly inventory levels—traditional and QR

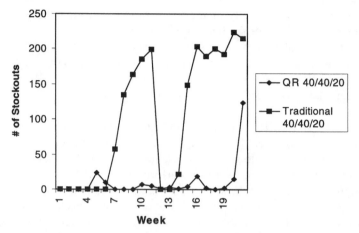

Figure 8.11   Stockouts—traditional and QR

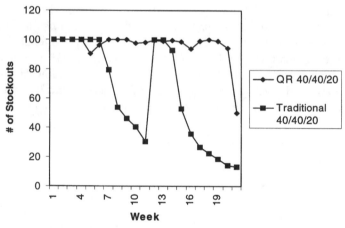

Figure 8.12   % Service levels—traditional and QR

It is not possible to achieve consistent, high levels of service by using traditional or VMI methods (Figure 8.12). The retailing industry is currently deeply involved in trying to provide a better service to its customers, levels of 95% being a popular target. QR provides a way of doing this. However, it should be noted that the service level falls off sharply once marking down starts, and certainly in the last 2–3 weeks of a season. It may be more realistic to think of the 95% level as applying to pre-markdown or, in the case of QR, prior to the last inventory replenishment. For the scenario examined here, the service levels prior to the end-of-season markdown event are 79%, 83% and 99% for traditional, VMI and QR, respectively.

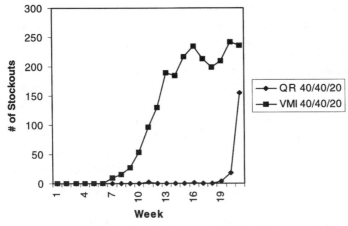

Figure 8.13   Stockouts—VMI vs. QR

The patterns are shown in Figure 8.13; stockouts for VMI and QR should be compared with those in Figure 8.11. The ability of the retailer to make some adjustments in the in-season orders produces a different pattern, but makes little difference to the cumulative data.

Table 8.4 shows the major performance parameters for the three methods of carrying out business over the 20-week season. We shall refer several times to the importance of Gross Margin Return On Inventory (GMROI) as a measure of performance. This is the gross margin divided by the average value of the inventory carried throughout the season, i.e. it is the amount of gross margin revenue generated per dollar investment in inventory. It is a prime financial indicator. QR is able to generate greater gross margin while requiring far less investment in inventory.

Another measure being discussed in the industry is GMROISL (GMROI adjusted for in-stock service level), i.e. GMROI multiplied by the average fraction of garments in stock prior to markdown. The purpose of this measure is to take into consideration that high GMROI values can be obtained by simply

Table 8.4   Performance comparisons

Measure	Traditional	VMI	QR
GMROI	2.3	3.8	5.0
Gross margin—$ thousands	53.5	48.3	57.3
Inventory turns	2.2	4.1	5.3
GMROISL	2.0	3.6	5.0
Service level—%	81	86	95
Lost sales—%	13	9	4
Liquidation—%	26	18	3

maintaining very low inventory levels and, in fact, being out of stock. GMROISL is more robust in this sense because it explicitly includes the in-stock level. QR maintains high in-stock levels so this measure favors QR even more than does GMROI.

The other data in Table 8.4 have been explained earlier in the chapter. There are no surprises here. VMI is superior to traditional, but the limited ability to manufacture in-season puts limits on the process. Notice the very low residual inventory (liquidation) levels under QR and that the gross margin is greater with QR even though the wholesale cost per garment is $2.00 more. The question of how much more the retailer should be willing to pay for a garment from a QR vendor to get the same gross margin, or GMROI, as with a traditional vendor or exporter will be discussed in Chapter 9.

8.4.3   Impact of Errors in Stock Keeping Units Mix

No matter how carefully a demand forecast is made, it will contain errors. Here we look at three types—color mix, style mix and size mix errors. For traditional, importing and, to a major extent, domestic VMI operations, the buyer plan freezes the SKU mix. QR differs in that the SKU mix is checked against demand through the season and shelf stocks are adjusted to match the requirements of the consumer.

Earlier in this chapter, we discussed the definition of SKU mix error used in the book. We now use three mix error levels: 0/0/0%, 20/20/10% and 40/40/20% (style/color/size) to look at their impact on QR and traditional retail results.

A glance at Table 8.5 shows that QR is relatively insensitive to error level, whereas for % Lost sales, % Service level and % Liquidated, traditional shows a marked deterioration in performance. The same is true for GMROI and Inventory Turns, but to a lesser extent.

Figure 8.14 takes one of the measures, stockouts, and traces it through a 20-week season for traditional and QR, each at two levels of mix error. The ways in which stockouts increase with increasing error is apparent. Even with large errors QR performs extremely well until the very end of the season.

Table 8.5   Impact of mix error

Measure	Traditional			QR		
	0/0/0%	20/20/10%	40/40/20%	0/0/0%	20/20/10%	40/40/20%
GMROI	3.3	2.9	2.3	5.1	5.1	5.0
Inventory turns	2.5	2.4	2.2	5.4	5.4	5.3
Lost sales—%	4	11	21	3	3	4
Service level—%	95	84	71	96	96	96
Liquidated—%	1	8	19	1	1	1

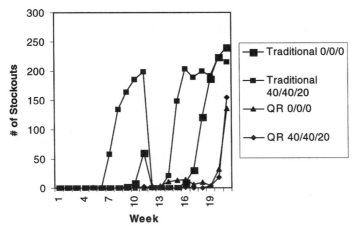

Figure 8.14   Stockouts for zero and high error levels

8.4.4   Impact of Volume Error

Perhaps the biggest problem facing the retail buyer is the estimation of total demand for a product line. This is particularly true for imported goods, as a firm contract is drawn well ahead of a season and an irrevocable letter of credit issued. In the case of domestic supply (traditional, VMI or QR), there is more room for adjustment if the season turns out to be better or worse than expected.

We looked at two cases: one where demand was 75% of expected, and a second where demand was 125% of forecast. The outcomes were evaluated in terms of the major performance indicators. Table 8.6 shows the results for the QR, VMI and traditional cases. Here we made the following assumptions about adjustments to the original buyer order:

- QR, full adjustments dictated by the re-estimation/reorder process.
- VMI can produce 10% more than plan.
- For traditional, there is no ability to manufacture in-season.

Table 8.6   Impact of volume forecast error on performance

Forecast errors	QR			VMI			Traditional		
	−25%	0%	+25%	−25%	0%	+25%	−25%	0%	+25%
GMROI	3.7	5.0	6.2	2.0	3.8	5.9	1.6	2.3	3.2
Turns #	4.0	5.3	6.5	2.8	4.1	6.0	1.8	2.2	2.6
Service level %	97	96	96	86	74	61	83	71	61
Lost sales %	3	3	3	8	19	31	11	21	31

QR takes greater advantage of the opportunities presented by higher-than-expected demand than does traditional retailing. This is reflected in inventory turns, and GMROI, with little loss of performance in the service measures.

When demand is less than expected QR maintains its advantage, but the differences in performance are not as large as when the demand is forecast more accurately. This is due to the excess stock that is present under traditional or VMI when demand is overestimated.

A point worth making may be somewhat obvious but is often not noted. It is that the greater the uncertainty associated with consumer demand, the greater the advantage of QR. Another way of looking at this is that the kind of supply chain that best supports retailing is highly dependent upon the level of uncertainty. This will be discussed in more detail in Chapter 11.

8.4.5   Cost to the Retailer of Errors in Size Mix

Everyone has experienced the irritation that follows when a product is selected but is not available in the required style, color and size combination, i.e. SKU. As an example consider apparel where color and style are notoriously difficult to forecast, but there are fewer excuses for making mistakes in the distribution of sizes. PoS data are widely available, and tracking these over, say, the first half of a season will give information on consumer preferences. In the second half of a season, stockouts will begin to give a distorted picture of preferences. Over 2–3 seasons, preferences should be well established.

If QR is the modus operandum for the store, the required stocks of the various sizes, together with appropriate reorders on the vendor, helps keep any given size from running out of stock. In this way, the distribution of sizes

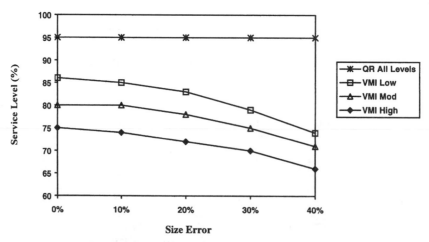

Figure 8.15   Impact of size error on Service level

preferred by the store's customers is quickly learned and used in future ordering of merchandise.

We considered two levels of style and color error; a low level (20% each), and a high level (40% each). For each level, we added size errors of 0%, 10%, 20%, 30% and 40%. The retail strategy used was VMI, and the garment had a shelf life of 10 to 20 weeks. Although we looked at both variations in the initial inventory and the seasonality of business; i.e. early, mid-season and late sales peaks, neither had a meaningful effect on the results.

Figure 8.15 shows the patterns involved for VMI. As expected, increasing size error decreased the % Service level. For a 40% size error with low style and color errors, the Service level dropped to about 76% from the 88% found for the 0% error. Under QR, however, there is no deterioration in Service level from about 96% regardless of the style/color/size error.

In Table 8.7 we show the impact of size error on other performance measures. In the cases of Revenue and Gross Margin, values are scaled to QR 0% error (20/20% style/color error) = 100. The results are self-explanatory.

8.4.6 Season Length and Quick Response Performance

When the first studies were carried out on QR, it was suspected that for very short seasons—eight to ten weeks—QR had little or nothing to offer the retailer. The problem was simple, there was not enough time to re-estimate demand and have reorders met by the vendor. At that time, three- to four-week reorder times seemed very short. This is not the case today; many manufacturers have gone to Just-in-Time production and very short order lead-times are common.

In order to investigate the impact of season length, we studied 8, 12, 16 and 20-week seasons using VMI and QR vendors. For the results presented below

Table 8.7 Size error and performance—QR vs. VMI

	VMI		QR	
Measure	0% size error	40% size error	0% size error	40% size error
Low style/color error (20/20%)				
Lost sales—%	9	18	3	3
Revenue	95	86	100	100
Gross margin	95	86	100	99
GMROI	4.3	3.8	5.1	5.1
High style/color error (40/40%)				
Lost sales—%	17	24	3	3
Revenue	87	80	100	100
Gross margin	86	79	100	99
GMROI	3.9	3.4	4.1	4.9

we assumed the following. The initial inventory, as a percentage of the total estimated demand, was 50%, 45%, 40% and 35% with 3, 7, 10 and 14 in-season replenishment orders for the 8, 12, 16 and 20 week seasons, respectively. A two-week lead-time was assumed for QR. VMI was the same, except that the lead-time was one week. For either vendor type, there was a single planned markdown of 25% about two weeks from the end of the season. As with the initial study of Table 8.4, the volume forecast was assumed to be 'perfect', and the mix error used was 40/40/20%.

Figures 8.16 and 8.17 show how season length affects % Service level and GMROI for QR, traditional and VMI. VMI Service level is relatively insensitive to season length while, for QR, as the season length increases to about 16 weeks, performance improves. Beyond 16 weeks, it is stable. GMROI increases with season length, though this is primarily a function of increased

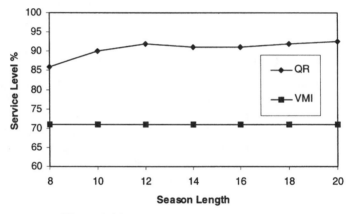

Figure 8.16   Service level vs. Season length

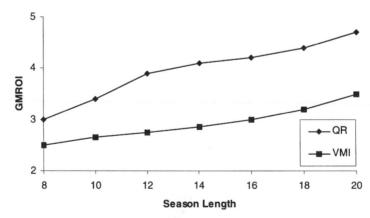

Figure 8.17   GMROI vs. Season length

Table 8.8   Effect of season length on performance

Scenario	Method	# Inventory turns	% Lost sales	% Liquidated
20 weeks	QR	5.3	3	1
	VMI	4.1	19	7
16 weeks	QR	4.6	4	2
	VMI	3.7	20	7
12 weeks	QR	4.4	5	2
	VMI	3.5	20	6
8 weeks	QR	3.7	10	4
	VMI	3.1	21	6

turns. However, due to the specified initial stocking levels, more inventory is on the shelf at the start of the season with longer season lengths. In fact, this can be reduced significantly and still yield high service levels. This last point is discussed below.

Other performance measures are considered in Table 8.8; Inventory turns, % Lost sales, and % of end-of-season goods that must be liquidated. Clearly, provided the vendor can meet orders in two weeks, QR can more than hold its own for season lengths of eight weeks.

8.4.7   Impact of Number of Stock Keeping Units on Number of Items

The breadth of a line, i.e. the number of SKUs, and the number of items for sale, have an impact on retail performance. Details of the various scenarios that have been examined can be found in Hunter et al. (1996), but the results are summarized as follows:

- For a given demand volume, performance declines as the number of SKUs increases. Similarly, for a given number of SKUs, there is a drop in performance with increasing volume. Figure 8.18 illustrates this behavior for % Service level in the case of QR. Figure 8.19 combines the three curves in Figure 8.18, adds the equivalent traditional data, and shows how the % Service levels behave for different values of Average Volume/SKU.
- For both QR and traditional, as the volume/SKU decreases, fewer customers find the item they want, thus increasing the Lost sales, and Liquidation percentages, and decreasing Service levels, Inventory turns and GMROI.
- With QR, the impact of smaller samples is relatively greater than for traditional, because re-estimation of remaining demand is less reliable, being based on fewer sales. Thus QR's advantage over traditional vanishes at around 15 units/SKU.

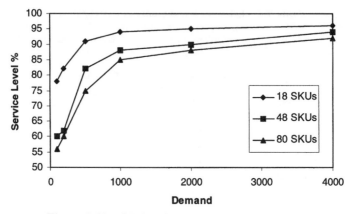

Figure 8.18   QR Service level vs. demand volume

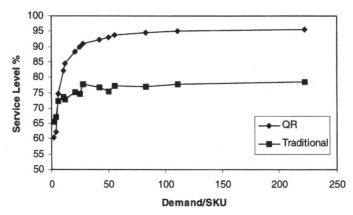

Figure 8.19   Service level vs. items per SKU—QR and traditional

These results raise several questions about the design and purchase of product lines. For example, what would be the full impact of adding another color or size? We have seen that performance would improve in a mechanical sense, but the impact could well be greater still as color is the prime motivator in garment purchase. The results also shed some light on 'boutique' performance, where stockouts are common.

8.4.8   Impact of Quick Response Initial Inventory Level

The percent of a season's goods shipped to the store before the season opens can be anywhere from, say, 50% to 100% in the case of traditional marketing. For QR, we have claimed that far less is needed (with VMI following suit).

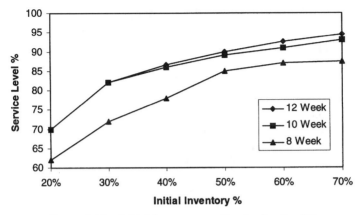

Figure 8.20   Initial Inventory vs. Service level—QR

How much is less? Figure 8.20 shows the impact of varying the initial shipment from 20% to 70% of a season's order on % Service level for 8, 10 and 12 weeks—the critical season lengths. Obviously, more inventory must be loaded up front when the seasonality sales demand pattern is skewed towards the early weeks.

8.4.9   Markdowns

This is one of the most controversial aspects of retailing. It is an art form, and particularly so if promotional sales are included in the term. Some retailers have two markdown periods at, say, 25% off, followed by 45% off. Others go to a 45% discount when 85% of the goods have been sold at first price. It would be tedious to try to give the results on performance measures of a broad range of discount strategies. Suffice it to say that the Sourcing Simulator model has recently been revised to provide greater flexibility to its users in exploring different markdown scenarios.

A major indicator of retail buyer performance is % Sell through. This measures the percentage of goods sold during a season at 'first price'. However, the Sell Through percentage is dependent on the markdown or sale policy of the store. If goods are not moving well, there will be pressure to reduce price in order to move them. The buyer is partly responsible for this circumstance, but his or her performance assessment must clearly spell this out.

8.5   TRANSITION TO QUICK RESPONSE

Although we urge full implementation of QR, including frequent reorders based on PoS data, it must be recognized that this is a lot to take on in one step.

A major US retailer recently asked the question:

'Is it possible to make significant improvements in performance by placing a single, mid-season replenishment order based on PoS data that covered the first few weeks of sales?'

The question was asked in the context of a line of merchandise sold over a 39-week season and normally handled traditionally, i.e. 100% of the goods delivered ahead of time. Subsidiary questions included:

'How much initial inventory should be carried?' and, *'When should the reorder be delivered?'*

Some sales data were provided, and the Sourcing Simulator was used to analyze a variety of scenarios. Without going into details, the results proved to be of interest and show that a profitable partial transition to QR is well worth while.

Because the accuracy of the buyer's plan is unknown, reordering strategies were tested under conditions where the actual customer demand varied from 25% under to 25% over the expected demand. The product mix error was set at 20%—believed to be typical for this product line. Also, the retailer and manufacturer agreed that the first feasible reorder period should be week 6 of the season, although this was examined in two-week increments.

The amount of inventory to stock at the start of the season is another important input. This is especially true if the first reorder is not made fairly early in the selling period. The initial inventory can be approximated for a desired customer service level (in this case 98% was chosen) using the Poisson density function (see Maddalena, 1998, for details).

The reordering strategies used in the analysis were:

- No reorders (traditional); 100% of expected sales delivered prior to the start of the season.
- One reorder during the season.
- Two reorders during the season.
- Every four weeks, and weekly reorders, both made on regular schedules.

The primary measures used in judging the relative performances of the different strategies were Gross Margin (GM), Gross Margin Return On Average Inventory Investment (GMROI), and GMROI times the average in-stock percentage, referred to here as GMROISL. These measures are discussed further in Chapter 9.

Typical results obtained for GMROI during the study (King and Maddalena, 1998) are given in Table 8.9. Here the values for demand errors of +25%

Table 8.9   GMROI values for reorder strategies

Reorder strategy	Reorder period (week)	Volume error (average)	Overall average	Increase vs. no reorder
No reorder		1.79	1.77	—
1 reorder	12	3.02	3.65	95%
2 reorders	10 & 23	4.42	5.37	195%
Monthly	6–26	5.72	6.74	277%
Weekly	6–27	6.02	7.14	297%

through to −25% are averaged, though when demand exceeded expectation, the GMROI values were greater than the average values.

8.6   COMMENTS

This chapter has provided some clear insights into the advantages that QR provides when applied to a supply pipeline dealing with seasonal goods. The lower inventory levels and stockouts can be contrasted with the marked higher all-round customer service provision of a QR operation. By comparing the operational achievements of 'Traditional', 'Vendor Managed Inventory' and QR approaches, it is clear that manufacturers and retailers using QR platforms can achieve substantial advantages.

The Sourcing Simulator model has begun to provide a fascinating insight into the potential opportunities for optimal operation that QR could bring to most industry supply systems. As a cost/benefit analytical tool, the Sourcing Simulator gives senior management detailed feedback of various 'what-if' scenarios. The ability to examine specific parameters or attributes of an organization's current operation and then contemplate the vast array of differing outcomes should one individual facet be changed, is a crucial strategic route to competitive edge.

9
RETAIL SOURCING AND PERFORMANCE

In this chapter we address a question related to the one that initiated the original enquiry into QR:

'Is there a way of combating imports?'

We now ask:

'Is there any financial, or other performance justification for sourcing off-shore?'

Many retailers claim that there is more than just money involved in the decision to import. They cite not only low unit costs, but the very high service levels of such places as Hong Kong, the willingness to co-operate with buyers, and the wide variety of materials and designs or styles available in the Far East at very short notice. Some of these claims are undoubtedly true, but as we will show here, there are very few retail performance measures that support the import choice.

Strategic Sourcing Decisions—LL Bean

LL Bean* is a US catalog retailer providing, among other products, a wide range of flannel and cotton garments. Prior to 1996, the fabric for these garments was sourced totally from Portugal—mainly because of the competitive price and high quality. This was shipped to the USA and cut and sewn into shirts by a third party manufacturer. The off-shore delivery process involved long lead-times (10–14 weeks) and an order commitment well in advance of the sale season. The latter involved predicting the SKU mix quantities, and percentages of patterns and

continues

colors in advance of sale. The Northwoods line is a fashion responsive item and has significant variances in color and plaid pattern every year.

In 1995, LL Bean used their normal ordering procedures for the major sale period at Christmas. This was their 'cash cow' and confidence was high. That year, however, the flannel shirt market collapsed, leaving LL Bean with nearly a year's worth of inventory at the end of the season. They were forced to cancel all commitments to their Portuguese supplier who, faced with a year of spare production capacity, retaliated by refusing to supply LL Bean ever again. The search began for a new supplier.

In the past, cost had been the main criterion upon which to select source of supply. Now they had to cast the net wider and considered all options. A detailed and extensive cost/benefit exercise was completed, and finally it was decided to source from Cone Mills—a domestic vendor! After lengthy negotiations a partnership between the two firms was embarked upon; one that was open and based upon full information disclosure. The result being that Cone has managed to drastically reduce the original (Portuguese) shipping time from 30 to two days. The yarn-dyed fabric production time is reduced to four weeks and costs are only marginally higher due to the influence of Quick Response and a proper understanding of the costs of imports. The following replenishment schedule shows how the operation is more flexible and responsive. It encourages smaller shipments when demand is low, and reduced reliance upon forward commitments based upon forecast.

LL Bean Replenishment Schedule

	Cone Mills replenishment schedule		Portuguese replenishment schedule	
Order date	Percentage of total order for season	Cumulative total (%)	Percentage of total order for season	Cumulative total (%)
February	30	30	100	100
April/May	30	60	0	100
Mid-June	10	70	0	100
Mid-July	10	80	0	100
Mid-August	10	90	0	100
Mid-September	10	100	0	100

Decisions can now be made later in the season in 'real-time' mode when demand is known. For example, LL Bean now use early season

continues

sales from their catalog as an indication of later activity. Consequently their sales have increased and customer service levels on all measures are markedly better.

For Cone Mills the arrangement to provide fabric for the Northwood line has doubled their business with LL Bean. It amounts to nearly two months full capacity for one of their mills. The increased confidence that LL Bean now have in delivery has meant that they have increased their orders and in return Cone has been able to offer price concessions.

The partnership has been built upon freely available electronic data sharing. The timely flow of product, order and inventory information enables both firms to make faster, more accurate decisions and reduce the pipeline delays. Interestingly, both parties are free to interrogate the other's major databases and pull files back and forth using the Internet and a secure software operation called TEXNET; surely this is the future for many firms.

* Our thanks to Jim Lovejoy, DAMA Project Director, for help with this example.

The information we present shows that QR and, to a lesser extent VMI, gives retail performance measures superior to those for Imports with the single exception of the financial ratio GM/Sales. The issue then is how should performance be measured—in terms of solid financial measures (GMROI, Inventory turns); % Customer Service level; % Sell through; $ Sales; or a convenient and easy to measure ratio?

9.1 SCOPE OF THE STUDY

We made use of the Sourcing Simulator to compare three strategies for sourcing a line of merchandise using various measures of performance available to the retailer. The strategies are common to most large retailers and represent the major choices open to a 'progressive' buyer. They are termed 'Off-shore'; 'Domestic with the vendor assuming much of the inventory responsibility' (referred to here as Vendor Managed Inventory, VMI); and 'Domestic using Quick Response (QR) methodologies'.

We say 'progressive' buyer because there is a fourth alternative, the 'Traditional' procedure which makes little analytic use of PoS data, takes a large percentage of a season's goods up-front and then asks for delivery of the rest in one or more deliveries later in the season. Volume and SKU mix are more or less fixed by the original buyer plan and most, or all, of the season's goods are made ahead of time. This 'Traditional' procedure was used widely until just a few years ago, but we have ignored it because some variation of VMI is now in common use. Also, as we noted in Chapter 8, there is little real difference in operational characteristics between importing and traditional marketing. The biggest difference is, of course, the product cost.

In the analysis that follows, off-shore sourcing is supported by only one of the performance measures generally used (see Table 9.1 below)—the ratio of Gross Margin $ to Sales $ (GM/Sales). The very low purchase prices obtainable off-shore yield gross margins that outweigh the poor sales levels associated with imported merchandise. However, there are serious problems associated with the use of a simple dollar ratio to make important sourcing decisions.

GM/Sales excludes any consideration of investment or the value of money. It is not a financial measure in the way that Gross Margin Return On Inventory (GMROI) in particular is. The number of times inventory turns during the season is also excluded from consideration as is the customer service level, the percentage sell through (the percentage of units sold at first price), and the volume of merchandise left over at the end of the season.

Further, a full analysis of all the hidden costs of imports—irrevocable letter of credit charges, delays at the port of entry, last minute use of air freight, expensive administrative travel, quality problems, early manufacturing commitment before purchasing trends are clear, little ability to change the order in terms of mix or volume—among others, has still to be undertaken. Despite these arguments against importing, retailers stress that the low off-shore prices allow 'specials' or promotions at below traditional price points, while still giving attractive markups.

Variations of VMI have become increasingly popular among retailers in the last couple of years as a way of reducing in-store stocks. In our analysis, we consider a form of VMI such that the vendors assume more responsibility for the store inventory by simply holding stock in their own warehouses and shipping it when the retailer asks for it. However, vendor production is based upon the pre-season estimate of demand, i.e. the buyer's plan. It entails minimal shipments at the start of a season, followed by frequent, small, PoS driven replenishments. Here we have been kind to the retailers. In fact, few of them have the ability to analyze PoS data, re-estimate demand, and place informed reorders. For the most part, they use a kind of minimum stock triggering mechanism to judge when more of an SKU is needed and later in the season many orders cannot be filled.

In the analysis that follows, VMI yields better performance than importing (except for GM/Sales) but falls short of QR. Its main attraction is that it serves as a necessary first step toward implementing QR; the drawback is the heavy load it places on the manufacturer, lacking as it does any SKU sales (PoS) information to allow intelligent production planning and finished goods inventory management.

In our analysis, QR leads to superior retail performance in all measures except GM/Sales. The underlying reasons include the realization that all forecasts are wrong and it is only during the season, when customer demand is revealed, that intelligent supply decisions can be made. These decisions can make full use of PoS data to re-estimate volume and SKU demand to issue frequent, small, EDI reorders on the vendor, i.e. QR.

As we have stated repeatedly, only a minimum percentage of the initial plan should be made ahead of season and the balance manufactured when sales trends have been made clear. Retail reorders are then met using rapid and flexible manufacturing processes. In this way, the volume and mix of goods on the retail shelf is continually adjusted to reflect true demand, while keeping inventories (retail and vendor) at any desired level consistent with the desired service levels.

This work was summarized in King and Hunter (1997), but for a more complete analysis, Pinnow and King (1997) should be consulted. The latter study leans over backward to show the disadvantages of domestic sourcing by imposing on the QR scenarios very low initial inventories; sufficient only to yield 95% service levels instead of the usual 100% for the first few weeks of the season.

9.2 METHODOLOGY

The results presented here were obtained using the Sourcing Simulator (see Chapter 8).

Prior to the start of the selling season, the retail buyer specifies a plan consisting of an estimate of the total demand for the merchandise, along with estimates of the percentage of total sales in each stock keeping unit (SKU).

For the off-shore strategy, the vendor produces and ships 100% of the buyer's plan prior to the start of the selling season.

Under QR, the vendor ships a portion (say 40%) of the buyer's plan prior to the start of the selling season. However, in-season manufacture is based upon a re-estimation of the actual demand using PoS data obtained by the retailer. The 'engines' of this strategy are the re-estimation and reorder algorithms that turn PoS data into information and allow interaction between retailer and supplier in a QR partnership.

Under VMI (as with QR), a portion of the buyer's plan is shipped prior to the start of the season. The retailer then makes weekly replenishment orders based on the re-estimation and reorder algorithms mentioned above—not a common procedure. However, shipments may be short since the vendor produces the goods according to the buyer's plan ahead of the selling season and simply holds in anticipation of retail reorders—as the season progresses, an increasing number of SKUs will be stocked out.

9.3   SCENARIOS

For each sourcing strategy, we examined a garment selling for $30.00 and bought for $10.50 off-shore, $14.50 domestically. These are typical values. In addition, we looked at the impact of reduced sales pricing—$25.50 for special promotions. Season lengths from eight weeks to 20 weeks were considered; i.e. from Fashion to Seasonal, although the majority of the results were tabulated for a 16-week season as these differ by only small amounts from those for shorter seasons. The volume of merchandise varied with season length: roughly 20 dozen for each week of the season.

Markdowns of 45% were scheduled when approximately 90% of the season's customers had come into the store, according to the buyer's plan. However, if in the second half of the season the actual sales fell below 85% of the expected sales, a 45% markdown was put into effect.

There are many possible seasonal sales patterns, and we looked at three: early peak in sales (normal for most lines); mid-season peak; and late season (e.g. swimwear). However, the early peak season was found to give the most representative results.

If the buyer is able to forecast demand perfectly, then the best strategy would probably be to use off-shore sourcing because of the lower per garment costs. However, errors in estimating the total volume of demand, as well as style/color/size SKU mix, certainly occur. We fixed the SKU mix error (Nuttle et al., 1991; Hunter et al., 1996) at 'moderate' levels and examined the impact of the buyer under- and overestimating the total volume of demand.

Finally, breakeven points were examined; i.e. how low must the cost of an imported garment be to match a QR garment for GMROI, and what must the cost of a QR garment be to match an import for GM/Sales.

9.4   RESULTS

9.4.1   Measures of Performance

Table 9.1 summarizes the primary results for a 16-week selling season. The Sales $ and Average Inventory data were scaled to QR = 1 for ease of comprehension. Among the other performance measures, % Sell through is the proportion of a season's merchandise that sells at first price; % Liquidated refers to the units remaining at the very end of the season and which must be disposed of at low prices; % Service level is the percent of times a customer finds his or her first choice SKU in stock; and % Lost sales refers to the percent of customers finding none of their preferences (first, second, etc. choice).

In all measures except GM/Sales revenue, QR is clearly best, followed by VMI. The power of Inventory Turns, or inventory 'velocity' has been addressed recently (Gilreath et al., 1995) and should be studied by retailers

Table 9.1   Retail performance measures

Measure	QR	VMI	Off-shore
GM/Sales revenue	0.49	0.48	0.60
GMROI	5.8	4.9	2.7
Turns	6.0	5.5	1.9
Average inventory	1.00	1.10	3.23
Sales revenue	1.00	0.94	0.89
Service level—%	93.2	85.6	72.7
Lost sales—%	5.1	10.7	17.0
Sell through—%	89.4	85.9	79.9
Job off—%	0.7	5.8	14.1

interested in true financial performance. Clearly, if VMI were to be taken to its logical conclusion, i.e. QR, the benefits to the retailer would be enormous in terms of all measures, except GM/Sales.

9.4.2   Promotional Goods

One of the arguments used by proponents of importing is that the lower purchase prices allow promotions to take place without serious loss of income to the retailer, whereas domestic sourcing restricts this kind of activity.

Suppose that instead of putting the garments we have been studying on sale for $30.00, both the QR and imports are launched at $25.50. In this case, QR retains its lead in terms of GMROI (4.0 vs. 2.1), Inventory Turns (6.0 vs. 1.9), and Service level (93.2 vs. 78.3). Imports win out in terms of GM/Sales (0.54 vs. 0.40). Again, we are back to the question of what constitutes a meaningful measure of success.

9.4.3   Length of Season

In general, the performance of QR improves with increasing season length. This is because the demand re-estimation gets better with more PoS data. In the early days of QR research, it was believed that the methodology had little to offer for high fashion goods, i.e. those with a shelf life of 10 or fewer weeks.

More recent results, using a reorder lead-time of two weeks, have shown that QR retains its strong edge over imports in terms of GMROI, Inventory turns, Service levels, etc. down to an eight-week season, see Chapter 8. Figures 9.1 and 9.2 show typical results for Service level and GMROI—the two indicators that best summarize the differences between the two sourcing policies. In the case of GMROI, there is a partial closing of the gap between the two, but QR keeps its advantage down to eight weeks.

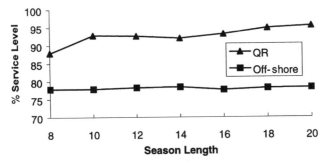

Figure 9.1   Service level vs. Season length

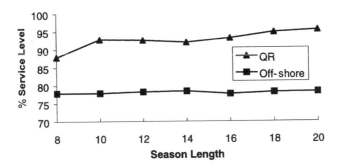

Figure 9.2   GMROI vs. Season length

9.4.4   Volume Error

Perhaps the biggest problem facing retail buyers is estimation of total demand for a line of merchandise. This is particularly true for imported goods as the number of units is fixed well ahead of the season. In the case of domestic supply, VMI or QR, there is room for adjustment and negotiation with the vendor. QR has the advantage in that the frequent re-estimations based on PoS data give early warning of demand trends. In the analyses described here, we assumed that under VMI sourcing, an additional 10% of the season's goods could be obtained in the second half of the season, should demand be underestimated. The QR vendor, on the other hand, could react to increased demand accordingly. We looked at two cases: one where demand was 75% of forecast, and a second where demand was 125% of forecast. The outcomes were evaluated in terms of the major performance indicators.

Table 9.2 shows the results for QR and off-shore sourcing for a 16-week selling season. As before, the results for VMI lie in between. In both the 75% and the 125% scenarios, QR maintains its superiority except for the GM/Sales indicator. QR is particularly impressive when demand is less than expected.

Table 9.2   Impact of volume forecast error on performance

Demand as a % of forecast	QR			Off-shore		
	125%	100%	75%	125%	100%	75%
GM/Sales	0.49	0.49	0.49	0.63	0.60	0.51
GMROI	8.3	5.8	4.3	4.1	2.7	1.6
Turns	8.5	6.0	4.5	2.4	1.9	1.7
Service level—%	89.0	93.2	95.5	63.9	77.7	83.7
Lost sales—%	8.2	5.1	3.4	30.3	17.0	11.9

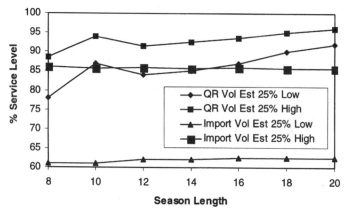

Figure 9.3   Service level vs. Season length: Impact of demand volume error

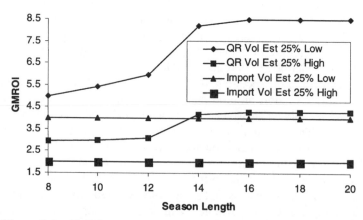

Figure 9.4   GMROI vs. Season length: Impact of demand volume error

This QR advantage holds for season lengths down to eight weeks. In Figures 9.3 and 9.4, the patterns for Service level and GMROI are presented, supporting the data in Table 9.2.

9.4.5   Stock Keeping Unit Mix Sensitivity

A further aspect of sourcing was next examined; that of the relative impacts of SKU mix errors on Service level, and GMROI for QR and imports. Figures 9.5 and 9.6 show the results obtained. Following everything said earlier, it is not surprising to find that QR is to be preferred over importing.

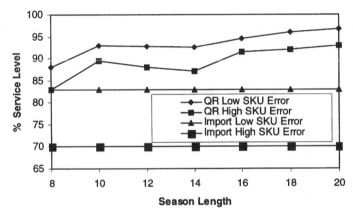

Figure 9.5   Service level vs. Season length: Mix error sensitivity

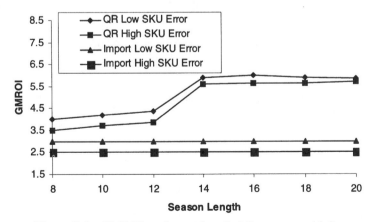

Figure 9.6   GMROI vs. Season length: Mix error sensitivity

9.4.6   Quick Response vs. Off-shore—Equivalent Costs

We have been discussing the meaningfulness of a non-financial measure of retail performance vs. a variety of indices related to financial excellence and customer service. One question remains:

'How would an import have to be priced to give a GMROI equal to that of the same product under QR?'

For completeness, we also answer the flip side of the question:

'What QR sourcing price would be needed to give GM/Sales ratios equal to those of Imports?'

Table 9.3 below shows the GMROI obtained with a QR product costing $14.50 and the Import GMROI for a range of off-shore costs. The data show that the Import would have to cost less than $5.50 (vs. the $10.50 used in this study) for season lengths greater than 12 to match QR's performance. This value increases for shorter seasons.

Table 9.4 shows the equivalent information, matching QR costs with the GM/Sales ratio obtainable for Imports. From this table, it can be seen that a domestic cost of $11.50 matches an import cost of $10.50 in this measure, although a domestic cost of $12.50 is quite close.

9.5   MIXED SOURCING STRATEGY

It should be possible to take advantage of both low off-shore costs and QR operational benefits by employing a mixed sourcing strategy.

Suppose that for a seasonal good, the first 40–50% of expected demand is met from overseas. The items are shipped ahead of the season and consumer

Table 9.3. GMROI for QR (Domestic cost $14.50) vs. Import at various cost levels

Season length (weeks)	QR $14.50	Import $10	Import $8	Import $7	Import $6	Import $5
8	3.9	2.3	3.3	4.1	5.1	6.5
10	4.2	2.3	3.7	4.1	5.1	6.5
12	4.4	2.3	3.4	4.1	5.1	6.5
14	5.9	2.3	3.3	4.1	5.1	6.5
16	5.8	2.3	3.3	4.1	5.1	6.4
18	5.8	2.3	3.3	4.1	5.1	6.5
20	5.9	2.3	3.3	4.1	5.1	6.4

Table 9.4 GM/Sales for off-shore (Import cost $10.50) vs. QR at various cost levels

Season length (weeks)	Import $10.50	QR $14.50	QR $13.50	QR $12.50	QR $11.50	QR $10.50
8	0.60	0.49	0.52	0.56	0.60	0.63
10	0.60	0.49	0.53	0.56	0.60	0.63
12	0.60	0.50	0.53	0.57	0.60	0.64
14	0.60	0.50	0.53	0.57	0.60	0.64
16	0.60	0.50	0.53	0.56	0.60	0.63
18	0.60	0.50	0.53	0.56	0.60	0.63
20	0.60	0.50	0.53	0.57	0.60	0.64

demand is closely monitored via PoS. After the first few weeks, volume and mix of merchandise are re-estimated, and reorders covering the balance of the season are placed on a domestic vendor in the regular QR manner. The average gross margin (GM) per item would be higher than for QR alone, demand would be matched with supply and there would be none of the drawbacks of end-of-season markdowns.

To date, only one analysis of a mixed strategy has been carried out (Lovejoy, personal communication). Here the importing of the goods fell under Section 807, a procedure in which end-product parts (such as cut fabric, as in this case, TV parts, car components, etc.), are made domestically (low labor, but high technical content) and assembled off-shore (high labor content, but low wages), then re-imported with duty being paid on the assembled costs, or added value. Section 807 is a US regulation and covers assembly in the Caribbean and Mexico, for example. The EU has similar procedures for activities in North Africa and Eastern Europe, while Hong Kong marketers use Chinese production before 're-exporting' to Europe.

The product line was a T-shirt in seven colors and five sizes with planned sales of 8000 dozen over a 20-week season. The cost of imports was 65% of that for domestic goods.

The scenarios were played out for pure QR and pure imports. For the mixed sourcing study, QR and 807 volumes were split evenly and weekly reorders were placed for the former roughly half way through the selling season. The results of simulation runs using the Sourcing Simulator are shown in Table 9.5. They suggest clearly that this area of retail sourcing strategy is well worth further investigation. However, there needs to be a better understanding of the procedures that would be required. Typical questions are:

- How feasible is it to have two raw material suppliers—one off-shore and one domestic in the case where 807 is not evoked?
- How much experience with the line would the domestic manufacturers need prior to reorders being placed upon them?

Table 9.5   Impact of a Mixed sourcing strategy on retail performance

	QR	807[1]	QR/807
Sales[2]	126	100	127
GM[3]	95	100	110
GM % of sales	47	63	55
Inventory turns	4.5	2.0	3.7
Service level—%	97	68	97
Lost sales—%	2	29	2
GMROI	4.0	3.3	4.5

[1] US terminology for off-shore assembly of components manufactured in America and re-imported with duty paid only on the added value. Similar arrangements are found in the EU and between Hong Kong and China.
[2] Indexed to import only values = 100.
[3] Indexed to import only values = 100.

- What are the benefits to the domestic up-stream supply system? Would they see it as half the business being better than none?
- How difficult would it be to effectively integrate the operations of these two distinct sources of supply?
- What is the optimal share of expected business going overseas?

Despite these unknowns, it seems likely that some kind of mixed sourcing will be attractive to retailers in a number of industries, especially if they are prepared to put in the necessary effort.

9.6   COMMENTS

The level of imports is a concern for the industries forming the Fast Moving Consumer Goods sector. We have long suspected that many retail sourcing decisions do not take into account the true costs of importation. Further, the continued application of aged and inadequate performance measures fails to recognize a fundamental advantage of using local QR vendors: product velocity. A properly organized QR manufacturer can provide retailers with a superior service to that of foreign imports, despite charging a higher unit cost. The savings to a retailer, in a number of areas, can be dramatic, and easily offset the cost disadvantage: providing the correct measures of performance are applied (ones that reflect modern, supply pipeline requirements).

One step in this direction is now being seen in the use of a Mixed Sourcing strategy. Here, the strengths and benefits of both on-shore and off-shore supply can be optimized.

10
THE MANUFACTURING MODEL

Once the Sourcing Simulator had been developed and exercised (Chapter 8), it became necessary to extend the modeling work to include up-stream processes. The first of these was manufacturing, where there was a need to answer questions about the kind of production system that could respond to a retailer employing a QR strategy. Later, this work was expanded to include other up-stream processes and will be summarized later. A good deal of this work is still being refined and QR linkages between the up-stream entities have yet to be clarified to the extent we hope to achieve. One of its principal merits is that it forms part of the program to develop an Interactive MIS (Chapter 5) for use by first and second tier suppliers who wish to examine the consequences and benefits of changing their way of doing business to accommodate down-stream QR procedures—particularly manufacturing assembly. It has also raised questions about inventory policy, optimal capacity utilization and the impact of product diversity on plant operations.

The Sourcing Simulator assumed either a perfect supply of merchandise; i.e. whatever was requested of the vendor arrived on the retail shelf complete, and on time or that the vendor has some relatively static fill rate. The first assumption is unrealistic, unless the vendor carries very large stocks, and it prompted the development of a supply system compatible with QR retail requirements. The second does not capture the characteristic that the supply system tends to be disrupted when things are most critical. An essential feature of the system is that it incorporates a responsive raw material, or component supply (Hunter et al., 1992). Version 2.0 of the Sourcing Simulator incorporates an explicit model of the vendor and is described below.

10.1 PRINCIPAL VENDOR FEATURES

These include:

- Ability to specify the vendor's production plan for pre-season and, if desired, in-season.

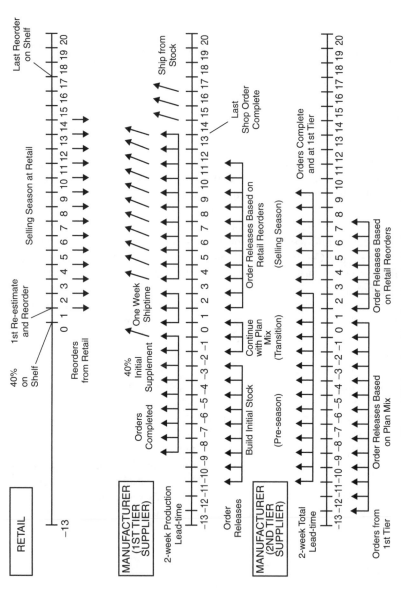

Figure 10.1 Combined schedule for 20-week season

- Specification of orders and deliveries for the primary raw material or component.
- Shops orders releases considering minimum lot sizes, capacity availability and raw material/component availability.
- Continual reshaping of the SKU mix in the working inventory as reorders are processed depending upon the relationship with the retailer (Traditional, VMI, QR, etc.).
- Dissolution of any remaining inventory in the last few weeks of the season.

10.2   EXAMPLE SCENARIO

As an example, consider the following scenario involving apparel, which is illustrated as a time line in Figure 10.1:

- Twenty-week retail-selling season.
- Initial retail inventory = 40% of the expected season's sales.
- Fourteen retail reorders.
- Three-week vendor-retail lead-time—two weeks' manufacture, one week shipping.
- Three-week transition inventory build.
- Final three retail reorders met from stock.
- Two-week raw material inventory built pre-season and used against last two shop orders.
- Two-week raw material lead-time.

Figure 10.1 shows the timing of reorders from retail, the release and completion of shop orders at manufacture broken down by phase of the manufacturing cycle (described above), shipments to retail, and the release and shipment of raw material orders.

The manufacturing cycle is made up of the three phases outlined below.

10.2.1   Pre-season

In this phase, items are manufactured at a steady rate for the number of weeks needed to accumulate and ship the initial (beginning-of-season) inventory as requested by the retailer. The volume and SKU mix are specified by the retail buyer's plan. Raw material is shipped weekly to the manufacturer in support of the build schedule. In addition, a small amount is shipped to serve as a working inventory. The mix of SKUs is determined by the buyer's plan.

10.2.2   Transition

Once the initial shipment has been made, manufacture continues at a steady rate, using the buyer plan to specify SKU mix, until the first reorder arrives. The working inventory accumulated during this period is used as a safety stock. Weekly raw material orders continue as for pre-season manufacture. The length of the transition phase equals the time required to manufacture and ship the order to the retailer.

10.2.3 Selling Season

With the arrival of the first reorder (shortly after retail sales begin), manufacture is driven by PoS information. Shop orders are issued that allow, to the greatest extent possible, shipments that correspond to the last reorder. Any shortfall is back-ordered for shipment as soon as possible. Similarly, material orders on suppliers reflect this PoS information.

As the season progresses, the mix of SKUs in the finished-goods inventory increasingly reflects the consumer-buying pattern. The last few reorders are met from the finished-goods inventory with no more goods being made during this period. Similarly, raw material stocks are dissolved during the last few weeks of manufacture.

The allocation of manufacturing capacity for the above scenario with a plan of 4000 items is calculated as follows. The initial inventory of 40%, i.e. 1600 items, leaves 2400 items to be manufactured during the transition period and the selling season. Dividing this by the number of retail reorders (14) gives a production rate of 171 items per week. With this production rate, just over nine weeks are required for the pre-season manufacture to build the initial inventory of 1600 items. The rate of in-season manufacture will, of course, be governed by the retail reorders and will be influenced in several ways, most notably by any change in the actual demand level. Table 10.1 shows the input and output variables for the manufacturing model beyond those described in Chapter 8. The ways in which these are used are described below.

10.2.4 In-season Manufacturing Shop-order Release

Within the selling season, manufacturing shop orders are released weekly with the number of releases fixed as the number of retail reorders, minus the number of weeks of working inventory built during the transition period which, for the example above equals $14 - 3 = 11$ (as shown in Figure 10.1).

The volume of the release is limited by the allocated weekly shop capacity. Reorders are shipped one manufacturing cycle after receipt. For the example, this cycle is two weeks, so within the season there will be typically two reorders received but not yet shipped.

The release quantities for individual SKUs for each shop order are determined by a two-step process (see Hunter et al., 1992) upon receipt of each retail

Table 10.1   Manufacturing input/output variables

Input	Output
Production plan (number and size of shop order releases and raw material reorder schedule)	Weekly:
Raw material usage factor	Retail reorder quantities
Minimum raw material order size and reorder lead-time	New production requirements
Raw material wholesale cost	Shop-order quantities
Manufacturing process time	Back-orders
Minimum lot size and maximum weekly capacity	Work in process
Shipping time to retail	Finished goods inventory Raw material reorders/receipts Raw material inventory @ 1st tier
	Full season: Retail reorder shortfall—% Unused raw material—% Finished goods surplus—%

reorder (available at the beginning of the week). This process considers:

- retail reorders received but not yet shipped
- back-orders (past due)
- work in process
- finished inventory
- availability of raw material
- any constraints on minimum release-batch size for individual SKUs or maximum number of SKUs in a shop order.

10.2.5   In-season Raw Material Reorders

Within the selling season, raw material reorders are also released weekly. The number of reorders is fixed as the number of shop orders minus the number of weeks of raw material inventory, minus the raw material-manufacturing lead-time. The reorder size and mix are determined by projected net raw material requirements. However, the reorder size is limited by the allocated weekly apparel shop capacity, as there is no need to order more fabric than can be used.

See Hunter et al. (1992) for a summarization of the procedures involved.

10.2.6   Results

Here we compare the results of 'perfect supply' to the retailer with those result-ing from the use of the manufacturing model. In summary, the differences are small and are of little consequence. In Tables 10.2 through 10.5, the first column refers to retail performance, the last three columns to manufacturing efficiency.

'Ship as per' refers to shipping only quantities ordered by the retailer, while 'Ship all' means shipping all remaining inventory against the final reorder.

In Table 10.2, the manufacturing system is shown to be capable of providing 'close to perfect supply' with only 3.5% of SKU specific retail reorders not sat-isfied with either Ship as per or Ship all. Also, the amount of raw material left over is trivial.

Other trials were carried out to investigate the impact of buyer SKU mix error as well as volume error on the manufacturer response. The results are uniformly gratifying.

In Tables 10.3 and 10.4, the effect of season length is examined. This is a critical scenario for QR manufacturing. The data illustrate the impact of going from 20 weeks to 10 weeks with lead-times of three and two weeks. Note that a 15-week season allows only nine retail reorders, six shop orders and two raw material reorders, thus reducing the ability of the manufacturer to supply the changing stream of reorders and shape the working inventories to match consumer demand.

When, for the same pattern of lead-times, the selling season is decreased to 10 weeks, only five retail reorders, two shop orders and no raw material

Table 10.2   Base case

Scenario	% Lost sales	% Reorder shortfall	% Raw material excess	% Merchandise surplus
Perfect supply	4.2	—	—	—
Ship as per	6.2	3.5	1.4	2.8
Ship all	5.0	3.5	1.4	—

Table 10.3   Effect of season length

Season length (weeks)	% Lost sales	% Reorder shortfall	% Raw material excess	% Merchandise surplus
20	6.2	3.5	1.4	2.8
15	9.0	7.3	4.9	5.6
10	21.0	14.7	4.1	12.3
10*	8.5	5.1	3.6	7.8

* Reduced lead-times.

Table 10.4   Details of trials

	15 weeks	10 weeks	10 weeks*
Number of items	3000	2000	2000
Number of retail reorders	9	5	6
Number of shop orders	6	2	1
Retail lead-time (weeks)	3	3	2
Finished goods inventory (weeks)	3	3	2
Raw material inventory (weeks)	2	2	1
Raw material lead-time (weeks)	2	2	1
Number of raw material reorders	2	0	2

* With reduced lead-times.

reorders are possible. Not surprisingly, there is a significant degradation in most performance measures. If, however, the manufacture-to-retail lead-time is reduced to two weeks, and the raw material-to-finished goods lead-time to one week, an additional retail reorder is introduced, shop orders are increased to four, and there are two opportunities to reorder raw material. The effect of these changes is shown in the last two rows of Table 10.4.

At this time, we should point out something of particular significance to the manufacturer. All the results mentioned above assumed a minimum manufacturing batch size of one. Table 10.5 introduces half-dozen and one-dozen minima. The restriction to a minimum SKU batch size of six has no impact on supply. Raising the minimum to 12 has an impact but this is small. The importance of these restrictions is largely academic, as the plant will, in fact, be manufacturing much larger quantities.

When a minimum batch size is introduced, there are two ways to handle it. First, and this is the way used in obtaining the tabulated results, the manufacturer does not issue a shop order until the net production requirement for an SKU is at least the minimum batch size. The second approach is for minimum batch size shop orders to be issued when the net production requirement is smaller than the minimum batch size. The former method is more convenient for the manufacturer, while the latter is more suited to the needs of the retailer interested in maximizing customer service level.

Table 10.5   Effect of minimum batch size on performance

Minimum batch	% Lost sales	% Reorder shortfall	% Raw material excess	% Merchandise surplus
1	6.2	3.5	1.4	2.8
6	6.7	4.0	2.1	2.6
12	9.2	6.7	4.9	2.1

The results outlined above show there is a manufacturing strategy that is fully compatible with QR retailing. The % Lost sales values are very much in line with the retailing results given in Chapter 8, and the % Reorder shortfall, % Fabric excess and % Merchandise surplus levels are excellent. It is likely that there are other protocols that would give similar results, and these should be explored.

We are not yet certain that the model just described is fully suitable for tying into the up-stream models and Master Scheduler to be described in Chapter 11. However, the QR research group at NCSU has a close working relationship with the Textile Clothing Technology Corporation [TC]², a joint government (DoC)/industry sponsored research and trade education facility. It has developed detailed shop floor level models of three types of manufacturing production system: the Progressive Bundle System, Stand Up, Hand-Off Modular Manufacturing, and the Unit-Production Mover System, which can be used to provide production capability data for manufacturing plant simulations.

These models can also be used to generate the data for creating response surfaces to characterize and compare system performance under various demand scenarios. As many companies move away from high work in process, large-batch sizes, toward more flexible manufacturing, 'team production' has emerged as a transitional system.

Team production is characterized by smaller batches, lower work in process, and teams of operators with low to moderate levels of cross-training. The details and complexities of line balancing in these environments are now being addressed.

As we said earlier, there are at least two basic approaches manufacturers can use to provide QR replenishment. One is to become a true, make-to-order facility, shipping to order in a reasonable time. Very few manufacturers at present operate in this manner, though the number is growing. Many so-called QR manufacturers ship from built-up inventories (safety stocks) based on both pre-season forecasts and in-season PoS data.

For retailers, vendor reliability is an important issue, where reliability is defined as the percentage of goods shipped (including mix) vs. goods ordered. The inability to obtain and stock items in high demand results, of course, in lost sales and lower profits.

The service level provided to the retailers by the manufacturers is not only affected by the flexibility of their operations; equally important is their ability to obtain raw materials from their 1st tier suppliers as and when needed in suitable quantities. This can pose a problem and without good service the manufacturers will be unable to supply reorders as needed.

Here we look at the effect on the retailer's performance of the short shipments of goods (Maddalena, 1998). The work is an extension of that discussed in Chapter 8, where even one mid-season QR-type shipment gives superior performance to a 'Traditional' strategy. The shipping schedule for multiple reorders is also the same.

A simple but very conservative approach was taken to test the QR strategy while ordering from an unreliable vendor. One hundred percent of the reorders were assumed to be short by amounts ranging from 10% to 50%, and the demand volume was varied between 75% and 125% of buyer's plan. There was no back-ordering—shortages had to be made up in the next reorder.

As expected, as the shortage levels increase, gross margin (GM) decreases. When orders are short by 24% or less, the QR strategy with a single reorder gives a better GM than the Traditional strategy. With two in-season reorders, QR does slightly better, and with weekly reorders, a greater GM is realized with QR even when every delivery is almost 50% short (see Figure 10.2).

The results for Gross Margin Return on Inventory (GMROI) tell a similar story—an increase in the frequency of reorders increases this value. But, GMROI also increases as the shortage level rises—see Figure 10.3. This raises

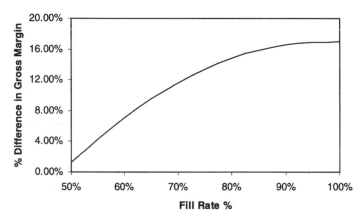

Figure 10.2   Impact of fill rate on gross margin

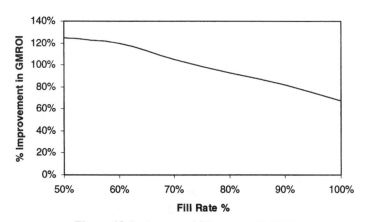

Figure 10.3   Impact of fill rate on GMROI

questions about the usefulness of GMROI. Recall that it is the result of dividing GM by the average inventory investment. Thus, even though GM decreases as the shortage level increases (i.e. the fill rate decreases), this is off-set by the lower inventory investment resulting from smaller deliveries. This question of what constitutes a 'super' financial performance measure will be discussed in Chapter 11.

10.3.   UP-STREAM MODELING

Here we shall only outline what is a very comprehensive program designed to investigate whether or not the processes involved in raw material and component manufacture are compatible with QR and specifically the manufacturing analyses carried out above. A full report of this work will be found in Hunter et al. (1993).

10.3.1.   Overall Approach

The manufacturing model just described, assumed perfect supply of raw material, i.e. the manufacturer received exactly what was ordered from all suppliers after a short, specified lead-time.

This is a major assumption. One of the most critical factors in the supply pipeline is, in fact, the speed with which raw materials or components can be supplied in the requested quantities and varieties. For example, in the textile industry, the normal practice is for the producer to ship large yardages ahead of, or early in, the season, based on the retail buyer position. Part of the reason for this is tradition, and part is fabric production (weaving, more so than knitting) times, which are long compared with cutting and sewing. A further factor is the additional cost to the textile producer of small yardages. But, QR requires that each part of the pipeline be responsive to its customers!

Accordingly, we undertook a program to model the up-stream processes— yarn spinning, knitting, weaving and fabric dyeing. The approach taken was to build stand-alone models for each of these entities, and then to link them together into a kind of integrated 'corporation'.

This work is incomplete, though the stand-alone models are well advanced and the prime results so far as QR is concerned are available. In addition to the entity models, there is a 'master schedule' generator that simulates the results of the booking of fabric orders placed by the corporation (called pipeline orders), as well as external or outside orders placed by other firms in the industry. The schedule provides inputs to the textile producing operations as a sliding 'x-week-ahead' view of orders, allowing them to develop their own production schedules. As consumer demand re-estimates and the resulting reorders change at retail, the master schedule changes too.

The master scheduling technique is of interest because it resembles closely the world of 'close partnerships' advocated by QR, thus allowing examination of the necessary elements of such partnerships, how they tie together, and their dependency, one on the other.

The plant models are data driven, i.e. they require inputs such as customer order streams, machine capacities and production rates. They produce the relevant output data, including empirical frequency distributions of order lead-times, back-orders and inventories by SKU. The plant models are also constructed in such a way that it is possible to explore alternate scheduling procedures—a very important part of the modeling paradigm—as well as the impacts of different capacity utilizations.

One important feature of the models is the considerable number of products they can handle. For example, the Spinning model was initially exercised using up to 36 different yarns, the Weaving model with up to 20 different fabrics, the Knitting model with as many as nine fabrics, and the Dyeing and Finishing model with an upper limit of 120 colors on a set of 20 fabrics (woven and knit). These are larger numbers than are met within most industrial operations; the models' scope is not trivial.

Similarly, when running the Master Schedule to drive the pipeline on behalf of the 4–5 manufacturing 'plants', a full range of fabrics suitable for Basic, Seasonal and Fashion merchandise were employed (see above).

Pipeline orders are referred to as 'contract' orders, i.e. those consisting of regular (random) weekly requirements for some known number of weeks or 'external' orders. External orders may also be contracted for either regular, on-going business or 'spot' orders that arrive randomly.

The daily plant activity is directed by routines that generate weekly or daily schedules for key processes, but the activity is also influenced by randomness in such factors as cycle times and yields.

These models provide vehicles for:

- understanding the interactions of decisions made within one firm with those in a supplier or customer
- analyzing operational practices within individual firms or across sub-sets of firms
- developing CEO-type information systems, and
- training personnel in making intelligent operational decisions.

10.3.2 Preliminary Results

Each model has a considerable number of both input and output variables. To handle the interactions among them, the practice has been to exercise the models using partial factorial designs, including numbers of products to be manufactured. These are ideal for developing the neural networking procedures used in the prototype MIS studies (see Chapter 11), but they make the reporting of results in graphical form laborious and, to many, confusing. They will not be presented here. Instead we will summarize the findings of the studies as they are pertinent to QR operations:

- All the models operate under wide ranges of conditions, i.e. they are robust.
- Extensive work on the spinning/raw material model has shown that standard inventory control procedures will probably not be optimal, though they work quite satisfactorily.
- All the models are responsive to changes in seasonal demands for different products as called for by the Master Scheduler, with no decline in customer responsiveness. They also handled complicated product lines devoted to outside 'spot' orders with little difficulty, even though satisfying internal orders took priority.
- From a QR point of view the prime question was, *'Can the up-stream companies meet the short order lead-times needed in order for their immediate customers to meet frequent reorders?'* The measures of this are the percentage of orders met in one, or two weeks. The Spinning/Primary, Knitting/Secondary and Dyeing/Tertiary models gave excellent service, for the most part, in one week. The Weaving model—much the most complicated and demanding of fabric preparation time—worked much better than expected and, in fact, matched or exceeded the performance of the others. Over a wide range of input variables, and with few exceptions, well over 95% of the internal orders were met in one week. When the lead-time was two weeks, this figure rose to 98% or better. For outside orders, the performance was not as good; 83–91% for one-week lead-times and approximately 87–94% for two weeks. Some of this difference is due to the lack of input from a Master Scheduler, the rest to the priority given to internal vs. spot orders.

These results are extremely encouraging. They suggest that with good information flow to up-stream entities, the requirements of the manufacturer and retailer can be met with a good level of confidence.

10.3.3   Primary or 1st Tier Manufacturing Model

We will describe only one of the plant models in this section. Yarn spinning has been chosen because it is close to being typical of many manufacturing operations, i.e. it is essentially generic. Also, spun yarns are found in most consumer, and many industrial, products from tarpaulins, tents, shoes and boots, apparel, carpets and rugs, to home furnishings. Essentially, spun yarns are collections of fibers that are aligned through a variety of preliminary processes, and then simultaneously drawn and twisted to give them the desired strength, twist level and thickness. Yarns vary depending on their end-use, from very fine yarns used in expensive shirtings or sheets, to coarse yarns used in floor coverings

(Lord, 1978), and are characterized by their 'count' or thickness, and their twist level. The spinning plant need not be concerned with the size, color or style of the garment in which the yarn will be used.

The purpose of this model was to analyze the relationships between input control parameters and plant performance, to determine optimal operational policies, and to study the impact of QR on a cotton spinning factory. By operational policies, we mean such management guidelines as: capacity utilization, scheduling procedures, number of products, minimum order size and order lead-times.

The model simulates the basic activity of a plant capable of producing around 25 million pounds of cotton yarn per year (Powell, 1993). The plant capacity can include up to 100 frames producing up to 36 different yarn counts. Blended yarns, e.g. polyester/cotton, were excluded because they gave complications in the fiber preparation stages, which were assumed to provide a perfect supply of roving to the spinning frames.

The activities include spinning frame scheduling, schedule execution, changeovers, coning (winding), inspection and shipping. At present, spinning is modeled as a make-to-stock operation (as opposed to made-to-order), with about 50% of the demand coming from external, non-pipeline customers. Orders are either call-outs against contracts, randomly generated on a weekly basis, or spot orders generated on a daily basis. Orders vary as to yarn count and quantity. The count mix and average weekly volume can be varied throughout the year to reflect seasonality in the use of different yarn weights. The plant is assumed to operate 24-hours per day, six days a week, although this can be changed.

So far, we have modeled two alternative strategies for controlling the inventory levels of finished yarns; a 'max/min' system and a 'target level' system (Clarke, 1995). Under the max/min system, which is widely used in industry, if the inventory level of a yarn rises above its nominal maximum level, then production is curtailed until the actual inventory level falls to its nominal minimum level. Spinning frames are loaded or scheduled based on management's knowledge or forecast of demand volume and mix. A management-specified portion of the frames is dedicated to specific high-volume yarn counts, which are produced continuously until otherwise indicated by the inventory control system. Dedication may be adjusted to reflect shifts in demand mix. The remaining frames are regarded as 'flexible capacity' and are scheduled reactively based on current need. For algorithms that generate the desired number of 'dedicated' frames, see Powell (1993).

With the target level system, production is incrementally raised or lowered periodically in order to try to maintain a specified inventory level using the concepts of Proportional Integral Derivative process control (Olsson and Piani, 1992). All frames are scheduled, one relative to the other. Orders are shipped daily, five days per week, limited by shipping capacity. Priority is given to blanket orders. Measures of performance include production levels, order response times, inventory levels, frame utilization, and margin (see Table 10.6).

Table 10.6 below gives some idea of the detail required for a meaningful simulation model if useful results are to be obtained—results useful to management and the operation of a plant. For those readers interested in such matters, Appendix I to this chapter gives information on the structure of the model.

The spinning model is ideal for the development of an interactive CEO information system. Decision surfaces, or simulation meta-models, have been fitted to the outputs of simulation runs to relate plant performance (inventory, order response times, etc.) to important input and operating parameters. The objective of decision surface modeling is to develop an interactive information system that captures the essential features of each plant model in strict (mathematical) relationships between plant performance and key decision parameters

Table 10.6   Input and output variables—spinning model

Inputs	Outputs
Number of frames	Weekly average lead-time for contract orders
Number of yarn counts	Weekly average lead-time for spot orders
Spindle efficiency	Weekly average lead-time for all orders
Target capacity utilization	Overall average lead-time for contract orders
Average order size	Overall average lead-time for spot orders
Schedule re-evaluation period (AT)	Overall average lead-time for all orders
Minimum inventory target (if min/max)	Lead-time distribution for contract orders
Maximum inventory target (if min/max)	Lead-time distribution for spot orders
Target inventory level (if target)	Lead-time distribution for all orders
Percentage of contract orders	% of time on scheduled frames by yarn count
Number of dedicated frames	% of time spent changing over frames
Coning/packaging time	Number of frame changeovers
Production rate by yarn count	% of time dedicated frames shut down
% of demand by yarn count	Weekly average inventory level by yarn count
Average daily demand	Overall average inventory level by yarn count
Inventory holding % by yarn count	Inventory distribution by yarn count
Inventory carrying cost rate	Revenue generated by yarn count
Production cost rate by yarn count	Total poundage shipped by yarn count Inventory carrying cost

(product mix, number of machines employed, etc.). These meta-models have the capability of providing senior managers with rapid, easy-to-use capability to predict the impact on a system's performance under various 'what-if' scenarios such as:

- 'What are the consequences of increasing the breadth of my product line?'
- 'What are the consequences of reducing my minimum order quantities?'
- 'What are the costs/benefits of reducing my order lead-times?'
- 'What is the break even cost of a new piece of equipment if it will reduce a particular process time?'
- 'What capacity utilizations are required for me to best serve my customers?'

We have developed sequential estimation procedures for fitting and testing the adequacy of classical response-surface meta-models involving polynomial functions up to a third order in the plant's key decision parameters. The main objective of this sequential approach is to obtain the simplest approximation to the performance of the simulation that is sufficiently accurate and that is based on feasible, cost effective sets of experimental runs.

An alternative to the above analytical approach, a pilot study on the use of neural networks for the spinning model, has proved extremely promising, see Wu et al. (1995a,b; 1997). It will be examined in Chapter 11.

10.4 COMMENTS

QR in the supply pipeline relies upon the optimal contribution of all stages: the retailer, 1st tier manufacturer, 2nd tier manufacturer, etc. Through the use of the Sourcing Simulator, this chapter has shown how a QR manufacturer can build a responsive and flexible architecture in-line with demand requirements. We have attempted to show the utility of QR to the manufacturing strategy by the use of a number of differing lead-times, season lengths and batch sizes. In this way, we hope the reader will realize that all sections of an industry supply complex, whether it be concerned with food, clothing, toys or automobiles, have to be properly aligned and integrated in order to satisfy demand. This wider viewpoint is explored in Chapter 11.

10
APPENDIX I
SPINNING MODEL STRUCTURE

The spinning plant produces n different yarn types. Each product is specified by a given yarn twist and thickness. The plant has m spinning frames each with s spindles that are operated h hours a day, d days a week. Yarn type i is produced on a spinning frame at a rate of r_i lb/spindle/day. Upon doffing there is a d_c day coning/inspection delay. The yarn is then placed into inventory and is ready to ship. Spinning frames can be either dedicated or scheduled. A dedicated frame is assigned a yarn type at the start of the simulation, and will only produce that yarn. A scheduled frame is re-assigned a yarn type periodically (every Δt time units) based on whichever product needs more inventory at that moment. A changeover delay is incurred on scheduled frames when switching from one yarn type to another. Both dedicated and scheduled frames may be idle or busy.

The rate of customer orders arriving each day is λ. Each order is randomly assigned a yarn type from a yarn mix distribution and an order quantity from an order size distribution with average order size O. There are two types of customer orders: contract orders and spot orders. The value K represents the percentage of total orders that are contract orders. Contract orders are placed by the plant's regular customers and arrive once per week on Monday mornings. Spot orders are generated by infrequent customers and arrive at any time during the week according to a Poisson process.

Orders are filled each morning with a maximum of x orders filled per day to reflect shipment capacity. All remaining orders are filled on Friday mornings if stock allows. No shipping is done on weekends. Contract orders have priority over spot orders and older orders have priority over newer orders.

The plant is operated as a make-to-stock system where the user specifies the average safety stock in terms of days of supply D. From this, the overall desired yarn inventory level in pounds of yarn, Y, is calculated and a portion of it is assigned to each yarn type i, y_i. The goal is to satisfy customer orders within a target lead-time, as well as keep the inventory at the user-specified level. It is important for a spinning plant to control accurately the amount of yarn in stock because it incurs carrying costs as well as acting as safety stock in cases of demand variations or machine failures.

The inventory problem involves trying to maintain the actual inventory level at the desired level. As already noted, one approach is to use max/min control, i.e. maintain the level of inventory within a specified range. The user inputs the range in terms of days of safety stock (D_{max}, D_{min}). From this, the maximum and minimum desired total inventory levels in terms of pounds of yarn (Y_{max} and Y_{min}) are calculated. Any dedicated frames producing yarn type i are shut down when the yarn inventory for type i is above its maximum level $y_{max,i}$ and production is allowed to resume when the inventory falls below its minimum $y_{min,i}$. Scheduled frames are re-allocated based on need.

An alternative to the max/min system is a single target level. This is a simpler concept for the user as only one value, the target level (D_{tar}), is specified. PID (Proportional Integral Derivative) process control is used to keep the inventory level for type i as close as possible to $y_{tar,i}$. It is implemented using all frames as scheduled frames (Clarke and King, 1993).

We dwell on this scheduling process because it is difficult to evaluate alternative procedures in a real plant, or in an analytic fashion, whereas the modeling paradigm allows a detailed examination.

To control the inventory level, both approaches monitor the net inventory position (NIP). This is the level of inventory assuming all Work in Process (WIP) has been completed and all back-orders β have been filled. By regulating NIP, the algorithms control the yarn in stock (finished yarn plus WIP).

PART IV
RESEARCH DIRECTIONS

It isn't that they can't see the solution. It is that they can't see the problem.

GK Chesterton

11
RESEARCH DIRECTIONS

In earlier chapters, we have made it clear that a great deal of work will be required before pipeline dynamics are completely understood. Computer simulation has proved to be a very effective research tool in many ways but it will not solve all the problems. Here we look at some of the research opportunities that remain.

11.1 SLIP INTERACTIONS

We have discussed in a QR-specific way, the need for caution in pushing store inventories back up-stream so as to minimize retailer-carrying costs. Here, we wish to take this idea a stage further.

A moment's thought will reveal that four fundamental quantities are involved in any part of a supply pipeline. The first is the customer Service level that is impacted by the Lead-time for supply and the Inventory on hand. The fourth quantity is the time taken to Process raw materials or components into finished goods. These quantities interact and it may be useful to think of the implied value of one given the values of the other three. For, example, what is the achieved customer service level given the level of inventory carried (raw and/or finished), the lead-time from the vendor and the process time? Alternatively, we could ask what level of inventory should be carried in order to achieve some customer service level given the process time and lead-time to get raw material?

An often overlooked factor that greatly affects the answers to the questions above is that of uncertainty or variance. A simple example which illustrates this is a queuing system. Consider an information booth at a tourist spot manned by one person. Assume first that the time to answer any question takes exactly the same amount of time, say 60 seconds (standard deviation is 0), and further that the time between tourists walking up to the booth is exactly 65 seconds (standard deviation is 0). Clearly, in this case, a tourist walking up to the booth will never wait for service since the service time is 5 seconds less than the inter-arrival time. However, if we add uncertainty to the process things change. Assume now that the time to answer a question is exponentially distributed still with an average of 60 seconds but with a standard deviation of 60 seconds. Similarly, the time between arrivals of tourists is exponentially distributed with an average of 65 seconds and standard deviation of 65 seconds. In this case tourists would expect to wait for about 12 minutes before being serviced (using Little's Equation from Queuing Theory, see for example Winston, 1994).

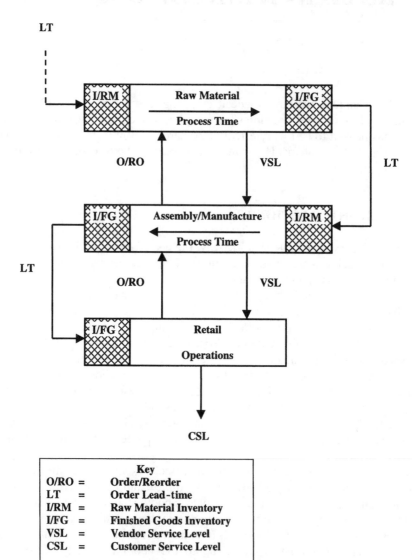

Figure 11.1   SLIP connections

Uncertainty in retailing can come from many sources. Some examples include:

- Inability to forecast consumer demand
- Complexity of the manufacturing process
- Primary and secondary tier manufacturer reliability/quality
- Transportation system reliability
- Inaccuracies in PoS data or bar-codes.

As pointed out by Fisher (1997), speed and flexibility of the supply system can help overcome the impact of uncertainty but typically at a cost. QR is probably overkill in well understood and well behaved systems.

Figure 11.1 sketches the SLIP connections between pipeline segments in a simple way, and from a QR point of view.

In Figures 11.2 and 11.3 are shown the kinds of relationships that intuitively come to mind when thinking about a retail operation. In the first, customer service level is related to store inventory for short, medium and long reorder lead-times. In Figure 11.3, the same variables are looked at in terms of the vendor service level. Note, however, that there are no values on the axes—those are what we need to know.

A similar graph is shown in Figure 11.4 that sketches the expected relationships between manufacturing process time and the inventory of finished goods for low, medium and high vendor service levels.

This approach to pipeline thinking has received little or no attention in the literature, but it seems to be of crucial importance to pipeline planning and

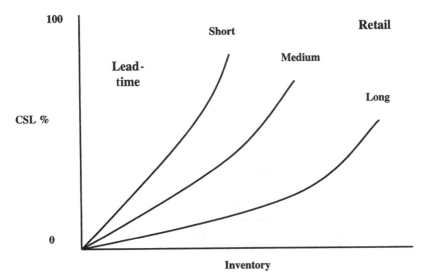

Figure 11.2   Inventory vs. Customer service levels by reorder lead-time

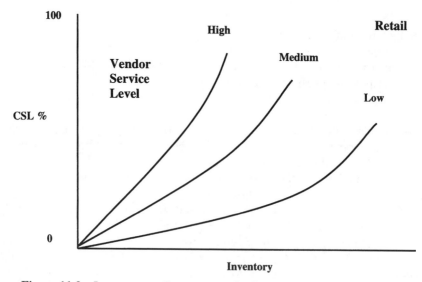

Figure 11.3   Inventory vs. Customer service levels by Vendor service level

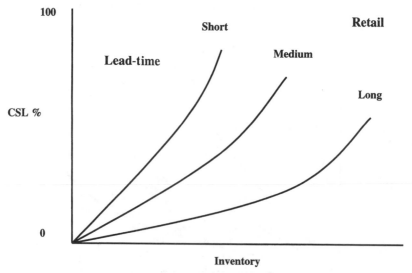

Figure 11.4   Process time vs. finished goods inventory by Customer service level

analysis. One of the reasons for the lack of interest is that the problem(s) is difficult to handle analytically. Dealing with one entity, for example retail, should be tractable, but hooking two entities together presents greater difficulties. The answer is believed to lie in intelligent stochastic modeling of the system. Such an approach would yield valuable insights into pipeline dynamics and help answer several questions now unresolved.

When QR was first promulgated, a question was asked by up-stream members of the pipeline, and it is still unresolved. The question was:

'*How do we share the financial benefits of QR—the retailer gets all the rewards?*'

On the face of it, the question is reasonable, and such answers as,

'*You stay in business,*'

are not satisfactory. For example, under QR, the manufacturers should receive small shipments from their suppliers as needed to respond to PoS driven reorders. But, short runs and frequent small shipments cost the up-stream suppliers money. At present, neither they nor the manufacturers are rewarded by the retailers for their demand responsiveness. There must be an overall view of pipeline dynamics that justifies up-stream profit sharing through higher pass-through prices or smaller inventory carrying costs.

Assume a manufacturer has been supplying a retailer in the traditional way. The company has built inventory and then shipped a significant part of the forthcoming season's order. They then continue to manufacture, building more inventory, and hoping it will be required by the retailer. The manufacturing processes are cost-minimal, but not necessarily the feed stock costs which are low on a per-unit basis, but which will almost certainly lead to end-of-season surpluses and liquidation.

Now the firm switches to QR. Their unit manufacturing costs could well increase as they move to modular (or something similar) production. Because they now have PoS data—or the equivalent, intelligent reorders—they can drastically reduce their finished goods inventories, and their costs, both pre-season and mid-season. They would like to keep raw material inventories to a minimum through frequent, small reorders on their supplier. The question is:

'*How much can I afford to pay the supplier for this service?*'

Certainly the company is in a position to pay something, but how much is simply not known.

This kind of question is important to the future of QR, and we use the term 'sharing the gravy' to describe the entire problem of re-costing or profit sharing within the pipeline and not letting the profit advantage go only to the retailer[1].

A second problem is of interest. The Japanese, and to a certain extent the Europeans, farm out the manufacture of basic products to off-shore suppliers, while retaining manufacture of short season goods for domestic manufacture. In North America, the common practice is the opposite. The major difference between Japan and the USA is that the former is vertically integrated to a high degree, while the latter tends to be laterally organized. Vertical organization usually implies that overall financial judgement is sounder. It is quite possible that SLIP modeling would throw light on this difference.

11.1.1   Initial Inventory vs. Service Level

We now return to the questions raised, and only partly answered, in Chapter 8, Section 8.5. The study (King and Maddalena, 1997) was undertaken at the request of a retailer who sources off-shore and who asked:

> *'with QR is it really necessary for me to place so many reorders for seasonal goods; won't one or two suffice; and if I do place fewer orders, how much initial inventory should I have in place to achieve a high % Service level?'*

To answer these and a number of related questions, the following scenarios were adopted. As is usual, the off-shore sourcing scenario assumes that 100% of the buyer's plan is purchased and shipped ahead of the selling season. In line with this, the initial inventory (initial delivery percentage) is set at 100%. For the QR scenarios, we set the initial inventory—expressed as a percentage of the expected season's sales—at a sufficiently high level to provide a high probability that customers would find the item in stock (a given probability of, for example, 0.95). Setting the initial inventory in this way biases the results toward the traditional case where 100% of the inventory is received up front and all customer demand is assumed to be satisfied in the initial weeks.

The demand volume as a percentage of the buyer's plan varied between 75% and 125% and the average was taken. The SKU error was set at 20% (a level widely used in industry). A 39-week season was used, with the first reorder delivered in week 12 for a one drop scenario (several side runs suggested this was close to optimal), and weeks 10, and 20 for a two drop scenario, etc.

It is assumed that the demand in any given week follows a Poisson distribution, thereby allowing the required initial inventory to be calculated directly by a convolution of the presumed demand over the lead-time weeks using the Poisson density function to calculate probabilities (Maddalena, 1998).

---

[1] The QRRP at Cardiff Business School is currently examining this and other areas as part of its Added Value Assessment (AVA) project. Some details are provided in Section 11.4 of this chapter.

Table 11.1   Inventory vs. % Service level vs. number of reorders for seasonal goods

% of traditional average inventory

Target customer service level (%)	No. of reorders			
	1	2	4	10+
75	41	27	18	14
80	42	27	19	15
85	43	28	20	16
90	45	30	22	17
95	47	32	23	18
99.8	59	42	33	26

Based on the summed SKU-level requirements for a range of target service levels, the values in Table 11.1 below show the inventories required in terms of traditional initial (100%) drop levels.

Two comments are in order. First, in one version of traditional marketing, about 40% of a season's goods are delivered before selling starts, with the rest delivered in weeks 8–10 of a 20-week season. We know that such a procedure gives low customer service levels and this is confirmed by the values in the first inventory column. Second, the information contained in the Table 11.1 must be treated with caution:

- The inventory levels are only those required for the period from the season opening to the arrival of the first reorder. We assume that after this, the re-estimation/reorder process will ensure optimal operating results.
- The results will be affected by the buyer forecast error levels and the timing of the first reorder.
- Most importantly, the appearance of the store—the stock presentation level—is paramount.

Thus the very low inventories shown in Table 11.1, and the accompanying performance results (GMROI, etc.) may well not be achievable for all types of merchandise. In other words, the results shown are bounded. However, a start has been made on resolving some of the problems associated with SLIP interactions.

11.2   SYSTEM DYNAMICS

Before going on to other research topics, we wish to mention System Dynamics (SD) as a possible input to SLIP thinking.

Jay Forrester developed SD in the late 1950s and totally changed the way people think about industrial systems. In his book, *Industrial Dynamics*, he examined supply chains, with their typical inventories, order lead-times and delays, unfilled order levels, etc. He then showed the impacts of changes in demand levels on these variables—huge and fluctuating wildly as enterprises struggled to control the dynamics of the system. He then went on to look at such corrective factors as reduced information flow times, reduced tiers in the pipeline stages and different management policies. However, as we noted earlier in this book, there were problems with his approach. First, he underestimated the impact of intelligent and aggressive managers who would jump in to dampen the wide oscillations in inventories, etc. Second, the products he examined were 'widgets'—uniform products with unlimited shelf life. Before long, SD became the preserve of environmental, ecological, planning and strategic analysts (for example, see Lyneis, 1980 and Roberts, 1981).

Lately, however, there has been a resurgence of 'modern', industrially oriented thinking regarding SD. Wickner et al. (1991) and Towill (1991) have reported studies in which they fine tuned ordering policy parameters, changed supply chain decision rules, and made better use of information flows.

These works, however, still concern 'widgets', service levels are not considered, and the focus is upon manufacturing. A change may at last be available. The latest 'Stella 5' software[2], which was originally designed for the Macintosh, now has a Windows version and can handle multiple SKUs simultaneously. This will allow such things as buyer error and SKU mix to be introduced into SD research. Such approaches could also provide alternative techniques for estimating the impact of QR on pipeline performance, and throw light on SLIP interactions.

11.3 LOGISTICS

Earlier in the book, we reviewed the place of logistics thinking in the broader context of recent business methodology. Here, we would like to become more specific, both in terms of QR versus traditional environments, and total logistics costs. For the textile and clothing industry a start was made in Hunter (1990), but the data are over 10 years old and badly need bringing up-to-date. Further, we now have a better idea of the important cost elements affecting QR and its competitors.

Below is a sampling of the things we do and do not know about the costs of doing business in the two environments, remembering that there are many others:

---

[2] 'Stella 5' software from high Performance Systems Inc., Hanover, NH, USA 03755 or http://www.hps-inc

- Though retail cost analyses of QR vs. traditional operations in the real world are known only vaguely, the modeling work described in earlier chapters has allowed good approximations of the benefits of QR in terms of revenue, margin, return on inventory investment, markdown and lost sales.
- The full costs of doing business off-shore have not been well defined. Executive travel, trips to check merchandise quality, the costs of irrevocable letters of credit, the costs on the retailing system of having fixed volumes and SKU mixes delivered to the stores with little chance of change, are some of the factors. Handling at the DC, and re-ticketing are others. This aspect of business requires a great deal more information if the buying decision is to be optimized.
- There are costs associated with short, flexible production runs, and with operating at lower than maximum capacity utilizations, though these may well be required to give the kind of service levels necessary for rapid supply of goods to the consumer.
- There are also costs associated with delivery of goods. Short lead-times generally mean higher costs. United Parcel Service in the USA claim, rightly, that goods can be delivered to any place in the country within three days. However, their shipping charges are considerably higher than those of the traditional local truckers who move things at a low cost, but with long delivery times. Similarly, drop shipping direct to stores, as opposed to DC deliveries, is likely to increase, and will require a premium. However, there is some reason to believe that the saving in time and inventory levels off-sets the additional shipping costs.
- On the positive side, EDI offers considerable cost savings. Rapid transmissions of orders, invoices and Advance Ship Notices (ASNs) save time and money. Also, if the information is entered directly into the recipient's information or operational procedures system, human errors can be avoided. Too little study of these advantages has been made.
- Streams of PoS information have value to everyone in the pipeline. The manufacturers can plan their production more intelligently and control their inventories of both raw materials and finished goods optimally. Similarly, the 1st tier raw material producers benefit from having improved understanding of the way demand is shaping up in the retail store; they can schedule yarn or fabric production to reflect this. But, again, research into the financial consequences of these aspects of the business is spotty at best.

A research project to address the total logistics package in the more modern sense of the word (see Copacino, 1997) is underway at NCSU. The purpose of the project is to provide detailed scheduling and logistical co-ordination in the supply chain in order to maximize consumer satisfaction and minimize operating costs.

11.4 PERFORMANCE MEASURES

Increasingly, retailers are looking to measure the performance of their suppliers in order to 'grade' them. Interest is focusing on such measures as order lead-times, percentage orders shipped on time, percentage fill rate (how much of the order was actually shipped on time), and back-order fill rate. This means, of course, that vendors must measure their own performance in these terms, as well as those of their suppliers. This is to be welcomed, as it is an important step in implementing QR (see Chapter 6 and in particular Section 6.8 on Benchmarking).

Equally important is that the retailers themselves adopts new performance measures. We have referred to this earlier, and in Chapters 9 and 10, looked at relatively new measures of financial performance—GMROI (Gross Margin/Average Inventory Investment) and GMROISL (GMROI* Adjusted for In-stock %). Although these measures have much to recommend them, they are not perfect. Orders with a low fill rate will give misleading values of GMROI because stocks are artificially kept low. In the case of GMROISL, the value may look satisfactory but stockouts will lead to poor customer service.

Industry and management theorists need to give thought to meaningful performance measures that will be used in-house as well as by suppliers and customers. One of the difficulties to be overcome is that until PoS data are routinely collected and properly analyzed, new measures are hard to find—there is a shortage of information. For example, in this book we have routinely written of stockouts, % lost sales and % customer service level with values coming from simulation models. In fact, only the most sophisticated retailer has any good information in these areas. Which values to choose, and how best to quantify and apply them is an important area of supply chain research.

In addition to the need for new performance measurements, their application is also the subject of research. At Cardiff Business School, under the auspices of the Quick Response Research Programme (QRRP), we are examining ways of applying agreed performance measures to the whole supply pipeline. The research takes as its starting point the importance of performance measures external to the firm. Methods are being examined whereby such measures of operation can be jointly agreed between a retailer, assembly or 1st tier manufacturer, and raw material processor (2nd tier manufacturer). Further, as part of an Added Value Analysis (AVA) collective reward systems are imposed whereby actions adding value throughout an integrated supply system are rewarded, while those continuing to subtract value are penalized. In this way there is an increased motivation on the part of all enterprises in the system to consider activities beyond their boundaries and impacts throughout the pipeline.

11.5   INFORMATION FLOWS

In earlier chapters we have suggested algorithms for retailer reorders on vendors, and raw material reorders on suppliers. These were based in the first case on knowledge of store inventories, and in the second on knowledge of manufacturing finished goods inventories. Clearly it is possible to extend this kind of thinking to operations further up-stream. Is there an easier and more encompassing method of transmitting information necessary for a QR supply system to operate efficiently? In Nuttle et al. (1998), a Master Schedule for the pipeline that encompasses all the entities involved is described and illustrated. This schedule is set up at the beginning of a season then modified as consumer preferences become clear.

This kind of 'supply chain' view is being incorporated in advanced planning and scheduling (APS) software (for example, see Hicks, 1997 and Dullin, 1998). However, other solutions must exist and the questions remain—what are the critical factors involved? What is acceptable to the various members of the supply chain? Which methods give maximum returns?

11.6   NEURAL NETWORKING FOR MANAGEMENT INFORMATION SYSTEMS

One of the prime objectives of the modeling program at NCSU was to develop techniques that would allow senior managers to obtain immediate answers to questions about their operations—a kind of Interactive Management Information System (MIS). Using the spinning model described in an earlier chapter, a variety of approaches have been taken to meet this objective. Decision surfaces, or simulation meta-models, have been fitted to the outputs of simulation runs to relate plant performance (inventory levels, order response time, etc.) to important input and operating parameters (e.g. product mix, number of machines). One of the drawbacks to this approach is the large numbers of products involved in a company's operations, making analytic or statistical treatments difficult to carry out. An index of diversity (for example, see Piellou, 1977) for the product mix in a complex plant that can be used effectively as a predictor, would simplify this kind of analysis, but to date nothing has surfaced.

A different approach has recently shown considerable promise—that of using artificial neural networks to investigate and present the complex sets of relationships between input and output variables, without recourse to analytic methods.

An excellent account of the methodology of neural networking and its applications is given in Masson and Wang (1990), where it is shown that the numbers, types and applications of artificial neural networks have increased enormously in the last 10–15 years. It is important reading for those whose interests lie in the field of Interactive MIS, as are ours. Other references include Kosko (1992), Zimmermann (1988) and Zurada (1992).

An artificial neural network is made up of a series of small processing units linked by connections that are weighted and directed. Units receive input signals via the connections and send output signals in a like way. In the approach discussed here, the units are assembled in three layers: one for inputs, one for outputs, and a third layer of 'hidden' (perceptron) units situated between the other two. A schematic of a neural network is shown in Figure 11.5.

Basically, if we define fields of input and output variable quantities, we would like the neural network to 'learn' the interactions between the input and output sets and produce n-dimensional relationships between the two through a large number of iterations. Results obtained from running the model are used to form a 'training' set of input/output relationships. This set is used in the network learning phase by applying a rule that uses the squared differences between the actual and desired outputs as an error measure to be minimized.

The weighting factors mentioned above as 'joining' the processing units are now adjusted using the measures of error in a reverse fashion until the input layer has been processed (so called back-propagation). The scheme being described is also classified as 'supervised' because the training set includes the outputs—'unsupervised' training makes use of input vectors only. It should be noted that the training sets should include full ranges of the variable values likely to be encountered in any CEO interaction.

Following a sufficient number of training runs to give errors of a desired (small) size, the program is exercised using other sets of variables in order to validate the net's performance.

In addition to the scheme outlined above, it is possible to invoke an additional process. If the 'fuzziness' implicit in the relationships is recognized and

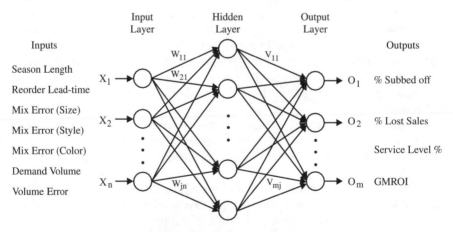

Figure 11.5   Structure of a neural network

applied, then uncertainties between the variables can be assessed and used to keep to a minimum the number of iterations, or 'epochs' needed to get useful results; i.e. relationships between input and output variables. Thus, with the use of a fuzzy learning rate controller, the number of epochs can be substantially reduced—in the example outlined below, to 950 epochs from the 10 000 needed without it.

The neural network technique has so far been tried out on the Sourcing Simulator and the spinning model outlined in Chapter 10 and graphical user interfaces have been developed in both 2-D and 3-D for each.

For the retail model, the key outputs were % Liquidated, % Lost sales, GMROI, and % Service level. Earlier work had shown that the input parameters most affecting these outputs are the season length, reorder lead-time, SKU mix error, volume error and demand volume. Therefore, for the three layer neural network, there are seven input nodes (three factors in the SKU mix error) and four output nodes. In addition, 10 neurons were used in the 'hidden' layer. Similar to a 3^k factorial, each input parameter was fixed either at the lowest, the center or the highest value to create samples for the runs. The input/output parameter sets provided 83 training patterns for the network. For each sample, the retail simulation was replicated 10 times to obtain the mean and variance of each output parameter. For testing, as opposed to learning, purposes, two input parameters were fixed at their middle values, setting the remaining three parameters at the highest and lowest values to generate an $8*10 = 80$ pattern (see Table 11.2).

For the four predictors, the combined mean error of the outputs was 1.35%, with % Liquidated contributing most of this (% Liquidated is small—normally less than 20%) (see Table 11.3).

Table 11.2   Input parameters

	Lowest	Medium	Highest
Season length	10 weeks	15 weeks	20 weeks
Reorder lead-time	2 weeks	3 weeks	4 weeks
Mix error	0% 0% 0%	20% 20% 10%	40% 40% 20%
Demand volume	S.L. × 50	S.L. × 100	S.L. × 150
Volume error	−20%	0%	+20%

Table 11.3   Training patterns

	% Liquidated	Lost sales	GMROI	Service level
Mean error—%	1.49	0.54	−0.32	−0.02
Error variance	69.54	84.67	8.11	0.33
Max. error	26.37	31.78	6.18	1.26
Min. error	−24.69	−36.36	−8.44	−1.79

Table 11.4 Validation

	% Liquidated	Lost sales	GMROI	Service level
Mean error—%	−0.71	0.99	−0.12	−0.01
Error variance	82.16	110.63	7.45	0.59
Max. error	27.94	28.56	9.02	1.69
Min. error	−19.11	−31.07	−6.55	−2.55

When the network was validated, the combined mean error of the four predictors fell to 0.15%, an excellent result, qualifying the neural network as a good tool for the prediction of retail performance (see Table 11.4).

For details of the application of a 'fuzzy' controller to modulate the learning rate of each input neuron throughout the training process, the original paper should be consulted (Wu et al., 1995c). The combined mean square error of the four predictors drops to 0.99% for the training results, and 0.87% for the validation sample, though the number of iterations was decreased by over 90%.

These kinds of results have encouraged us to explore the usefulness of neural networking for the other manufacturing models, including the spinning model. In the latter, we looked at the numbers of yarns produced, ranging from six to 18; the number of frames from 15 to 45; percentage plant utilization from 82% to 88% in one-unit increments; the agreed on or blanket orders from 40 to 100%; the inventory stocks from six to 12 days; and the average order size from 5K to 15K pounds. The results were equally as impressive for the spinning as the retail model.

In order to make the outputs from the Neural Network model more comprehensible, a program was developed to show surfaces graphically; for example, the relationship between % Service level, % Machine utilization and the number of spinning frames used for a particular scenario. It has been incorporated in the Sourcing Simulator Version 2.0.

11.7 SHORT SEASON AND FASHION GOODS

We have discussed the reduced utility of QR for short season goods as the selling season decreases to eight weeks or less. It is now time to examine recent trends in retailing, where season lengths are heading, and ways to adapt.

The movement to shorter seasons is partly a result of consumer pressures for increased variety and convenience—the preponderance of perishable foods and chilled ready-meals with a shelf life of only days is a stark example of the latter, and partly the result of designers seeking to increase market share. By designers, we mean the pure boutique, including the 'fashion chains', the 'boutique within the (department) store' design houses, as well as higher priced house brands. The former have led the way and are capable of 4–6 week shelf lives or less and there is some indication that they are considering 'continuous' fashion—continually topping up the in-store merchandise with new colors, styles, etc. and removing the slow moving lines on, say, a weekly or bi-weekly basis. Such a trend will trickle down to mid-price and lower price fashion goods, for competitive reasons and also because the public demands this availability.

This kind of development toward shorter shelf lives is now evident in a number of consumer sectors. It will not occur overnight and will probably not affect more than a small proportion of merchandise, even when in full swing. But, it is far removed from the re-estimation/reorder world of QR.

Here is one possible scenario—there are others, including the old-fashioned one of making sample goods and walking them around the buyers. To make very short season merchandise work to its fullest, the pipeline will need CAD/CAM and new product development taken a step beyond its current evolution. Imagine a manufacturer (domestic or off-shore) who has designed a line of short season products using a state-of-the-art CAD system. Let him or her be linked to buyers and his or her important customers through high fidelity imaging. The buyer can ask for changes in styling or color, using EDI or any other method, and, when happy, can order some volume of merchandise. This technology is available to the adventurous, but our interest focuses on the question of how much to order initially, remembering that the likelihood of reorders is very small.

The first thing the buyer should do is to use PoS information at his or her disposal to make sure that the mix he or she orders is as correct as possible. We have discussed this earlier. However, we now raise an important point: there is a well known, but not well quantified, correlation between attributes of a SKU. A particular example is depth of color and size preference in apparel. Among women, the darker shades are preferred by customers buying the larger sizes. We urge retailers to make use of PoS information to pin down this relationship as it relates to their customers. All it takes is (say) a 3×3 grid with colors broken down into Light, Medium and Dark, and sizes into Small, Medium and Large. The entries would be % Sales or units. This grid would then be applied to the SKU order mix.

The buyers of short season goods should accumulate as many goods sales data as possible, showing volumes sold over the short seasons they are interested in—preferably broken down into distribution frequencies. Then they are essentially involved in a News Boy or News Vendor problem (Morton, 1971).

As was discussed in an earlier chapter, the name derives from a news vendor who orders, and pays for, papers for resale the same day. Demand is uncertain; any papers left over have no value—only a cost. If papers are under-ordered, profit (and customer goodwill) are lost. Calculation of the optimal order quantity is an Operations Research problem and relies on the use of a demand distribution function based on the news vendor's (or equivalent) experience.

There is a growing body of research into the applicability of News Boy and related theories—see Bradford and Sugrue (1990), Clark and Scarf (1960), Crowston et al. (1973), Murray and Silver (1966), Schmidt and Nahmias (1984), and Zachs, (1981). In Chapter 8 we discussed, though only briefly, a News Boy approach to Basic goods and compared it to both the K_s 'weeks supply' method of re-estimation/reorder, and a Morton's Curve Approximation (MCA) strategy (Martin, 1997). Indications are that both have merit. When both a Distribution Center and individual stores are involved, it seems that combinations of K_s and one of the other two could well improve on K_s alone (Reynolds, 1995). The strongest argument for using News Boy or MCA is that they consider, implicitly, the economic implications of inventory carrying costs, and can be driven by pre-determined 'Target service levels'. The drawbacks to the two methods include the computing required under certain circumstances, and the fact that they are not as intrinsically 'understandable' to the industry as the 'Weeks of Supply' methodology (see Chapter 5).

We argue that further investigation into these and other re-estimation/ reorder processes will be of benefit to the industries involved, and particularly so when they are evaluated in conjunction with the simulation techniques described in this book.

The position of the short season goods buyer is much more complicated than most others, mainly because she has several disposal options—her goods have a value at the end of a season (day). She can mark them down, she can dispose of them through an outlet store, or she can sell them to a jobber—frequently all at different prices. For these reasons, an analytic (mathematical) solution to the problem of how many items to buy is likely to be extremely difficult. At NCSU we are, therefore, looking at the possibility of developing a generalized News Boy model, suitable for the retailer of short season merchandise, which allows inputs of the kinds of variables mentioned above.

The main obstacle to progress in this area is the lack of data. PoS information is quite new and very few people, it seems, have even started to build historical series that could be applied to new and sophisticated analytical tools.

A second obstacle has to do with a long-standing personnel practice. The average junior buyer spends less than two years in a department. It has been said that she or he spends the first year learning the job and the second one angling for a move. The more senior people have a well-developed appreciation for their products, but their responsibilities are broader. Any aid can only help their performance.

It should be noted here that there is a growing body of literature concerning optimal procedures in industry for solving manufacturing problems and exact solutions for individual manufacturing companies. Of importance is the *Harvard Business Review* article on Obermeyer, a ski-wear manufacturer and the analytic back-up review (Fisher et al., 1994). We would like to see a heavier emphasis on the retailing function (where exact solutions are much more difficult to come by), and more generalized solutions, i.e. those not restricted to a single operation.

11.8   PROPORTIONAL INTEGRAL DERIVATIVE (PID) SCHEDULING

In Chapter 10, while discussing a spinning plant model, we introduced an alternative to the popular max/min scheduling procedure. Proportional Integral Derivative process control is used to keep inventory as close as possible to a target set by management. Appendix I shows how PID operates.

The Target Inventory algorithm tends to have an average inventory that is slightly larger than the target level. The max/min algorithm, on the other hand, tends to keep the average inventory level closer towards the minimum level. These characteristics are most obvious in cases with a large number of different products (18–36 yarns). Because of this, a simulation using the max/min algorithm cannot be accurately compared to a simulation using the Target Inventory algorithm with a target level half-way between the min/max levels.

In order to compare performance measures such as percentage of on-time orders and the variance of the inventory level, only simulations which have approximately the same average inventory level are compared regardless of their user-specified target or min/max levels. The data presented in this section was collected in five-year simulation runs using the 18 yarn base case.

11.8.1   Percentage of Orders Shipped on Time

The target algorithm gives an average inventory level that is comparatively less than the max/min algorithm while maintaining the same performance in shipping. Figure 11.6 shows, for one simulation, the average inventory levels needed for each algorithm to achieve a certain percentage of overall orders shipped within five days. For 80% on-time shipping, the Target Inventory

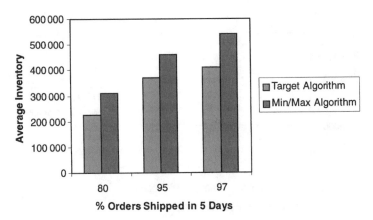

Figure 11.6   Comparison of inventory level required to meet shipment schedules

algorithm gives an average inventory of approximately 77 000 lb less than the max/min algorithm. At 95%, the Target Inventory algorithm gives 100 000 lb less than the max/min algorithm, and at 97%, the difference is approximately 130 000 lb. From these data, it appears that as a higher percentage of on-time shipping is desired, the larger the difference is between the inventory levels of the two algorithms.

The better performance of the PID algorithm is not without its problems; it requires considerably more frame changes than the max/min algorithm. In an extensive series of runs, the PID algorithm led to approximately nine changes per day vis-à-vis 5.0 to 5.5 for max/min.

11.8.2   Standard Deviations of the Inventory Level

The reason behind the better performance of the Target Inventory algorithm is its comparatively lower inventory standard deviations. The graph in Figure 11.7 shows how the inventory standard deviation changes with respect to the average inventory level for both algorithms. Since inventory under PID control does not fluctuate as much, more orders can be shipped at the same average inventory level as opposed to the max/min algorithm. (Again, the importance of uncertainty or variance is highlighted.)

As an example, below are the actual inventory levels recorded over a one-year simulation period for both the Target Inventory algorithm (Figure 11.8) and the max/min algorithm (Figure 11.9) using an 18-yarn scenario. The statistics are for each week: the average inventory, the maximum inventory and the minimum inventory.

Both simulations have an average inventory level of approximately 316 000 lb. The Target Inventory algorithm has a standard deviation of 21 000 lb as opposed to 33 000 lb for the max/min algorithm. The lower inventory standard deviation for the Target Inventory algorithm is visually

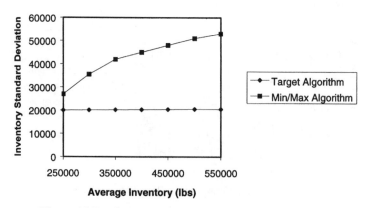

Figure 11.7 Comparison of inventory standard deviation

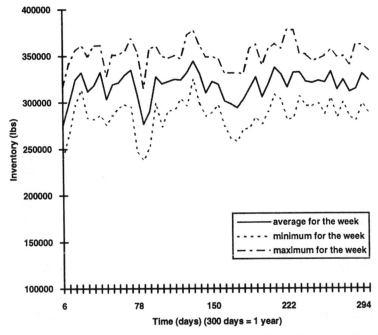

Figure 11.8   Actual inventory over time under the Target Inventory algorithm

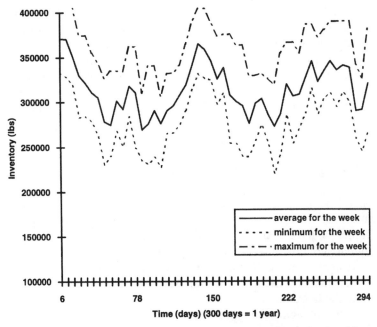

Figure 11.9   Actual inventory over time under the max/min algorithm

detectable from the graphs. The target algorithm shipped 92% of its orders on time as opposed to the max/min algorithm that shipped only 80%.

11.9   COLOR

There is no shortage of research topics that would benefit QR. Here we will mention briefly just one more.

The first thing a shopper does on entering a store is to look around for color. Color is the prime attractor, and even slight differences in shade or depth can be important within a color group. After that the customer will look at different designs, styles, shapes, etc. The primacy of color applies to garden furniture, automobiles in a display room, apparel, home furnishing, food, carpets— almost any consumer purchase. Further, color preferences change rapidly as new fashion images appear and vanish.

Colors can be described precisely using the CIE system (Commission International de l'Eclairge) which defines them as vectors in a three dimensional space based on three primary colors. And yet the retailer still uses an antiquated, purely descriptive system—Kola Nut and Chocolate are two descriptors—which precludes any building of databases or exchange of quantitative information. Thus, no use of CIE information is made when buyers and manufacturers are planning for a new season.

A simple piece of software should be developed which would allow discussion and modification of colors between their respective computers instead of the time consuming process of walking around of trial products or prototypes. As an adjunct to a CAD/CAM system, such software would allow buyers to input their views on color very early in the design process.

We realize that there remain problems of color perception between a cathode ray tube and the actual good, but much progress has been made toward ironing out these differences. However, every effort must be made to reduce the time taken to design a product and have it approved by the purchaser.

11.10   THE QUICK RESPONSE DOMAIN

Earlier in the book we noted that QR is not a universal panacea for management problems. Some industries, for example certain kinds of household furniture (see Chapter 5), have characteristics that prevent them from enjoying the benefits brought about by QR system technologies and procedures. In order to get a better grasp of what are the limits to QR we have undertaken a joint research program to characterize, in a general way, these limitations. This we call delineating the QR domain.

In brief, for all significant consumer goods service industries, we assemble the following sub-sets of information or characteristics that indicate the complexity involved (something other approaches often fail to recognize), and thereafter, the QR approach necessary.

- Economic features (sales, time series of sales, inventories, etc.).
- Distribution systems for goods or services and their channels.
- Seasonality features, including shelf lives, importance of peak selling periods.
- Retail operational procedures, including PoS analyses.
- Promotional profiles such as known cannibalization, etc.
- Manufacturing characteristics/procedures.
- Operational performance measures.
- Consumer requirements.
- Et al.

The program then calls for investigation of the relationships and correspondences between these sets of characteristics as a route to delineating the QR boundaries and exploring possible new areas of QR activity. In this way we are able to appreciate generic demand uncertainty, product attributes and customer type. A grouping or mapping of the corresponding sets allows application of QR strategy to particular flow characteristics and a move toward customization of approach to demand profile.

11.11   COMMENTS

By its very nature, the QR methodology must be capable of adaptation and growth. We have discussed the increasing trend toward short season goods in both Europe and North America. This is perhaps one of the greatest challenges facing firms operating in volatile consumer markets. A number of approaches to the problem are possible, however we are convinced that only those methods that consider the whole pipeline will be truly effective. In this vein, a better understanding at an inter-industry and pipeline level of logistics flows and SLIP interactions may prove the most fruitful for short season categories. Similarly, the new research to understand the customization of demand flows by product and customer sets will possibly prove a future paradigm shift in logistics thinking.

QR is, as we are fond of saying, almost totally dependent upon data and information flows: without these, companies will continue a 'myopic' response to demand challenges. The continued development of MIS and neural networking models will be of prime importance in this area.

We hope the reader, no matter what her or his interest or background, will have found something of value in this book. For us it has been a sharp learning curve and an unforgettable experience. Two invaluable lessons have, however, become clear: first, the futility of attempting to offer all things to all people, the subject area is far too broad and our omissions will be obvious. Second, the simple elegance of QR, and indeed its main strength, is the strong adherence to a philosophy of customization, uniqueness and individuality, as well as continual development or improvement. What we advocate for one firm will not necessarily apply to another, and certainly will not be applicable in another industry (beware the catholicon peddling such wares). Customers and consumers are unique, so must be the firms that serve them. It is in this light that we, the authors, are continually learning and attempting to refine QR.

We have still a great deal to do and learn—why don't you join us—we need all the help we can get. Any comments, observations and criticisms (providing they are constructive) would be most welcome. At stake is a greatly improved pipeline performance and a better chance for domestic suppliers to thrive! We can *all* be contacted using any *one* of the following e-mail addresses:

Bob_Lowson@msn.com
King@eos.ncsu.edu
Nimrod@netrover.com

11
APPENDIX I
THE PID ALGORITHM

The Target Inventory algorithm is implemented every Δt time units. It calculates yarn i's *NIP* value, NIP_i, and compares it with its target level, $y_{tar,i}$. The difference is called the error, e_i. By adjusting the number of frames running each yarn type, the Target Inventory algorithm attempts to alleviate the error within a user-specified amount of time. The Target Inventory algorithm uses process control to regulate the inventory. Process control involves influencing one variable (the controlled variable) by changing the value of another variable (the controlling variable) (Johnson, 1984).

Because the Target Inventory algorithm regulates *NIP* in its attempt to influence the yarn stock, *NIP* is the controlled variable. For each yarn type i, $NIP_i(t)$ is effectively a continuous function of time, the current number of running frames, $N_i(t)$, spindle efficiency, E, frame setup times, S, and customer order attributes, F_o, (number of customer orders, order sizes, product demand mix), i.e.

$$NIP_i(t) = F(N_i(t), F_0, E, S) \text{ for yarns } i = 1 \dots n$$

Variation in these variables is responsible for creating error (actual level—desired level) in *NIP*. Because of uncontrollable demand variations, it is virtually impossible for the system to be error-free. Thus, the objective is to minimize the error.

The number of frames running type i ($N_i(t)$) is the controlling variable for $NIP_i(t)$ because it is the only variable which influences $NIP_i(t)$ and which can also be altered by the simulation model. There is a separate control equation for each yarn type. Since there is a limited number of spinning frames, contention may occur when the total number of frames required for all yarns exceeds m.

Process control uses a repetitive procedure that involves feedback. Figure 11.4 is a diagram of the steps involved. The model attempts to control a

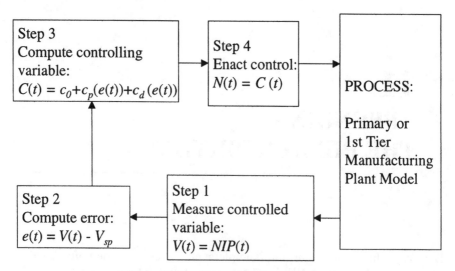

Figure 11.10 Steps in the control process

continuous variable ($NIP_i(t)$) using a discrete, capacitated control variable ($N_i(t)$). Steps 1 through 4 are repeated every Δt time units.

The formulae in Figure 11.10 are the relationships used in implementing the Target Inventory process. Rather than go into details of the processes involved, we recommend that the reader consult the original papers.

LIST OF ACRONYMS

AAMA	American Apparel Manufacturers Association
ACR	Automated Consumer Response
AMTEX	American Textile Partnership
ANSI	American National Standards Institute
ANSI ASC X12	American National Standards Institute Accredited Standard Committee
APP to APP	Application to Application
ASN	American Standard Number
ASN	Advanced Shipping Notice
ATC	Apparel and Textile Challenge
AVA	Added Value Assessment
BCG	Boston Consulting Group
CAD	Computer Assisted Design
CAM	Computer Assisted Manufacture
CEO	Chief Executive Officer
CIE	Commission International de l'Eclairage
CMT	Cut, Make and Trim
CNC	Computer Numerically Controlled
DAMA	Demand Activated Manufacturing Architecture
DC	Distribution Center
DoC	US Department of Commerce

DRP	Distribution Resource Planning
EAN	European Article Number
ECR	Efficient Consumer Response
EDI	Electronic Data Interchange
EDIFACT	Electronic Data Interchange for Administration, Commerce and Transport
EoS	End of Season
ERDF	European Regional Development Fund
ERP	Enterprise Resource Planning
EU	European Union
FIFO	First in First out
FMCG	Fast Moving Consumer Goods
GEIS	General Electric Information System
GM/S	Gross Margin to Sales
GMROI	Gross Margin Return on Inventory
GMROISL	Gross Margin Return on Inventory Service Level
HBR	*Harvard Business Review*
IBM	International Business Machines
IMIS	Interactive Management Information System
IS	Information System
I/S	Inventory to Sales Ratio
IST	Information Systems Technology
IT	Information Technology
JIT	Just-in-Time
KSA	Kurt Salmon Associates
MAX/MIN	Upper and Lower Inventory Controls
MIS	Management Information System
MRP	Materials Requirement Planning
MRPII	Manufacturing Resource Planning
NCSU	North Carolina State University

NIP	Net Inventory Position
NRF	National Retail Federation
NTC	National Textile Centre
PID	Proportional Integral Derivative
PoS	Point of Sale
PS	Presentation Stock
QFD	Quality Function Deployment
QM	Quality Management
QR	Quick Response
QRRP	Quick Response Research Program
R&D	Research and Development
SCM	Supply Chain Management
SD	System Dynamics
SKU	Stock Keeping Unit
SLIP	Customer **S**ervice level, **L**ead time, **I**nventory and **P**rocessing time
SME	Small to Medium-sized Enterprise
SRC	Supplier–Retailer Collaboration
SS	Sourcing Simulator
TAPS	Textile/Apparel Process Simulator
[TC]^2	Textile/Clothing Technology Corporation
TLC	Total Logistics Cost
TQM	Total Quality Management
TRADACOMS	UK version of ANSI
UPC	Universal Product Code
UPC/A	Symbology interchangeable with UPC, i.e. a bar-code
VAN	Value Added Network
VAP	Value-Adding Partnership
VICS	Voluntary Industry Communications Standards

VMI	Vendor Managed Inventory
WIP	Work in Progress (or Process)
WWW	World Wide Web

BIBLIOGRAPHY

AAMA (1996), *Measurements For Excellence*, Quick Response Leadership Committee. This report was published via the Internet—http://www.tc2.com/qrlc/QRLCMEAS/.

Abbeglen J and Stalk G (1985), *Kaisha: the Japanese Corporation*, Basic Books: NY.

Arthur Andersen Consulting (1998), *Quick Response: A Study of Costs and Benefits to Retailers of Implementing QR and Supporting Technologies*, Technical Report, New York, NY, USA.

Attenborough R (1982), *The Words of Gandhi*, Newmarket Publishing, New York, NY, USA.

Benjamin DM and Mazzioti BW (1996), *Enterprise Modeling Tool*, [TC]^2, Cary, NC.

Benjamin DM, Mazziotti BW and Armstrong FB (1994), *Issues and Requirements for Building a Generic Animation*, Proceedings of the Winter Simulation Conference, Tew JD et al. (Eds) IEEE, Piscataway NJ.

Bertalanffy L von (1950), *Theory of Open Systems in Physics and Biology*, Science 3.

Bertalanffy, L von (1956), *General Systems Theory*, General Systems, 1.

Boisot M (1994), *Information and Organizations: the Manager as Anthropologist*, Harper Collins.

Borsodi R (1927), *The Distribution Age*, Appleton & Co.

Bradford JW and Sugrue PK (1990), *A Baysian Approach to the Two-period Style-goods Inventory Problem with Single Replenishment and Heterogeneous Poisson Demands*, J. Operational Soc., Vol. 41, No. 3.

Brain LA (1994), *PID Based Inventory Control of a Textile Spinning Plant*, Master of Science Thesis, Operations Research Program, NC State University.

Braithwaite AJ (1990), *Management of Quick Response*, Textile Asia, Vol. 21, No. 5, 134–137.

Brusco S (1982), *The Emilian Model: Productive Decentralization and Social Integration*, Cambridge Econ. Vol. 6, 167–184.

Burrell G (1997), *Pandemonium*, Sage, NY.

Chen Y (1994), *A Generalized Simulation Model of Weaving Mill Operations*, Operations Research Program, NSCU, July.

Clark AJ and Scarf H (1960), *Optimal Policies for a Multi-Echelon Inventory Problem*, Management Science, Vol. 6, No. 4.

Clarke LAM (1995), *Development and Comparison of Yarn Inventory Control Algorithms in a Textile Spinning Plant*, Operations Research Program, NCSU, Raleigh, NC.

Clarke LAM and King RE (1993), *PID-Based Inventory Control of a Textile Spinning Plant*, NCSU-IE Technical Report, Raleigh, NC.

Clarke S (1990a), *The Crisis of Fordism or the Crisis of Social Democracy?*, Telos, Vol. 83.

Clarke S (1990b), *New Utopias for Old: Fordist Dreams and Post-Fordist Fantasies*, Capital and Class, 42.

Collins RS and Schmenner RW (1993), *Perspectives for Managers*, IMD Number 1.

Coase RH (1937), *The Nature of the Firm*, Economica, Vol. 4.

Copacino WC (1997), *Supply Chain Management, The Basics and Beyond*, St Lucie Press, Boca Raton, FL.

Crowston WB, Hausman WH and Kempe WR (1973), *Multistage Production for Stochastic Seasonal Demands*, Management Science, Vol. 19, No. 8.

Cunning J, Ingle A and Winchester S (1995), *The Future will not be a Replica of the Past: Pooling Creative Talents to Help See Round Corners*, 76th World Conference of the Textile Institute, Istanbul.

De Meyer A (1992), *Creating the Virtual Factory*, Insead Research Report.

Douglas M (1982), *In The Active Voice*, Routledge, London.

Drucker P (1962), *The Economy's Dark Continent*, Fortune, April.

Dullin E (1998), *Enterprise and Plant-Centric Scheduling*, IIE Solutions, February, pp. 16–20.

ECR Europe (1997), *The Official European ECR Scorecard*, ECR Europe.

EDI World Institute (1995), *The Why EDI Guide*, World Trade Center, 380, rue Saint-Antoine Ouest, Bureau 3280, Montreal, Quebec, Canada H2Y 3X7.

Eldredge N and Gould SJ (1972), *Punctuated Equilibria: An alternative to Phyleticgradualism* in Schopf TJM (Ed.), *Models in Paleobiology*, Freeman, Cooper & Co.

Fisher ML (1997), *What is the Right Supply Chain for your Product?* HBR, March–April.

Fisher MM, Hammond JH, Obermeyer WR and Raman A (1994), *Making Supply Meet Demand in an Uncertain World*, HBR, May–June.

Foxall J (1981), *Strategic Marketing Management*, Halstead Press.

Forrester JW (1961), *Industrial Dynamics*, The MIT Press, Cambridge, Mass.

Fralix M and Off J (1994), *Agile Manufacturing within a Demand Activated System*, Quick Response Proceedings, Chicago, IL.

Frazier RM (1986), *QR Inventory Replenishment*, paper presented at the 75th National Retail Merchants Association Conference.

Giffi CA, Roth AV and Seal GM (1990), *Competing in World Class Marketing: America's 21st Century Challenge*, Business One Irwin, Homewood, IL.

Gilreath TL, Reeve JM and Whalen CE Jr (1995), *Time is Money: Understanding the Product Velocity Advantage*, Bobbin, March.

Goddard T, Realff ML and Realff MJ (1996), *Modeling and Analysis of Weaving-Preparation Systems with Respect to Small Lot Manufacturing*, J. Text. Inst., Vol. 87, Pt. 2, No. 1.

Godet M (1982), *From Forecasting to La Prospective—A New Way of Looking at Futures*, J. of Forecasting, Vol. 1.

Goldman SL and Nagel RN (1993), *Management, Technology and Agility: The Emergence of a New Era in Manufacturing*, Int. J. Techn. Manag., Vol. 8, pp. 18–38.

Gramsci A (1971), *Americanism and Fordism*, in Hoare Q and Nowell-Smith G (Eds.), *Selections from the Prison Notebooks of Antonio Gramsci*, Lawrence and Wishard, London.

Gunston R and Harding P (1987) *QR: US and UK Experiences*, Textile Outlook Int., (10), 43–51.

Hall TC (1991), *Evaluation of Demand Re-estimation Methods for Seasonal Apparel using a Simulation Model*, Master of Science Project Report, Industrial Engineering Dept., NCSU.

Hamel G and Prahalad CK (1990), *Strategic Intent*, HBR, May–June.

Harding PW (1985), *QR in the Soft Goods Pipeline*, paper presented at the Conference on Computer-Aided Manufacturing in Textiles, Clemson University, Clemson, SC.

Hayes RH (1981), *Why Japanese Factories Work*, HBR, July–Aug.

Hayes RH, Wheelwright SC and Clark KB (1988), *Dynamic Manufacturing*, The Free Press, New York.

Hewitt WC Jr, Hodgson TJ, Hunter NA and King RE (1991), *Analysis of the Benefits of Quick Response Implementation for the Domestic Retail, Apparel and Textile Industries*, NCSU, Ind. Eng. Technical Report.

Hicks D (1997), *The Manager's Guide to Supply Chain and Logistics Problem-Solving Tools and Techniques*, IIE Solutions, September, 43–47.

Hinshaw JC and McGoogan AC (1993), *Modeling and Analysis of a Textile Knitting Plant*, Dept. of Ind. Eng. NCSU.

Hunter NA (1990), *Quick Response in Apparel Manufacturing*, The Textile Institute, Manchester.

Hunter NA (1996), *A Quick Response Feasibility Study of Selected Companies in the Estrie*, (unpublished study on behalf of MICT, Govt. of Quebec).

Hunter NA, King RE and Nuttle HLW (1992), *An Apparel Supply System for QR Retailing*, J. Text. Inst., Vol. 83, No. 3.

Hunter NA, King RE and Nuttle HLW (1996), *Evaluation of Traditional and Quick Response Retailing Procedures by Using a Stochastic Simulation Model*, J. Text. Inst., Vol. 87, Pt. 2, No. 1.

Hunter NA, King RE, Nuttle HLW and Wilson JR (1993), *The Apparel Pipeline Modeling Project at North Carolina State University*, J. Clothing Science Techn, Vol. 5, No. 3/4.

Hunter NA and Valentino P (1995), *Quick Response—Ten Years Later*, Int. J. Clothing, Science Techn, Vol. 7, No. 4.

Johnson CD (1984), *Microprocessor-Based Process Control*, Prentice Hall, Europe.

Johnson G and Scholes K (1997), *Exploring Corporate Strategy*, Prentice Hall, Europe.

Johnson R and Lawrence PR (1988), *Beyond Vertical Integration—the Rise of the Value-Adding Partnership*, HBR, July–August.

Kaplan RS and Norton DP (1992), *The Balanced Scorecard—Measures that Drive Performance*, HBR, Jan–Feb.

Kanter RM (1989), *When Giants Learn to Dance*, Unwin.

Kincade DH (1995), *Quick Response Management System for the Apparel Industry: Definition through Technologies*, Clothing Textiles Res. J., Vol. 13, No. 4, 245–251.

King RE and Hunter NA (1996a), *The Impact of Size Distribution Forecast Error on Retail Performance*, NCSU-IE Technical Report, Department of Industrial Engineering, NCSU, Raleigh, NC.

King RE and Hunter NA (1996b), *Demand Re-Estimation and Inventory Replenishment of Basic Apparel in a Specialty Retail Chain*, J. Text. Inst. Vol. 87, No. 1.

King RE and Hunter NA (1997), *Quick Response Beats Importing in Retail Sourcing Analysis*, Bobbin, Vol. 38, No. 7.

King RE and Maddalena RP (1998), *Replenishment Rules*, Bobbin, May.

King RE and Poindexter ML (1990), *A Simulation Model for Retail Apparel Buying*, (NCSU-IE Tech Report 90–9), Ind. Eng. Dept., NCSU, Raleigh, NC.

King RE and Zozom A (1997), *Customer Behavior upon encountering a Stockout*, Working Paper, NCSU.

Ko E (1993), *A study of relationships between organizational characteristics and QR adoption*, Masters Abstracts Int., Vol. 31, 1529.

Ko E and Kincade DH (1997), *The Impact of Quick Response Technologies on Retail Store Attributes*, Int. J. Retail Distribution Manag., Vol. 25, No. 2.

Kosko B (1992), *Neural Networks and Fuzzy Systems*, Prentice Hall.

Kübler-Ross E (1970), *On Death and Dying*, Tavistock/Routledge Publications, London.

Kuhn T (1962), *The Structure of Scientific Revolutions*, Int. Encyclopaedia of Unified Science, Vol. 2, No. 2, University of Chicago.

Kurt Salmon Associates (1988), *Quick Response Implementation—Action Steps for Retailers, Manufacturers and Suppliers*, Technical Report, New York, NY.

Kurt Salmon Associates (1989), *Implementing VICS Technology and QR*, Technical Report, New York, NY.

Kurt Salmon Associates (1993), *Efficient Consumer Response: Enhancing Consumer Value in the Grocery Industry*, Food Marketing Institute, Washington, DC.

Kurt Salmon Associates (1995), *Efficient Consumer Response*, Food Marketing Institute, Washington, DC.

Kurt Salmon Associates (1997), *The Official European ECR Scorecard*, Atlanta, GA.

Kurt Salmon Associates (1998), *Consumer Outlook '98*, Technical Report, New York, NY.

Langton CG (1992), Life at the edge of chaos, in Langton CG, Taylor C, Dayne Farmer J and Rasmussen S (Eds.), *Artificial Life II, Santa Fe Institute Studies in the Sciences of Complexity*, Vol. 10.

Levy S (1992), *Artificial Life: The Quest for a New Creation*, Pantheon Books, New York, NY.

Lord PR (1978), Spinning *Conversion of Fiber to Yarn*, School of Textiles, NCSU.

Lowson B (1995), *A Rent in the Fabric*, Textiles Institute Conference on QR, Istanbul.

Lowson B (1998a) *Quick Response for SMEs: A Feasibility Study*, Textile Institute, UK.

Lowson B (1998b), *The Role and Outlook for the SME in the Manufacture and Distribution of Clothing and Footwear*, Int. J. Text. Inst., Vol. 89, No. 2, Part 1.

Lowson B (1998c), *Quick Response and Performance Measurement for Retailing*, Int. J. Text. Inst., Vol. 89, No. 2, Part 2.

Lowson B and Hunter NA (1996), *Quick Response: A Platform for Operational Diversity*. Text. Inst. World Conference, Tampere, Finland.

Lyneis JM (1980), *Corporate Planning and Policy Design*, Massachusetts Institute of Technology Press.

Maddalena RP (1998), *The Transition from Traditional to Quick Response Apparel Retailing: A Case Study*, Dept. Ind. Eng., NCSU, Raleigh NC.

Manning S and Nuttle HLW (1993), *Master Schedule Generator*, Dept. of Ind. Eng., NCSU.

Martin CR (1997), *Analysis of Sourcing Strategies for Seasonal Apparel*, Unpublished Master's Thesis, Dept. Ind. Eng., NCSU.

Masson E and Wang YJ (1990), *Introduction to Computation and Learning in Artificial Neural Networks*, Eur. J. Operational Res., Vol. 4, 47–62.

Mazziotti BW (1993), *Modular Manufacturing's New Breed*, Bobbin, April.

Mazziotti BM (1995), *Simulation and Analysis of Team Sewing*, Textile/Clothing Technology Corporation, [TC]^2, Cary, NC.

Mazziotti BW and Armstrong FB (1994), *Creating a Focussed Application Simulator with Flexible Decision Making Capability*, Winter Simulation Conference, Tew JD et al. (Eds.), IEEE, Piscataway, NJ.

Meadows DL, Behrens III WH Meadows DH, Naill RF, Randers J and Zahn EKO (1975), *The Dynamics of Growth in a Finite World*, Wright-Allen.

Morton TE (1971), *The Near-Myopic Nature of the Lagged-Proportional-Cost Inventory Problem with Lost Sales*, Operations Res, Vol. 19, No. 7.

Murray GR and Silver EA (1966), *A Baysian Analysis of the Style Goods Inventory Problem*, Manag. Science, Vol. 12, No. 11.

Nagel RN and Dove R (1991a), *21ˢᵗ Century Manufacturing Enterprise Strategy, Volume 1: An Industry Led-View*, Agile Manufacturing Enterprise Forum in co-operation with the Iacocca Institute, Lehigh University, Bethlehem, PA.

Nagel RN and Dove R (1991b), *21ˢᵗ Century Manufacturing Enterprise Strategy, Volume 2*, Agile Manufacturing Enterprise Forum in co-operation with the Iacocca Institute, Lehigh University, Bethlehem, PA.

NCSU (1995), *Neural Network Graphical User Interface*, Dept. Ind. Eng.

Nuttle HLW, King RE and Hunter NA (1991), *A Stochastic Model of the Apparel-Retailing Process for Seasonal Apparel*, J. Tex. Inst., Vol. 82, No. 2.

Nuttle HLW, King RE, Wilson JR, Hunter NA and Fang SC (1998), *Simulation modeling of the textile supply chain*. Int. J. Tex. Inst., Vol. 89, No. 2.

Ohmae K (1982), *The Mind of the Strategist: the Art of Japanese Business*, McGraw-Hill.

Ohno T. (1978), *Toyota Production System*, Productivity Press.

Olsson G and Piani G (1992), *Computer Systems for Automation and Control*, Prentice Hall.

Piellou EC (1977), *Mathematical Ecology*, John Wiley & Sons.

Pinnow AD and King RE (1997), *Break-even Costs for Traditional vs. Quick Response Apparel Suppliers*, NCSU-IE Dept. Technical Report #97–4.

Piore MJ and Sabel CF (1984), *The Second Industrial Divide: Possibilities for Prosperity*, Basic Books, NY.

Porter ME (1985), *Competitive Advantage: Creating and Sustaining Superior Performance*, The Free Press, Macmillan.

Porter ME (1996), *What is Strategy?* HBR, Nov–Dec.

Powell KA (1993), *Interactive Decision Support Modeling for the Textile Spinning Industry*, Master of Science Thesis, Ind. Eng. Dept., NCSU.

Quinn, JB, Doorley TL and Paquette PC (1990), *Beyond Products: Services-Based Strategy*, HBR, March–April.

Reynolds SA (1995), *Analysis of Reordering Strategies for Seasonal Style Goods*, Working Paper, Dept. Ind. Eng. NCSU.

Roberts EB (Ed.), (1981), *Managerial Applications of System Dynamics*, Massachusetts Institute of Technology Press.

Rowse AL (1950), *The England of Elizabeth*, Oxford University Press.

Schein E (1985), *Organisational Culture and Leadership*, Jossey-Bass.

Schmidt CP and Nahmias S (1984), *Optimal Policy for a Two-stage Assembly System under Random Demand*, Operations Res., Vol. 33, No. 5.

Shah Idris (1980), *The Way of the Sufi*, Octagon Press.

Shippey SA and Sands CA (1993), *Modeling and Analysis of the Textile Knitting Component of an Integrated Fiber-Textile-Apparel Manufacturer*, Dept. Ind. Eng., NCSU.

Skinner W (1974), *The Focused Factory*, HBR, Vol. 52, No. 3.

Stalk G and Hout TM (1990), *Competing Against Time*, The Free Press, NY.

Stalk G and Webber AM (1993), *Japan's Dark Side of Time*, HBR, July–August.

Stacey R (1996), *Emerging Strategies for a Chaotic Environment*, Long Range Planning, Vol. 29, No. 2.

Sullivan PC (1992), *A study of the adoption of Quick Response in the United States apparel manufacturing industry*, Unpublished doctoral dissertation, New York University, NY.

Textile Apparel Linkage Council (1988), *Getting started with piece goods linkage*, American Apparel Manufacturers Association, Arlington VA.

The Apparel and Textile Challenge (1996), Benchmaking Seminar, 22 October, London.

Towill DR (1991), *Supply Chain Dynamics*, Int. J. Comp. Integrated Manu., Vol. 4, No. 2.

Wagner H (1975), *Principles of Operations Research*, Prentice Hall, NY.

Ward J, Griffiths P and Whitmore P (1990), *Strategic Planning for Information Systems*, John Wiley & Sons.

Whittington R (1993), *What is Strategy—and Does it Matter?* Routledge.

Wickner J, Towill DR and Naim M (1991), *Smoothing Supply Chain Dynamics*, Int. J. Prod. Econ., Vol. 22.

Williamson OE (1981), *The Modern Corporation: Origins, Evolution, Attributes*, J. Econ. Lit., Vol. XIX.

Winston WL (1987), Operations Research, PWS-Kent.

Winston WL (1994), *Operations Research, Application and Algorithms*, Wadsworth Publishing, Belmont, CA.

Womack JD, Jones D and Roos D (1990), *The Machine that Changed the World*, Rawson Macmillan, NY.

Wu P (1997), *Neural Networks and Fuzzy Control with Applications to Textile Manufacturing and Management*, unpublished PhD dissertation, Department of Industrial Engineering, North Carolina State University, Raleigh, USA.

Wu P, Fang SC, King RE and Nuttle HLW (1995b), *Decision Surface Modeling of Textile Retail Operations using Neural Networks*, Joint Conference on Information Sciences.

Wu P, Fang SC, King RE and Nuttle HLW (1995a), *Decision Surface Modeling of Apparel Retail Operations using Neural Network Technology*, Int. J. Operations Quant. Manag, Vol. 1, 33–47.

Wu P, Fang SC, Nuttle HLW, Wilson JR and King RE (1995c), *Guided Neural Network Learning Using a Fuzzy Controller with Applications to Textile Spinning*, Int. Trans. Operations Res., Vol. 2, 389–404.

Zachs S (1981), *Statistical Problems in the Control of Multi-Echelon Inventory Systems*, in Schwartz L (Ed.), *Multi-Level Production/Inventory Control Systems: Theory and Practice*, North Holland.

Zimmermann HJ (1988), *Fuzzy Set Theory and its Applications*, Kluwer Nijhoff Publishing.

Zurada JM (1992), *Introduction to Artificial Neural Systems*, West Publishing Company, US.

INDEX